I0868488

Islamic Law and the Crisis of the Reconquista

Studies in Islamic Law and Society

Founding Editor

Bernard Weiss

Edited by

Ruud Peters and A. Kevin Reinhart

VOLUME 39

The titles published in this series are listed at *brill.com/sils*

Islamic Law and the Crisis of the Reconquista

The Debate on the Status of Muslim Communities in Christendom

By

Alan Verskin

BRILL

LEIDEN | BOSTON

Library of Congress Cataloging-in-Publication Data

Verskin, Alan, author.
Islamic law and the crisis of the Reconquista : the debate on the status of Muslim communities in Christendom / by Alan Verskin.
pages cm. — (Studies in Islamic law and society ; v 39)
Includes bibliographical references and index.
ISBN 978-90-04-28319-0 (hardback : alk. paper) — ISBN 978-90-04-28453-1 (e-book) 1. Islamic law.—History. 2. Malikites—Spain—History. 3. Muslims—Non-Islamic countries. 4. Muslims—Legal status, laws, etc. 5. Spain—History—711–1516. I. Title.

KBP56.V47 2015
297.1'401813—dc23

2014040635

ISSN 1384-1130
ISBN 978 90 04 28319 0 (hardback)
ISBN 978 90 04 28453 1 (e-book)

Copyright 2015 by Koninklijke Brill NV, Leiden, The Netherlands.
Koninklijke Brill NV incorporates the imprints Brill, Brill Nijhoff and Hotei Publishing.
All rights reserved. No part of this publication may be reproduced, translated, stored in a retrieval system, or transmitted in any form or by any means, electronic, mechanical, photocopying, recording or otherwise, without prior written permission from the publisher.
Authorization to photocopy items for internal or personal use is granted by Koninklijke Brill NV provided that the appropriate fees are paid directly to The Copyright Clearance Center, 222 Rosewood Drive, Suite 910, Danvers, MA 01923, USA.
Fees are subject to change.

This book is printed on acid-free paper.

For Sara

الرفيق قبل الطريق

∵

Contents

Acknowledgments

This book would not have been possible without the help of my teachers, friends and family. I owe a great debt to Michael Cook and Muhammad Qasim Zaman. Michael Cook was the first to open the fascinating world of classical Islamic sources to me and I continue to benefit from his guidance. Muhammad Qasim Zaman's insightful comments and suggestions often led me to pursue new and productive areas of research. While at Princeton, I gained much from my conversations with Lawrence Rosen who offered a fresh and enlivening perspective on the functioning of Islamic law. At Princeton, I benefited from the expertise, mentorship and encouragement of Nancy Coffin, Michael Barry, Mark Cohen, Andras Hamori, M. Şükrü Hanioğlu, Bernard Haykel, Norman Itzkowitz, Bernard Lewis, Abraham Udovitch and Aron Zysow. At Brill, I would like to thank my editors, Nienke Brienen-Moolenaar and Nicolette van der Hoek, as well as the two anonymous reviewers.

I would also like to thank my earlier academic mentors for giving me my first taste of the scholarly life and for the personal interest that they have taken in my intellectual development. Kenneth Green invited me to attend my first graduate seminar and, in so doing, set me on the path to academia. Harry Fox and Tirzah Meacham introduced me to the tools of linguistic textual analysis. With David Novak, I first explored the interactions of theology and law. At the University of Chicago, where I spent two critical years studying in the Divinity School, I would like to thank Paul Mendes-Flohr for exceptional mentorship; James Robinson for his infectious excitement for the study of medieval thought; and the late Farouk Mustafa for teaching me Arabic.

Much of this book was completed while I was the recipient of an ACLS New Faculty Fellowship at Columbia University. I would like to thank both ACLS and Columbia University for this opportunity. In particular, I would like to thank my colleagues, Gil Anidjar, Patricia Grieve, Najam Haider, Wael Hallaq, Mahmood Mamdani, Brinkley Messick and Timothy Mitchell. The final part of this book was completed at the University of Rhode Island. I am very thankful for the warmth and advice given to me by all my new colleagues: Bridget Buxton, Kathleen Davis, Rae Ferguson, Timothy George, Michael Honhart, Erik Loomis, Alexander Magidow, Rod Mather, Rosa Maria Pegueros, Miriam Reumann, Joëlle Rollo-Koster, Andrea Rusnock, Evelyne Sterne, James Ward, Robert Widell and Nancy Woyak.

My time has been made pleasurable and meaningful through the companionship and advice of my friends and colleagues: Khalil Abdur-Rashid, Yaron Ayalon, Franz Bibfeldt, Zachary Braiterman, Mehmet Darakioglu, Jonathan

Fluger, Elliot Hen-Tov, Kathi Ivanyi, Amanda Izenstark, Jessica Marglin, David Moore, Jacob Olidort, Helen Pfeiffer, Intisar Rabb, Uriel Simonsohn, Mark Sinyor, Mairaj Syed, Jack Tannous, Bella Tendler, Markus Wiener, Brett Wilson, Joseph and Judith Witztum, and Oded Zinger. I also gratefully acknowledge the generous support of the Social Sciences and Humanities Research Council of Canada, the Andrew W. Mellon Foundation, the American Council of Learned Societies, Princeton University and Columbia University.

I owe a great deal of thanks to my father for his unceasing nurturing of my intellectual development. He taught me languages, took me to the university library from the age of eleven, and has patiently read my work. I could not have reached this point without him. I would also like to thank my parents-in-law, Jerry and Sharon, and my grandparents-in-law, Henry and Bella, for the active interest and support that they have shown for my scholarly work. Thanks also to Maya, Hannah and Daniel who were always there to provide welcome diversions from research. Finally I would like to thank my wife Sara to whom this book is dedicated. Sara has been an intellectual and emotional companion closer than I could have ever imagined. Her contributions to my work are very great. In addition to giving me moral support, she has read and commented on everything I have written. From the time we met in a class on Averroes, she has immensely broadened my academic horizons leading me to pursue many avenues of intellectual enquiry of which I had previously been unaware. For all of this and more, my love and thanks.

Alan Verskin
March 2014
Providence, Rhode Island

Introduction

The Reconquista, or Christian conquest of Muslim Iberia, precipitated a great intellectual crisis for Muslims.[1] For most of Islamic history, the vast majority of Muslims had lived under some kind of Islamic ruler. Islam's religious and legal institutions, which had developed under such political conditions, had naturally taken a Muslim ruler as a given. As a result of the Reconquista, Islamic scholars had to contemplate what it would mean for Islam to be practiced without such a ruler. They had to determine whether a Muslim ruler was assumed in Islamic legal texts simply as a result of historical circumstances or because the ruler was an essential part of the Islamic legal system. This book examines the way in which jurists of the Mālikī legal school, the legal school which came to predominate in the Iberian Peninsula and the Maghrib,[2] developed Islamic law in response to the political, theological, and practical

1 The term "Reconquista" assumes a narrative of a unified Christian Spain which historians believe to be false. Since no convenient substitute term has emerged, most historians, retain it and I have reluctantly followed their lead. Interestingly, contemporary writings in Arabic on the Reconquista use the term *istirdād*, a direct translation of "reconquista," see Muḥammad al-Sharīf, *al-Maghrib wa-ḥurūb al-istirdād* (Tetouan: Jāmiʿat ʿAbd al-Mālik al-Saʿdī, Kullīyat al-Ādāb wa'l-ʿUlūm al-Insāniyya, 2005) and Nādiya Ḥusnī Ṣaqr, *Dawr ʿAbd al-Raḥmān al-Nāṣir fī irjāʾ ḥarakat al-istirdād* (Mecca: al-Maktaba al-Fayṣaliyya, 1985). The use of the term "Reconquista" is discussed in Peter Linehan, *History and the Historians of Medieval Spain* (Oxford: Oxford University Press, 1992), 5 ff. and Joseph F. O'Callaghan, *Reconquest and Crusade in Medieval Spain* (Philadelphia: University of Pennsylvania Press, 2003), 3 ff.

2 On the spread of Mālikism in Iberia, see J. López Ortiz, "La recepción de la escuela malequí en España," *Anuario de Historia del Derecho español* 7 (1930), 1–167; Hady Roger Idris, "Réflexions sur le Mālikisme sous les Umayyades d'Espagne," in *Atti del terzo congresso di studi arabi e islamici. Ravello, 1–6 settembre 1966* (Napoli: Istituto universitario orientale, 1967), 397–414; Alfonso Carmona, "The Introduction of Mālik's Teachings in al-Andalus," in *The Islamic School of Law*, ed. P. Bearman et al. (Cambridge: Harvard University Press, 2005), 41–56; Maribel Fierro, "Proto-Malikis, Malikis, and Reformed Malikis in al-Andalus," in *The Islamic School of Law*, 57–76; and Christopher Melchert, *The Formation of the Sunni Schools of Law, 9th–10th centuries C.E.* (Leiden: Brill, 1997), 156–64. On its spread in the Maghrib, see Mansour H. Mansour, *The Maliki School of Law: Spread and Domination in North and West Africa, 8th to 14th Centuries C.E.* (San Francisco: Austin & Winfield, 1995); ʿUmar al-Jīdī, *Mabāḥith fī al-madhhab al-Mālikī bi'l-Maghrib* (Rabat: al-Hilāl al-ʿArabiyya li'l-Ṭibāʿa wa'l-Nashr, 1993), 33 ff.; and Muḥammad b. Ḥasan Sharḥabīlī, *Taṭawwur al-madhhab al-Mālikī fī al-gharb al-Islāmī ḥattā nihāyat al-ʿaṣr al-Murābiṭī* (Rabat: al-Mamlaka al-Maghribiyya, Wizārat al-Awqāf wa'l-Shuʾūn al-Islāmiyya, 2000).

© KONINKLIJKE BRILL NV, LEIDEN, 2015 | DOI 10.1163/9789004284531_002

difficulties posed by the Reconquista. It shows how religious concepts, even those very central to the Islamic religious experience, could be rethought and reinterpreted in order to respond to the changing needs of Muslims. Although most of this book focuses on the Reconquista period, its final chapter examines how the legal positions formulated by the jurists of this period shaped nineteenth-century Muslim responses to French rule in the Maghrib.[3]

Extensive legal discussions about living under non-Muslim rule in the pre-modern period tend to occur only in the context of great political crisis and confrontation with non-Muslim societies. The formative texts of the Sunnī legal schools, most of which were written in the heartlands of Islamic territory, have very little to say about the matter. For them, Islamic territory (*dār al-Islām*)[4] was vast and expanding. The issues pertaining to life under non-Muslim rule were a rare exception to this rule to which they gave little, if any, attention. The limited territorial gains made by non-Muslim powers, for example, those made by the Byzantines or the Crusader kingdoms, were never dealt with extensively by jurists.[5]

The major exception to the silence of the jurists on questions pertaining to life under non-Muslim rule was their responses to the Reconquista.[6] The

3 Following J.M. Abun-Nasr, my use of the term Maghrib is intended to also encompass the area known in the medieval period as Ifrīqiya. I have chosen to use this term instead of North Africa as I do not extensively deal with the smaller Mālikī legal school located in Egypt, see J.M. Abun-Nasr, *A History of the Maghrib in the Islamic Period* (Cambridge: Cambridge University Press, 1987), 3.

4 For a recent discussion of this term and its opposite, the abode of war (*dar al-ḥarb*), see Muhammad Mushtaq Ahmad, "The Notions of *Dār al-Ḥarb* and *Dār al-Islām* in Islamic Jurisprudence with Special Reference to the Ḥanafī School," *Islamic Studies* 47 (2008), 5–37.

5 For a treatment of the scattered legal discussions on life under non-Muslim rule, see Khaled Abou El Fadl, "Islamic Law and Muslim Minorities: The Juristic Discourse on Muslim Minorities from the Second/Eighth to the Eleventh/Seventeenth Centuries," *Islamic Law and Society* 1 (1994), 141–187. For examples of Mālikī jurists who noted this dearth in the legal literature, see the statement of the Granadan judge Muḥammad b. Muḥammad Ibn ʿĀṣim (d. 829/1426) in Aḥmad b. Yaḥyā al-Wansharīsī, *al-Miʿyār al-muʿrib wa'l-jāmiʿ al-mughrib ʿan fatāwā ahl Ifrīqiya wa'l-Andalus wa'l-Maghrib*, ed. Muḥammad Ḥajjī (Rabat: Wizārat al-Awqāf wa'l-Shu'ūn al-Islāmiyya li'l-Mamlaka al-Maghribiyya, 1981), 2: 151. For a similar statement by al-Wansharīsī himself, see ibid., 2: 125.

6 Even regarding this issue, what survive are not the responses of jurists who lived under Christian rule, but those of jurists who lived under Muslim rule and responded to the situation. Jurists who lived in Christian Iberia may well have written *fatwās* about their situation, but if they did, none are extant. The only documented example of a *fatwā* by a Mudéjar jurist concerns whether the skins of animals which are not ritually-slaughtered can be used as prayer mats, see summary in Francisco Fernández y González, *Estado social y político de los*

Iberian Peninsula was an area with well-established Muslim communities, and its gradual reconquest over the course of several hundred years left an aftermath so great in human terms that it compelled the jurists to deal with it. It is therefore very often to this period that subsequent jurists turn in order to probe what little the tradition has to say about matters pertaining to life under Christian rule. As I will discuss, this act of juristic reflection occurred during the nineteenth-century French conquest of the Maghrib when Muslims again had to consider the religious and legal implications of living under a Christian government.

Historical Overview

The Muslim political presence in Iberia dates to 92/711[7] when Muslim armies seized control of the region excepting some small Christian enclaves in the north. Although skirmishes with Christian powers had occurred from the very inception of Muslim rule, the Reconquista itself is usually said to have begun towards the end of the fifth/eleventh century with the conquering of such significant Muslim centers as Toledo (478/1085) and Huesca (489/1096).[8] Further conquests, however, were deferred for over a century by the Almoravids and the Almohads, two consecutive Maghribī dynasties which held the Christians at bay and even recovered some lost territory. In the seventh/thirteenth century, the tide again turned in favor of the Christians. The Almohad dynasty weakened and then dissolved and Christians were once again able to gain several significant victories, including the capture of the Kingdom of Valencia (636/1238), which had a particularly large Muslim population. This momentum continued and, before the close of the ninth/fifteenth century, not only had Muslim rule entirely ceased in Iberia but Christians also occupied much of the Maghribī coast.[9]

Mudéjares de Castilla (Madrid: J. Muñoz, 1866), 393–94, referred to in Gerard Wiegers, *Islamic Literature in Spanish and Aljamiado: Yça of Segovia (fl. 1450), His Antecedents and Successors* (Leiden: Brill, 1994), 82. Unfortunately, the original *fatwā* is no longer extant.

7 Here as elsewhere, Gregorian calendar dates follow *hijrī* ones.

8 For a general history of the Reconquista, see Joseph F. O'Callaghan, *Reconquest and Crusade in Medieval Spain* and Derek W. Lomax, *The Reconquest of Spain* (London: Longman, 1978).

9 Andrew C. Hess, *The Forgotten Frontier: A History of the Sixteenth-Century Ibero-African Frontier* (Chicago: University of Chicago Press, 1978), 6 ff.

Many Muslims fled Iberia in the wake of its Christian conquest. Those who stayed came to be called "Mudéjars."[10] In return for their pledge of loyalty to the Christian king, Mudéjars were allowed to remain in their lands without changing their religion.[11] The conditions under which Mudéjars lived varied considerably. In newly conquered regions, the treatment of Mudéjars tended to be better as Christian rulers depended upon them to prevent depopulation.[12] Depopulation was a persistant concern for Christian rulers. Maintaining control over new territories was costly and, without a sufficient population, these territories could not be economically exploited. Thus while the rhetoric of the Reconquista pushed for an Iberia which was empty of Muslims, pragmatic considerations deferred expulsion. Instead, Mudéjar populations were jealously guarded by Christian rulers and came to be referred to in Latin sources as "royal treasures" (*thesauri regii*).[13] Strict punishments were imposed on those who harmed Mudéjars because doing so was injurious to royal revenue and, by extension, to the security of the kingdom. To further safeguard their Mudéjar populations, Christian rulers often prevented them from leaving their lands and sometimes even actively solicited new Muslim immigrants.[14]

The Mudéjars were often highly integrated into the Christian societies in which they lived. They were well represented in Christian armed forces, Mudéjar leaders became officials of Christian rulers and Muslim legal courts occasionally became branches of Christian government.[15] The result

10 The Arabic word for Mudéjars is *mudajjanūn* or *ahl al-dajn*. On the relationship between the terms in Spanish and Arabic, see Isidro de las Cagigas, *Los Mudéjares* (Madrid: Consejo Superior de Investigaciones Científicas, Instituto de Estudios Africanos, 1948), 1: 58 ff. and F. Maíllo Salgado, "Acerca del uso, significado y referente del término mudéjar," in *Actas del IV congreso internacional encuentro de las tres culturas, Toledo 30 septiembre–2 octubre 1985*, ed. Carlos Carrete Parrondo (Toledo: Tel Aviv University and the city of Toledo, 1988), 103–112.

11 L.P. Harvey, *Islamic Spain, 1250 to 1500* (Chicago: University of Chicago Press, 1990), 3.

12 For a further elaboration of this theme, see chapter 2.

13 Chancery of the Archive of the Crown of Aragon, C 913: 33, transcribed in John Boswell, *The Royal Treasure: Muslim Communities under the Crown of Aragon in the Fourteenth Century* (New Haven: Yale University Press, 1977), 471.

14 Robert I. Burns, "Immigrants from Islam: The Crusaders' Use of Muslims as Settlers in Thirteenth-Century Spain," *The American Historical Review* 80 (1975), 24.

15 For discussions of Muslim soldiers in Christian armies, see Hussein Fancy, "Theologies of Violence: The Recruitment of Muslim Soldiers by the Crown of Aragon," *Past and Present* 221 (2013), 39–73 and Ana Echevarría, *Knights on the Frontier: The Moorish Guard of the Kings of Castile (1410–1467)*, tr. M. Beagles (Leiden: Brill, 2009). On the court system, see Isabel O'Connor, "The Mudéjars and the Local Courts: Justice in Action," *Journal of Islamic Studies* 16 (2005), 339; and Boswell, *The Royal Treasure*, 111–12. Cf. Ana Echevarría Arsuaga,

was that the Mudéjar leadership enforced their community's compliance with Christian ordinances, collected taxes, and maintained public order. Extensive Christian involvement in Muslim religious institutions sometimes resulted in their undergoing considerable modification. In this regard, Brian Catlos makes this observation on Mudéjar institutions in Catalonia and Aragon:

> Anchored in institutions which were neither Islamic nor entirely Christian, the patrician families straddled a middle ground as the leaders of their community and affiliate members of the Christian administration. At times defending but frequently at odds with their own subjects, they comprised a pre-modern colonial native elite. Offices such as the *alcadia* and *çaualquenia*[16] were Muslim and Arabic in name but had been emptied for the most part of Islamic content, and deprived of the checks and balances which had guarded against abuse under Muslim rule.[17]

The features that Catlos describes were not exhibited by all Mudéjar institutions, but their existence is a testament to the precarious conditions under which the Mudéjars lived.

The growth of Christian populations in formerly Muslim Iberia set in motion the events which brought the era of the Mudéjars to a close. With the threat of depopulation removed, the Christian need for the Mudéjars diminished and their treatment worsened. Matters were brought to a head with the fall of Granada (897/1492), an event which marked the end of Muslim political power in the Iberian Peninsula. Although the Muslims of defeated Granada were initially granted Mudéjar status which allowed them to continue to observe their religion, this protection was soon rescinded.[18] In 1498, Francisco Jiménez de Cisneros, the archbishop of Toledo, introduced a program of forced

"De cadí a alcalde mayor. La élite judicial mudéjar en el siglo XV," *Al-Qanṭara*, 24 (2003), 139–168 and 273–289.

16 While the Arabic origin of this term seems clear, the Arabic upon which the term is based is obscure. Catlos suggests that it is derived from the term *ṣāḥib al-ḥukm*, see Brian A. Catlos, *The Victors and the Vanquished: Christians and Muslims of Catalonia and Aragon, 1050–1300* (Cambridge: Cambridge University Press, 2004), xviii. Catlos is likely correct, with a slight modification. This individual was usually referred to in al-Andalus as *ṣāḥib al-aḥkām*. My thanks go to the anonymous Brill reviewer for drawing my attention to this.

17 Catlos, *The Victors and the Vanquished*, 219. Cf. Tulio Halperin-Donghi, *Un conflict nacional: Moriscos y Cristianos viejos en Valencia* (Valencia: Institución Alfonso el Magnánimo, 1980), 97.

18 Miguel Angel Ladero Quesada, *Granada después de la conquista: repobladores y mudéjares*, 2nd ed. (Granada: Diputación Provincial de Granada, 1993), 435 ff.

conversion which sparked Mudéjar revolts that were then forcibly subdued by Christian armies.[19] Utterly defeated, the remaining Muslims of Iberia, under varying degrees of coercion, either converted to Christianity or emigrated.[20] By 1502, the practice of Islam was officially outlawed in all parts of Iberia and the Mudéjar era ended. Muslims who remained came to be known not as Mudéjars but as "Moriscos,"[21] a term which designates outward converts to Christianity who were able to practice Islam only in secret. By 1614, the Moriscos also ceased to exist, the victims of several waves of expulsion.[22]

The Jurists on Muslim-Christian Relations

Many jurists expressed their distrust of the Mudéjars. While some sympathized with their plight as the tragic victims of war, they were nonetheless suspicious of their collaboration with Christian authorities. Willingly or unwillingly, by providing economic and social stability, and occasionally military assistance,

---

19 Gerard Albert Wiegers, *Islamic Literature in Spanish and Aljamiado*, 9 and David Coleman, *Creating Christian Granada: Society and Religious Culture in an Old-World Frontier City, 1492–1600* (Ithaca: Cornell University Press, 2003), 6.

20 On migration to the Maghrib, see J. Vallvé, "La emigración andalusí al Magreb en el siglo XIII," in *Relaciones de la Península Ibérica con el Magreb*, ed. M. García-Arenal and M.J. Viguera (Madrid: Consejo Superior de Investigaciones Científicas, 1988), 87–129; Muḥammad Razzūq, *al-Andalusiyyūn wa-hijrātuhum ilā al-Maghrib* (Casablanca: Ifrīqiya al-Sharq, 1989) and M. Marín, "Des migrations forcées: les ulema d'al-Andalus face à conquête chrétienne," in *L'Occident musulman et l'Occident chrétien au moyen âge*, ed. M. Hammam (Rabat: Faculté des Lettres, 1995), 44 ff. On how this massive migration transformed the Maghrib, see John D. Latham, "Towards a Study of Andalusian Immigration and its Place in Tunisian History," *Les Cahiers de Tunisie* 5 (1957), 203–249. Cf. Linda Jones, "Retratos de la emigración: La (Re)conquista y la emigración de los ulemas a Granada, según *al-Iḥāṭa* de Ibn al-Jaṭīb," in *Biografías mudéjares o La experiencia de ser minoría: biografías islámicas en la España cristiana*, ed. Ana Echevarría Arsuaga (Madrid: Consejo Superior de Investigaciones Científicas, 2008), 21–58.

21 For the classic definition of this term, see Pascual Boronat y Barrachina, *Los moriscos españoles y su expulsión: Estudio histórico-crítico* (Valencia: Imprenta de Francisco Vives y Mora, 1901), 1: 423 ff. On why the use of the term is problematic, see L.P. Harvey, *Muslims in Spain, 1500 to 1614* (Chicago: University of Chicago Press, 2005), 3 ff. and Míkel de Epalza, "La voz oficial de los musulmanes hispanos, mudéjares y moriscos, a sus autoridades cristianas: cuatro textos, en árabe, en castellano y en catalán-valenciano," in *Sharq al-Andalus* 12 (1995), 280.

22 There are few references to Moriscos in juristic works, see L.P. Harvey, *Muslims in Spain, 1500 to 1614*, 64 ff.

to Christian regimes, Mudéjars strengthened them and placed neighboring Muslim lands in danger. Some jurists believed that righteous Mudéjars existed, others felt that Mudéjars were willing collaborators with the Christians, but the grave political implications of courtesies granted to Mudéjars, whether righteous or unrighteous, necessarily threw these questions into the background.[23]

The jurists' views on the Mudéjars should also be examined in the context of their views on Christian-Muslim relations in general. Jurists of Iberia had long contemplated the effects of living in al-Andalus which, although ruled by Muslims, had substantial Christian populations as well as powerful Christian neighbors. As they saw it, although the rule of al-Andalus by Muslims reduced the danger that contact with Christians would lead to the assimilation of their beliefs and customs, it did not eliminate this risk.[24] Abū al-Ḥasan Ibn Bassām al-Shantarīnī (d. 542/1147),[25] for example, writes regarding Muslim Andalusīs:

---

23 See, for example, al-Wazzānī, *al-Nawāzil al-jadīda al-kubrā fī mā li-ahl Fās wa-ghayrihim min al-badw wa'l-qurā al-musammā bi'l-Mi'yār al-jadīd al-jāmi' al-mu'rib 'an fatāwā al-muta'akhkhirīn min 'ulamā' al-Maghrib* (Rabat: Wizārat al-Awqāf wa'l-Shu'ūn al-Islāmiyya li'l-Mamlaka al-Maghribiyya, 1996), 3: 35. I henceforth refer to the latter work as *al-Mi'yār al-jadīd.* Abū al-Qāsim al-Burzulī (d. 841/1438) notes that the Muslims who lived on the Christian-controlled island of al-Qawṣara (Pantelleria), which lies off the coast of Sicily, did so of their own choice, see *Fatāwā al-Burzulī: jāmi' masā'il al-aḥkām limā nazala min al-qaḍāyā bi'l-muftīn wa'l-ḥukkām,* ed. Muḥammad al-Ḥabīb al-Hayla (Beirut: Dār al-Gharb al-Islāmī, 2002), 2: 23. Cf. Ibn Nājī, *Sharḥ Ibn Nājī al-Tanūkhī 'alā matn al-Risāla,* ed. Aḥmad Farīd al-Mazīdī (Beirut: Dār al-Kutub al-'Ilmiyya, 2007), 2: 485. Muslims continued live in Pantelleria until the late 15th century, see Henri Bresc, "Pantelleria entre l'Islam et la Chrétienté," *Cahiers de Tunisie* 19 (1971), 105–127.

24 Warnings against the dangers of close relations with non-Muslims appear frequently in Islamic literature from the time of the Qur'ān and are frequently referred to in the jurists' discussions of the Mudéjars. Examples in the Qur'ān include 5: 51, 5: 57 and 60: 1. On these and others, see Louise Marlow, "Friends and Friendship," *Encyclopaedia of the Qur'ān,* ed. Jane McAuliffe (Leiden: Brill, 2009), 2: 273. For examples in post-Qur'ānic literature, see al-Wansharīsī, *al-Mi'yār al-mu'rib,* 2: 140; Janina Safran, "Identity and Differentiation in Ninth-Century al-Andalus," *Speculum* 76 (2001), 581; Fernando de la Granja, "Fiestas cristianas en al-Andalus," *al-Andalus* 35 (1970), 135 and 139 and H.E. Kassis, "Roots of Conflict: Aspects of Christian-Muslim Confrontation in Eleventh-Century Spain," in *Conversion and Continuity: Indigenous Christian Communities in Islamic lands Eighth to Eighteenth Centuries,* ed. Michael Gervers and Ramzi Jibran Bikhazi (Toronto: Pontifical Institute for Medieval Studies, 1990), 154–55.

25 Mohamed Meouak and B. Soravia, "Ibn Bassām al-Šantarīnī (m. 542/1147): algunos aspectos de su antología *al-Ḏajīra fī maḥāsin ahl al-Ŷazīra,*" *al-Qanṭara* 18 (1997), 221–232.

> On account of their location in this clime, close to the Christian kingdoms (*ṭawāʾif al-Rūm*), in a land which is the last of those conquered by Islam and quite removed from the influence of Arab traditions, surrounded by the vast sea and the Christians ... they [the Andalusīs] reap nothing but perdition.[26]

The jurists believed that the dangers posed by living in close proximity to Christians were even greater for the Mudéjars because they lacked a Muslim ruler. Thus Ibn Miqlāsh (d. 794/1392)[27] declares that, as a result of living among Christians, the Mudéjars display an indifference to all things Islamic. This is manifested, he says, by the fact that they cavalierly participate in Christian ceremonies and festivals.[28] Muḥammad b. ʿAlī al-Ḥaffār of Granada (d. 811/1408)[29] describes how easily the customs of those who engage in the religiously forbidden can come to be adopted by those who live near them. It is for this reason, he says, that Muslims are prohibited from associating with those who drink wine, commit adultery, or engage in other such prohibited acts. How much greater, he says, is the prohibition against living among those who deny God and spread lies about His Prophet.[30] Aḥmad b. Yaḥyā al-Wansharīsī (d. 914/1508),[31] whom I will discuss in further detail, also comments on this phenomenon.[32] He says that as a result of societal pressures, Muslims living in Christian lands will find themselves seeing forbidden things, coming into

26 Ibn Bassām al-Shantarīnī, *al-Dhakhīra fī maḥāsin ahl al-Jazīra*, ed. Iḥsān ʿAbbās (Beirut: Dar al-Thaqāfa, 1979), 1: 14, quoted in Hanna Kassis, "Muslim Revival in Spain in the Fifth/Eleventh century," *Der Islam* 67 (1990), 83. For similar sentiments, see al-Wansharīsī, *al-Miʿyār al-muʿrib*, 2: 140 and Muḥammad b. ʿUmar Ibn al-Qūṭiyya, *Tārīkh iftitāḥ al-Andalus*, ed. Julián Ribera (Madrid: Revista de Archivos, 1926), 12.

27 The author's full name is Abū Zayd ʿAbd al-Raḥmān al-Ṣinhājī, usually known as Ibn Miqlāsh. On this jurist, see H. Buzineb, "Respuestas de jurisconsultos maghrebíes en torno a la inmigración de los musulmanes hispánicos," *Hesperis-Tamuda* 26–7 (1988), 62.

28 Biblioteca Nacional de Madrid, ms. 4950, 228 r, published in Hossain Buzineb, "Respuestas de jurisconsultos maghrebíes en torno a la inmigración de los musulmanes hispánicos," 63. On the issue of participation in Christian festivals, see Fernando de la Granja, "Fiestas cristianas en al-Andalus," 119 ff.

29 Aḥmad Bābā, *Nayl al-ibtihāj bi-taṭrīz al-dībāj* (Cairo: n.p., 1932), 282.

30 Biblioteca Nacional de Madrid, Ms. 5324 (fols. 47v–48v), published in Kathryn A. Miller, "Muslim Minorities and the Obligation to Emigrate to Islamic Territory: Two *Fatwās* from Fifteenth-Century Granada," *Islamic Law and Society* 7 (2000), 278.

31 His full name is Aḥmad b. Yaḥyā b. Muḥammad b. ʿAbd al-Wāḥid b. ʿAlī al-Wansharīsī. On his life, see Francisco Vidal Castro, "Aḥmad al-Wanšarīsī (m. 914/1508). Principales aspectos de su vida," *al-Qanṭara* 12 (1991), 315–52.

32 al-Wansharīsī, *al-Miʿyār al-muʿrib*, 2: 137–41.

contact with the impure (*najas*)[33] and eating forbidden food. This trend will first be seen among the weaker elements of society; the effect, however, will gradually spread to others, and eventually all Muslims in these lands will come to imitate Christians by speaking their language,[34] participating in their religious festivals, and wearing their clothes.[35] This cultural Christianization, he says, has already happened to the Mudéjars of Ávila[36] who have entirely lost their knowledge of the Arabic language, the loss of which has meant that their devotions (*mutaʿabbadāt*) have also died out.

The jurists also disliked the idea of Muslims living under Christian rule because they believed that doing so violated both their own personal honor and that of their religion.[37] Al-Wansharīsī, for example, says that living under Christian rule where Islam is denigrated can never be accepted by anyone

33 Z. Maghen, "Close Encounters: Some Preliminary Observations on the Transmission of Impurity in Early Sunnī Jurisprudence," *Islamic Law and Society* 6 (1999), 348–392; idem, "Strangers and Brothers: The Ritual Status of Unbelievers in Islamic Jurisprudence," *Medieval Encounters* 12 (2006), 173–223 and Janina Safran, "Rules of Purity and Confessional Boundaries: Mālikī Debates about the Pollution of the Christian," *History of Religions* 42 (2003), 204.

34 On the loss of the Arabic language, see Gerard Wiegers, "Language and Identity: Pluralism and the Use of Non-Arabic Languages in the Muslim West," in *Pluralism and Identity: Studies in Ritual Behaviour*, ed. Jan Platvoet et al. (Leiden: Brill, 1995), 303 ff. and John Boswell, *The Royal Treasure*, 381 ff. It is interesting to note that, elsewhere in his *al-Miʿyār al-muʿrib*, al-Wansharīsī cites a *fatwā* regarding whether prayers can be said in the Berber language. The answer of the anonymous jurist is that prayers may be said in any language because God knows every language, see al-Wansharīsī, *al-Miʿyār al-muʿrib*, 1: 186.

35 For other condemnations of Muslims who attend Christian festivals, wear Christian clothing or imitate Christians in other ways, see al-Wansharīsī, *al-Miʿyār al-muʿrib*, 11: 150–52; Abū al-Faḍl ʿIyād b. Mūsā al-Yaḥsubī, *Kitāb al-shifā bi-taʿrīf ḥuqūq al-Muṣṭafā*, ed. ʿAlī Muḥammad al-Bajāwī (Cairo: Maṭbaʿat ʿĪsā al-Bābī al-Ḥalabī, 1977), 2: 1072–73 and 1080, and L.P. Harvey, *Islamic Spain, 1250 to 1500*, 90. For an interesting parallel pertaining to the imitation of Jews, see al-Wansharīsī, *al-Miʿyār al-muʿrib*, 11: 111–12.

36 It has been suggested that the text refers not to Ávila but to Ayelo in Valencia, see P.S. van Koningsveld and G.A. Wiegers, "The Islamic Statute of the Mudéjars in the Light of a New Source," *al-Qanṭara* 17 (1996), 28. Scholarship on the Muslims in Valencia, however, has shown that they continued to extensively use Arabic in documents into the 15th and 16th centuries. See María del Carmen Barceló Torres, "Las cartas árabes de Vila-Real. (Revisión del panorama mudéjar valenciano)," *Estudios Castellonenses* 1 (1982), 367.

37 See, for example, Biblioteca Nacional de Madrid, ms. 4950, 228 r, published in Hossain Buzineb, "Respuestas de jurisconsultos maghrebíes en torno a la inmigración de los musulmanes hispánicos," 63.

who "possesses manliness (*muruwwa*)."[38] A man who is willing to live under Christian rule is one who takes no pride in protecting his family and those who depend upon him. He is one "who willingly throws himself, his wife and his children at their hands at the height of their power … while depending on them to fulfill their treaty." He is one who is not concerned to ensure the safety of "his daughter or pretty female relative" from the "enemy's vulgar dogs or foreign pigs coming across her."[39] The honor of Muslim women, al-Wansharīsī claims, is in constant danger when living in Christian society.[40]

Most *fatwā*s on the Mudéjars, however, deal not with the issue of the violation of personal honor, but with the issue of the violation of the honor due to Islam. For these jurists, Islam is the divinely decreed order. The order which Islam represents mandates that truth be elevated over falsehood and that belief be elevated over unbelief. Muḥammad b. Muḥammad Ibn al-Ḥājj (d. 737/1336)[41] summarized the matter by quoting the *ḥadīth*, "Islam is exalted and nothing is exalted above it."[42] For al-Wansharīsī, one of the primary ways in which Muslims honor this principle is through obedience to a Muslim ruler

38 al-Wansharīsī, *al-Miʿyār al-muʿrib*, 2:139–140. On this term, see Ignaz Goldziher, "Muruwwa and Dīn," in *Muslim Studies*, ed. S.M. Stern (London: George Allen & Unwin Ltd., 1967), 22.

39 al-Wansharīsī, *al-Miʿyār al-muʿrib*, 2:140–1. As an example, al-Wansharīsī makes reference to the daughter-in-law of al-Muʿtamid b. ʿAbbād (r. 462–84/1069–1091), the last ruler of the ʿAbbādid dynasty, who is reported to have become the mistress of King Alphonso VI of Castille and to have converted to Christianity. On this event, see E. Lévi-Provençal, "La 'mora Zaida', femme d'Alphonse VI de Castille et leur fils l'infant D. Sancho," *Hesperis* 18 (1934), 1–8.

40 There is no way of determining whether Muslim women were subject to greater risk of sexual assault in Christian-ruled territories, but there are Christian court records which document cases of assault on Muslim women by Christians, see Isabel A. O'Connor, "Muslim Mudéjar Women in Thirteenth-Century Spain: Dispelling the Stereotypes," *Journal of Muslim Minority Affairs* 27 (2007), 63–4. Documents also suggest that there were many Mudéjar prostitutes, see M. Meyerson, "Prostitution of Muslim Women in the Kingdom of Valencia: Religious and Sexual Discrimination in a Medieval Plural Society," in *The Medieval Mediterranean: Cross-Cultural Contacts*, ed. Marilyn J. Chiat and Kathryn L. Reyerson (St. Cloud: North Star Press of St. Cloud, 1988), 87–95 and F. Roca Traver, "Un siglo de vida mudéjar en la Valencia medieval (1238–1338)," *Estudios de Edad Media de la Corona de Aragón* 5 (1952), 161.

41 On this Egyptian Mālikī, Abū ʿAbdallāh Muḥammad b. Muḥammad ibn al-Ḥājj al-ʿAbdarī al-Fāsī, see Brockelmann, *Geschichte der arabischen Litteratur*, 2: 83 and Supplement 2: 95.

42 Muḥammad b. Muḥammad Ibn al-Ḥājj, *al-Madkhal* (Cairo: al-Maṭbaʿa al-Miṣriyya, 1929), 4: 53–54, quoting *Ṣaḥīḥ al-Bukhārī*, no. 1288: "al-Islām yaʿlū wa-lā yuʿlā." This *ḥadīth* is discussed in Yohanan Friedman, *Tolerance and Coercion in Islam: Interfaith Relations in the Muslim Tradition* (Cambridge: Cambridge University Press, 2003), 35 ff.

who ensures that society implements this idea. To instead give obedience to a Christian ruler is a dramatic inversion of the divine order. Even if a Christian ruler were to grant Muslim subjects the freedom to practice Islamic rituals, this would be insufficient as his rule over Muslims would still be in basic violation of this principle of religious hierarchy.[43]

The Works of al-Wansharīsī on the Mudéjars

Mālikī legal thought on living under non-Muslim rule was several hundred years in the making. In the Reconquista-era, the most extensive treatment of this issue occurred in the *fatwā*s of Aḥmad b. Yaḥyā al-Wansharīsī (d. 914/1508). Al-Wansharīsī was a very influential jurist, but it is impossible to determine the degree of influence of these particular *fatwā*s for a variety of reasons. First, he wrote them to respond to the situation of the Mudéjars whose era came to an end, and who therefore effectively ceased to exist, shortly after he wrote about them; for this reason the applicability of his *fatwā*s was sharply limited in time. It is possible that the *fatwā*s had an impact on the decision of Mudéjars regarding whether to migrate, but there is no documentary evidence to either support or refute this. His works on the Mudéjars are seldom referred to until the nineteenth century because, once the vast majority of Muslims had left the Iberian Peninsula, there was little need for jurists to deal with their anomalous legal situation. However, although the question of the influence of al-Wansharīsī's *fatwā*s on the Mudéjars cannot be resolved, they are an important example of the culmination of much legal reflection on this issue. Perhaps because they provide such a convenient overview of previous thought, they have been regarded by many scholars as the definitive Mālikī position on the matter.[44] I do not give them this pride of place, but since they contain the most extended discussion of the laws relating to the Mudéjars, I deal with them here and throughout the book in some detail and provide a full translation of al-Wansharīsī's major works on the subject in the appendix.

Al-Wansharīsī is now primarily known as the author of an influential anthology of Andalusī and Maghribī Mālikī *fatwā*s, entitled *al-Miʿyār al-muʿrib*

43 al-Wansharīsī, *al-Miʿyār al-muʿrib*, 2:137–38.

44 See, for example, Dominique Urvoy, *Le monde des ulémas andalous du V/XIe au VII/XIIIe siècle: étude sociologique* (Geneva: Droz, 1978), 138 and Jean-Pierre Molénat, "Le problème de la permanence des musulmans dans les territoires conquis par les chrétiens, du point de vue de la loi islamique," *Arabica* 48 (2001), 394.

wa'l-jāmiʿ al-mughrib, which I frequently draw upon.[45] He apparently began work on the anthology in 890/1485 after one of his students in Fez, Muḥammad Ibn al-Jardīs, gave him access to his enormous library which contained Andalusī and Maghribī legal manuscripts dating from the fourth/tenth century to their own time. He completed the anthology eleven years later in 901/1496, but continued to make revisions until his death in 914/1508. The anthology is carefully organized according to subject and includes his own occasional glosses and *fatwās*. Al-Wansharīsī describes his purpose in compiling the anthology thus:

> This is a book that I have entitled *The Clear Measure and the Extraordinary Collection of the Judicial Opinions of the Scholars of Ifrīqiya, al-Andalus, and the Maghrib*. In it, I have assembled *fatwās* [issued by] modern and ancient [scholars], including those which are the most difficult to find in their sources and to extract from their hiding places on account of their being scattered and dispersed and because their locations and the access to them are obscure. [I have assembled the book] in the hope that [it] will be of general utility ... I have organized it in accordance with the categories of the law in order to facilitate its use by whoever examines it, and I have specified the names of the *muftīs*—except on rare occasions.[46]

As al-Wansharīsī's remarks imply, the size and scope of the anthology is very great. Its modern edition spans twelve volumes and contains thousands of legal opinions. The anthology became influential as the definitive reference work of legal precedent among Mālikī jurists, and it continues to be frequently referred to in contemporary discussions.[47]

The *fatwās* by al-Wansharīsī on the Mudéjars are contained in the section of the work which deals with the laws of *jihād*. In addition to questions arising from the activity of *jihād* itself, this section also contains *fatwās* dealing with its aftermath, that is, on the laws of how Christians and Jews are to be treated once they have been conquered and have become subject peoples (*dhimmīyūn*).

---

45 On this work, see Francisco Vidal Castro, "El Miʿyâr de al-Wanšarîsî (m. 914/1508). I: fuentes, manuscritos, ediciones, traducciones," *Miscelánea de estudios árabes y hebraicos* 42–3 (1993–94), 317–62 and idem, "El Miʿyâr de al-Wanšarîsî (m. 914/1508) II: contenido," *Miscelánea de estudios árabes y hebraicos*, 44 (1995), 213–46. For an attempt to partially index the work, see Vincent Lagardère, *Histoire et société en occident musulman au moyen âge: analyse du Miʿyār d'al-Wanšarisī* (Madrid: Casa de Velázquez, 1995).

46 al-Wansharīsī, *al-Miʿyār al-muʿrib*, 1: 1, quoted in David S. Powers, *Law, Society, and Culture in the Maghrib, 1300–1500* (Cambridge: Cambridge University Press, 2002), 6.

47 On the influence of al-Wansharīsī, see Jacques Berque, "Ville et université, aperçu sur l'histoire de l'école de Fès," *Revue historique de droit française et étranger* 26 (1949), 89–90.

It was thus natural for al-Wansharīsī to include a subsection on the reverse situation, which he sometimes refers to as that of the "Muslim *dhimmīyūn*,"[48] those Muslims who were conquered by non-Muslims and continued to live in their territory as subject peoples.

Al-Wansharīsī's two *fatwās* on the Mudéjars are both responses to requests for *fatwās* from a single jurist, Abū ʿAbdallāh Ibn Quṭiyya, about whom nothing is known.[49] Al-Wansharīsī is aware that, in writing legal opinions dealing with the question of living under non-Muslim rule, he is filling a gap in the legal literature. He notes that the omission of this discussion is not to be regarded as evidence that the early jurists condoned the practice. Rather, he says that these jurists did not comment on the matter because it was not relevant during their lifetime. Muslim communities only came to live under non-Muslim rule several centuries later when the Christians captured Sicily and parts of the Iberian Peninsula in the fifth century after the *Hijra*.[50]

Al-Wansharīsī's longer *fatwā* on the legal ramifications of non-Muslim rule, written during the late Mudéjar period,[51] is entitled *Asnā al-matājir fī bayān aḥkām man ghalaba ʿalā waṭanihi al-Naṣārā wa-lam yuhājir wa-mā yatarratabu ʿalayhi min al-ʿuqūbāt waʾl-zawājir*.[52] This translates as "the most exalted of all transactions: a clarification of the laws pertaining to one whose land has been

48 al-Wansharīsī, *al-Miʿyār al-muʿrib*, 2: 137.

49 The precise vocalization of his name is also uncertain and the above vocalization is merely a conjecture.

50 Ibid., 2: 125. Here, al-Wansharīsī seems to be following the view of the Granadan judge, Muḥammad b. Muḥammad Ibn ʿĀṣim (d. 829/1426).

51 The date on which the *fatwā* was completed is given in the printed edition as Sunday, 19 Dhū al-Qaʿda 896 (approximately September 23, 1491). Van Koningsveld and Wiegers suggest that this date might be incorrect as the day of the week does not correctly correspond to the date—the 19th is a Friday, not a Sunday. This in itself would not be enough to reject the date recorded in the printed editions as such two-day discrepancies can occur in dating systems which depend on local sightings of the moon. Van Koningsveld and Wiegers do, however, cite the catalog of Michael Casiri who lists a version of this manuscript as having been composed in 898 (1493). This year has the advantage that 19 Dhū al-Qaʿda occurs on a Sunday. There is no satisfactory way of arbitrating between these two datings. Either date, however, firmly establishes the text as having been written during the late Mudéjar period. See van Koningsveld and Wiegers, "The Islamic Statute of the Mudéjars in the Light of a New Source," 53 and Michael Casiri, *Bibliotheca arabico-hispaña escurialensis* (Madrid: Antonius Perez de Soto, 1760–70), 2: 170, no. 1753.2.

52 This *fatwā* is contained in al-Wansharīsī, *al-Miʿyār al-muʿrib*, 2: 119–36. For the first Western attempt at an edition of the work, albeit one which contained only the question posed to al-Wansharīsī, see Marcus Joseph Müller, *Beiträge zur Geschichte der westlichen Araber* (Munich: G. Franz, 1866), 1: 42–44.

conquered by the Christians and has not migrated[53] and what punishments and restrictions apply to him." The word, *matājir* (sing. *matjar*), is difficult to translate. A. de Biberstein Kazimirski translates the word as, "1. Marchandise 2. Trafic, commerce."[54] I have opted for "transactions" as it conveys the word's dual connotations of commerce and exchange. The "most exalted of all transactions" is presumably that which is made by Muslims who exchange a life of physical comfort in Christian territory for a life of poverty as migrants in Muslim territory.[55] The *Asnā al-matājir* is the longer of al-Wansharīsī's two *fatwā*s on the Mudéjars and is the one to which subsequent jurists most extensively refer. Al-Wansharīsī intended it to deal comprehensively with the issue of living under Christian rule and ended the *fatwā* with the hope that it would be the last work which would have to be written on the subject.[56]

In the *Asnā al-matājir*, the petitioner, Ibn Quṭiyya, describes the situation of some Muslims who migrated to the Maghrib from Christian Iberia with the most noble of intentions. Out of "obedience to God and His Messenger," he says, they and their families abandoned their homes and much of their wealth in order to settle in the abode of Islam. However, once there, they regretted their decision as they found their new living circumstances to be very harsh. They experienced difficulty in obtaining a livelihood and regarded the inhabitants of the Maghrib as inhospitable.[57] Their complaints, Ibn Quṭiyya notes, did not merely reflect a materialistic mourning for the loss of the physical comforts of their former homes; rather, they involved a criticism of both Islam and of Islamdom. Their words, he says, indicate "their weakness of faith and their

53 Since the Arabic verb *h.j.r.* can mean either immigration or emigration, I have chosen to translate it as migration in order to avoid translating a single word in two different ways.

54 See *Dictionnaire Arabe-Français* (Paris: Maisonneuve et cie, 1860), 1: 246.

55 This is reflected in al-Wansharīsī's statement about preferring worldly goods to migration, see al-Wansharīsī, *al-Miʿyār al-muʿrib*, 2: 131. Something akin to this notion is also expressed in the Qur'ān, see, for example, 3: 177: "Those who buy unbelief at the price of faith will not hurt God in anything. They will have a painful punishment." All translations from the Qur'ān are taken, sometimes with modification, from *The Qur'ān*, tr. Alan Jones (Cambridge: Gibb Memorial Trust, 2007).

56 Van Koningsveld and Wiegers have suggested that much al-Wansharīsī's argument is taken largely from the work of Muḥammad b. Yaḥyā Ibn Rabīʿ, a thirteenth-century Malagan author whom al-Wansharīsī does not acknowledge as a source. I have not been able to access the manuscript which van Koningsveld and Wiegers describe as: "A set of photocopies in our possession of parts of a privately owned Arabic manuscript in a village in the surroundings of the Moroccan City of Tetuan." See van Koningsveld and Wiegers, "The Islamic Statute of the Mudéjars in the Light of a New Source," 20.

57 al-Wansharīsī, *al-Miʿyār al-muʿrib*, 2: 119.

lack of conviction in their beliefs." They publicly disparage the abode of Islam and praise the abode of war. Because of their reported love of the abode of war, one of them is reported to have provocatively asserted that the direction of the true *hijra* (religiously mandated migration) is not from the abode of war to the abode of Islam, but vice versa. Another is reported to have said that if the Christian ruler of Castille were to visit the Maghrib, they would ask him to take them back with him. The more cunning among them, he says, seek to find a legal ruse (*ḥīla*) which would allow them to return to Christian lands, although he does not mention what exactly this ruse involves. What, Ibn Quṭiyya asks, is to be done about these people, and how is one to respond to their claims?[58]

Al-Wansharīsī's shorter *fatwā* on the Mudéjars is untitled and undated. Since it deals with the Mudéjars of Marbella, I will henceforth refer to it as the Marbella *fatwā*. Its *terminus post quem* is 890/1485, the year in which Marbella fell to the Christians. Because it does not refer to the *Asnā al-matājir*, it is likely that it was written before it.[59] The Marbella *fatwā* involves the case of a man, known for his virtue and piety (*dīn*), who had been unsuccessfully looking for his brother who had gone missing while fighting against the Christians in Iberia. Once he had given up hope of finding him, the man wished to return to Muslim lands, but found another reason which prevented him from leaving. In the course of his travels, he had come across a Muslim community in the town of Marbella which continued to dwell there under Christian rule. This community, Ibn Quṭiyya says, is in dire need of this man's skills and leadership in order to survive because he had become a "spokesman (*lisān*) and helper for the Muslim *dhimmīyūn*," not just for those Muslims in Marbella, but for Muslims all over western Iberia. He advocates on their behalf before the Christian rulers regarding whatever hardships fate deals them (*nawāʾib al-dahr*) and saves them from many calamities. Most of the Muslims in this region, Ibn Quṭiyya says, are quite unable to deal with the Christians by themselves and would be

58 Ibid., 2: 119–20. Other sources indicate similar disatisfaction among Andalusian migrants to the Maghrib. See, for example, Shihāb al-Dīn Aḥmad b. Muḥammad al-Maqqarī al-Tilimsānī, *Azhār al-riyāḍ fī akhbār ʿIyāḍ*, ed. Musṭafā al-Saqqā et al. (Cairo: Maṭbaʿat lajnat al-taʾlīf waʾl-tarjama waʾl-nashr, 1939), 1: 68 and *Kitāb nubdhat al-ʿaṣr fī akhbār mulūk Banī Naṣr aw taslīm Gharnāṭa wa-nuzūl al-Andalusiyyīn ilā al-Maghrib*, in A. Bustani and C. Quirós, *Fragmentos de la época sobre noticias de los reyes nazaritas o capitulaciones de Granada y emigración de los andaluces a Marruecos* (Larache: Artes Gráficas Boscá, 1940), 44 and 56, referred to in van Koningsveld and Wiegers, "The Islamic Statute of the Mudéjars," 54.

59 The editor of the *al-Miʿyār al-muʿrib*, Muḥammad Hajjī, states that this *fatwā* was written after the fall of Granada. He does not, however, give a reason for this, see al-Wansharīsī, *al-Miʿyār al-muʿrib*, 2: 137.

helpless without him. If this man were to migrate, the Muslims of Marbella would not be able to find anyone to replace him and would suffer great harm. Given this state of affairs, he asks, is he permitted to stay in Christian territory even though such a course of action would not usually be permitted?[60]

Al-Wansharīsī appends the Marbella *fatwā* to the *Asnā al-matājir* in his anthology because it fulfills a slightly different rhetorical function. Whereas the *Asnā al-matājir* deals with those Muslims whose wish to return to Christian Iberia is motivated by impiety, the Marbella *fatwā* deals with an individual who is known to be of good character, but who wishes to stay in Christian Iberia because, by doing so, he believes that he is actually fulfilling his religious obligations as a Muslim. Whereas the claims of those who wish to return to the abode of war in the *Asnā al-matājir* are easy to dismiss as they are immediately discredited by the obviously impious character of those who advocate them, the virtuous man of the Marbella *fatwā* presents a more difficult challenge.

Although the arguments which al-Wansharīsī gives differ slightly between the two *fatwās*, his ultimate position remains the same. Regardless of the intentions of those who live in Christian territory, he says that there is an absolute prohibition on remaining there and a corresponding obligation to leave. He succinctly and unequivocally states his position thus:

> Dwelling among the unbelievers,[61] other than those who are protected and humbled peoples (*ahl al-dhimma wa'l-ṣaghār*), is not permitted and is not allowed for so much as an hour of a day. This is because of the filth (*adnās*), dirt (*awḍār*), and religious and worldly corruption which is ever-present [among them].[62]

Al-Wansharīsī therefore recommends the same course of action to the man of Marbella that he recommends in the *Asnā al-matājir*. Given the sinful nature of non-Muslim lands, he adds that there is no excuse which would allow a Muslim to live there:

---

60 Ibid., 2:137.

61 It is important to realize that when al-Wansharīsī uses the terms unbelievers and unbelief (*kufr*) in these *fatwās*, he is referring to Christians and Christianity. For the purpose of determining a Muslim's obligation to make *hijra*, no distinction between pagan and Christian lands is made. Christian lands are lands of unbelief for they are lands "in which the trinity is worshiped, bells are rung, Satan is venerated and the Merciful One is blasphemed against," see al-Wansharīsī, *al-Miʿyār al-muʿrib*, 2:131.

62 Ibid., 2:138.

> There can be no concession of any kind ... which would allow for a return [to the abode of unbelief] or for the abandonment of migration (*hijra*). [A person] cannot in any way be excused from this whether by claiming the presence of an oppressive difficulty or by making use of a delicate ruse (*ḥīla*). Rather, he must discover any means he can to release himself from the unbelievers' noose. [Even] under circumstances in which he cannot find a tribe to defend him and patrons to shelter him, and is [therefore] content to reside in a place in which religion is harmed and in which the public affirmations of Islamic norms are prohibited (*iẓhār shaʿāʾir al-muslimīn*), he [is considered to have] abandoned the religion (*māriq min al-dīn*) and set out upon the path of the apostates (*al-mulḥidīn*).[63]

Thus al-Wansharīsī clearly and unequivocally states the unacceptability of remaining under non-Muslim rule. To do so, he says, is to commit one of the greatest sins and is tantamount to affirming unbelief.[64] He adds that all Islamic rituals, including prayer and fasting on Ramaḍān, have no meaning when practiced in the abode of war.[65] His answer to the question of the man in Marbella differs only in its tone. Whereas the *Asnā al-matājir* is directed towards justifying severe punishments for those who choose to live in Christian territory or declare their wish to return there, the Marbella *fatwā* instead focuses upon the harm to Islam caused intentionally or unintentionally by those who live there. The Marbella *fatwā* thus reads more as a plea to the man himself to leave such territory than as a plea to other Muslims to force him to do so.

---

63 Ibid., 2: 124.

64 Interestingly, elsewhere in *al-Miʿyār al-muʿrib*, without making any adverse comment, al-Wansharīsī includes a fragment of an anti-Christian polemic by one such Mudéjar, Abū ʿAlī al-Ḥusayn Ibn Rashīq (d. 696/1297), who remained in the town of Mursiya (Murcia) with his father to assist Muslims with writing contracts and other legal matters, see al-Wansharīsī, *al-Miʿyār al-muʿrib*, 11: 155–8. On this polemic, see Hanna E. Kassis, "A 13th-Century Polemical Debate between Ibn Rashīq of Mursiyah and a Priest from Marrākush," *The Maghreb Review* 29 (2004), 8–21.

65 al-Wansharīsī, *al-Miʿyār al-muʿrib*, 2: 138–39. This view appears to be at variance with the majority Mālikī opinion that Islamic law applies in the abode of war, see David de Santillana, *Istituzioni di diritto musulmano malichita* (Rome: Istituto per l'Oriente, 1925), 1: 70 ff. and ʿUbaydallāh b. al-Ḥusayn Ibn al-Jallāb (d. 378/988), *al-Tafrīʿ*, ed. Ḥusayn b. Sālim al-Dahmānī (Beirut: Dār al-Gharb al-Islāmī, 1987), 1: 357–58.

Modern Analyses of the Mālikī Position on the Mudéjars

Although the issue of how Islamic law dealt with the Mudéjars has been frequently referred to by scholars, the discussion has seldom extended much beyond al-Wansharīsī's writings. Further, even the treatment of al-Wansharīsī's writings has rarely included much more than a cursory summary of their contents. Little attempt has been made to place these *fatwās* in the larger context of Mālikī legal thought, or even in the context of other relevant *fatwās* contained in al-Wansharīsī's *al-Miʿyār al-muʿrib*. This has often led to reductionist analyses which speculate on al-Wansharīsī's psychological motivations and, by extension, those of his contemporaries, rather than offering a thorough examination of his legal arguments and their historical context. The result has been a number of radically different interpretations of al-Wansharīsī's *fatwās*, sometimes accompanied by an unfavorable judgment of his moral character. Some scholars regard al-Wansharīsī's *fatwās* as an accurate reflection of Mālikī law, but see this position as morally reprehensible or lacking in human kindness. Ḥusayn Mu'nis, the author of the first critical edition of al-Wansharīsī's *fatwās* on the Mudéjars, says that they are a testament to the tragic state of intellectual decay which prevailed in the Islamic law of his day. The jurists of this era, he says, were entirely unwilling to engage in independent judical thought (*ijtihād*). He describes this era as being affected by a general malaise which meant that no one was capable of producing anything other than an unthinking reiteration of the works of their legal predecessors. He concludes his indictment of al-Wansharīsī by remarking on his extreme lack of empathy and compassion for the Iberian Muslims whom he says deserved greater sympathy.[66] Many scholars followed Mu'nis's lead. E. Molina López makes similar points when he accuses al-Wansharīsī of a rigid adherence to a legal formalism which makes him unsympathetic to the plight of the Mudéjars.[67] After making comparable remarks, F. Maíllo Salgado adds that jurists like al-Wansharīsī bear joint responsibility with the Christians for the exodus of Muslims from the Iberian Peninsula during the Reconquista.[68] More recently,

---

66 al-Wansharīsī and Ḥusayn Mu'nis (ed.), "Asnā al-matājir fī bayān aḥkām man ghalaba ʿalā waṭanihi al-Naṣārā wa-lam yuhājir wa-mā yatarattabu ʿalayhi min al-ʿuqūbāt wa'l-zawājir," *Revista del Instituto de Estudios Islámicos en Madrid* 5 (1957), 5 ff.

67 E. Molina López, "Algunas consideraciones sobre los emigrados andalusíes," *Homenaje al Prof. Darío Cabanelas* (Granada: University of Granada, 1987), 1: 425–6. This author also criticizes al-Wansharīsī for what he believes is poor Qur'ānic interpretation.

68 F. Maíllo Salgado, "Consideraciones acerca de una *fatwā* de al-Wanšarīsī," *Studia Historica* 3 (1985), 185.

the most articulate advocate of this view, Alejandro García Sanjuán, has made the case thus:

> Al-Wansharīsī completely disregards the historical environment in which Marbella's Muslims lived, formulating his legal ruling in a very strict tone based on the application of the precepts of the *Sharīʿa*. The jurist detaches himself from reality and issues his *fatwā* basing his judgment merely on the implementation of Islamic law and not on the specific circumstances of the period, hence its dogmatic undertones.[69]

Thus, according to these scholars, al-Wansharīsī lacked the emotional ability to step beyond the confines of the Mālikī legal system and give a ruling appropriate to the situation at hand. They believe that al-Wansharīsī's *fatwā*s reflect his belief that Islamic law is a rigid and unchanging entity which is unable to adapt to social circumstances or respond to human suffering.

Other scholars interpret al-Wansharīsī's *fatwā*s in a way opposite to the one outlined above—that is, they claim that they are harsh as a result of too much emotion and too little consideration of the legal tradition. Leonard Harvey accuses al-Wansharīsī of making a faulty legal analogy on the basis of Qur'anic passages. While it is true, Harvey says, that Muḥammad left the persecution of pagan Mecca for refuge in Medina, he argues that al-Wansharīsī is incorrect in understanding these passages as "relevant to the exile of Muslims who might think of leaving Christian Spain."[70] Another scholar, Farhat Dachraoui, speaks of the "caractère arbitraire de son jugement sur les émigrés au Maghreb," and describes al-Wansharīsī's legal reasoning as a "mauvais argument sans doute."[71] While he acknowledges that al-Wansharīsī's opinion is not without some legal precedent, he says that it is more the product of his great anger at the loss of Muslim Spain.[72] Similarly, Khaled Abou El Fadl sees al-Wansharīsī's position as being based less on previous legal thought than on "social and political considerations." He blames the harshness of al-Wansharīsī's *fatwā*s on "the

69 Alejandro García Sanjuán, *Till God Inherits the Earth: Islamic Pious Endowments in al-Andalus (9–15th Centuries)* (Leiden: Brill, 2007), 29. Cf. Idem, "Del Dar al-Islam al Dar al-Harb: la cuestion Mudéjar y la legalidad Islamica," in *Congreso conmemorativo del 750 aniversario de la Toma de Carmona* (Carmona: Diputacion de Sevilla, 1998), 177–188.

70 L.P. Harvey, *Islamic Spain, 1250 to 1500*, 60.

71 Farhat Dachraoui, "Intégration ou exclusion des minorités religieuses. La conception islamique traditionnelle", in *L'expulsió dels moriscos: conseqüències en el món islàmic i el món cristià* (Barcelona: Generalitat de Catalunya, Departament de Cultura, 1994), 200.

72 Ibid., 202.

intensity of the competition between Christians and Muslims and the deep sense of humiliation that al-Wansharīsī feels" which, he says, "is evident in his emotional language."[73] He excuses Mālikī jurists like al-Wansharīsī for their "uncompromising position" by arguing that it must be viewed "in the light of the humiliating defeats suffered in Andalus, Sicily, and Crete."[74] As Abou El Fadl sees it, were it not for the psychological pressure of Christian persecution, jurists like al-Wansharīsī would have arrived at rulings based on a level-headed analysis of Mālikī legal sources which would have been more permissive of Muslims living under Christian rule. He does not, however, specify to which Mālikī legal sources he refers.

Still other scholars have attempted to defend al-Wansharīsī by adopting interpretations which soften his message. Aboobaker Asmal, without explaining the reasons for his interpretation, suggests that al-Wansharīsī's main animus is directed not against those Muslims who live in Christian territory, but against those who openly declare their intention to move there. A blind eye could be turned to the former, but the latter have to be punished by the ruler.[75] Read thus, al-Wansharīsī is seen to have taken a relatively benign view of the Mudéjars. More recently, Kathryn Miller, at one point in her work, takes a similar position: "[Al-Wansharīsī's] prime target was not Mudéjars in Spain but emigrant Mudéjars to North Africa who regretted their emigration and so deserved 'God's condemnation and anger.' " The former, in her interpretation, were much less culpable than the latter and were therefore worthy of "the mercy of God and His generous forgiveness." On the basis of this analysis, she then asks, "Should al-Wansharīsī then be considered truly a rigorist?",[76] a term which she defines as a jurist who argues that "Mudéjars should not be permitted to live in Christian Spain."[77] Elsewhere in her book, however, Miller seems to reject this conclusion and says that al-Wansharīsī does indeed belong

73 Khaled Abou El Fadl, "Islamic Law and Muslim Minorities," 155.

74 Idem, "Striking a Balance: Islamic Legal Discourses on Muslim Minorities," in *Muslims on the Americanization Path?*, ed. Yvonne Yazbeck Haddad and John L. Esposito (Atlanta: Scholars Press, 1998), 51. Cf. Abraham L. Udovitch, "Muslims and Jews in the World of Frederic II: Boundaries and Communication," *Princeton Papers in Near Eastern Studies* 2 (1993), 83–4.

75 Aboobaker M. Asmal, "Muslims under Non-Muslim Rule: The *Fiqhi* (Legal) Views of Ibn Nujaym and al-Wansharisi" (Ph.D. dissertation, University of Manchester, 1998), 213, referred to in Lawrence Rosen, *The Justice of Islam* (Oxford: Oxford University Press, 2000), 196–7.

76 Kathryn A. Miller, *Guardians of Islam: Religious Authority and Muslim Communities of Late Medieval Spain* (New York: Columbia University Press, 2008), 193.

77 Ibid., 23.

to the “rigorist” camp.[78] Thus, according to Asmal, and one view of Miller’s, al-Wansharīsī tolerated those Muslims who wished to live under Christian rule and his views are therefore not to be viewed as harsh or unsympathetic. In my opinion, the flaw in this kind of analysis is that, although one of al-Wansharīsī’s *fatwās* is indeed directed at Muslims who regret their migration to the abode of Islam, as I will explain, he makes it abundantly clear that his remarks apply with equal force to Muslims who live in the abode of war. This point is further developed in other *fatwās* by al-Wansharīsī which are specifically directed towards Muslims who live in the abode of war.[79]

Like Asmal and Miller, Jocelyn Hendrickson does not see al-Wansharīsī as a “rigorist,” but reasons her position on different grounds. She says that al-Wansharīsī’s opinion is “not necessarily any more strict or rigorist than the opinions of al-Māzarī, al-ʿAbdūsī, or al-Wahrānī, the three jurists whose opinions are held most often to be more lenient or pragmatist than those of al-Wansharīsī.”[80] She further argues that al-Wansharīsī did not intend “to encourage Mudéjars to emigrate or to condemn those among them who could not or would not do so.” She says that to suggest that his *fatwās* are primarily concerned with an Andalusī context betrays a biased belief in the “exceptionalism of the Iberian Muslim predicament.”[81] She instead argues that al-Wansharīsī’s works were primarily intended to address local, Maghribī, concerns among which she thinks the foremost are Portuguese incursions on the Maghribī coast. It is difficult to accept this analysis. The questions which prompted al-Wansharīsī’s responses refer specifically to the situation of Andalusī Muslims. Al-Wansharīsī would no doubt have been well aware of

---

78 Ibid., 28.

79 al-Wansharīsī, *al-Miʿyār al-muʿrib*, 2: 137–41 and al-Wazzānī, *al-Miʿyār al-jadīd*, 3: 28–31. The latter *fatwā*, which does not appear in al-Wansharīsī’s *al-Miʿyār al-muʿrib*, was first noticed by al-Yūbī, see Laḥsan al-Yūbī, *al-Fatāwā al-fiqhiyya fī ahamm al-qaḍāyā min ʿahd al-Saʿdiyyīn ilā mā qabla al-ḥimāya: Dirāsa wa-taḥlīl* (Rabat: al-Mamlaka al-Maghribiyya, Wizārat al-Awqāf wa’l-Shu’ūn al-Islāmiyya, 1998), 206–207.

80 Jocelyn Hendrickson, “The Islamic Obligation to Emigrate” (Ph.D. Dissertation: Emory University, 2009), 100. At times, Hendrickson seems to vacillate. For example, she writes: “It is often contended in the literature that al-Wansharīsī’s *fatwās* were stricter than previous rulings, but if so—and the extent to which this is true is debatable—and if one or both of these fatwas actually circulated in the Iberian Christian kingdoms, it would have been only this degree of strictness which set al-Wansharisi’s opinions apart and which would have to account for any special impact of his writings on Iberian Muslims’ decisions.”

81 Hendrickson, “Muslim Legal Responses to Portuguese Occupation in Late Fifteenth-Century North Africa,” *Journal of Spanish Cultural Studies* 12 (2011), 321.

the Portuguese occupation of parts of the Maghribī coast and would have also been aware that they were very different in form from Christian conquests in the Iberian Peninsula.[82] Since the small and highly-fortified garrisons in which the Portuguese sequestered themselves were seldom in a position to exact more from the surrounding Muslim population than tribute, it was an open question whether the lives of these Muslims fell in the same legal category as those of the Mudéjars who were subject to much greater Christian governance. It is therefore possible that al-Wansharīsī did not view the Portuguese occupation as presenting the same legal predicament as the conquest of Iberia. The main difficulty with Hendrickson's argument, however, is that of why, if al-Wansharīsī's main intention had been to address the situation of the Portuguese occupation, he would have excluded all mention of it from these *fatāwā*. Surely, writing from Waṭṭāsid Fez which was openly at war with the Portuguese, he would have had no incentive to esoterically disguise his censure of those who lived under their rule as a response to a strictly Andalusī affair. It therefore seems more logical to view his *fatāwā* as being fundamentally about what he says that they are about, that is, Iberian Muslims.[83]

82 The difference is well-illustrated by looking at the fortified settlements which the Portuguese built in order to shelter themselves from the local inhabitants—a strategy unparalleled in Iberia. On this, see Martin M. Elbl, "Portuguese Urban Fortifications in Morocco: Borrowing, Adaptation, and Innovation along a Military Frontier," in *City Walls: The Urban Enceinte in Global Perspective*, ed. J. Tracy (Cambridge: Cambridge University Press, 2000), 349–85.

83 There is an additional difficulty in Hendrickson's article, "Muslim Legal Responses to Portuguese Occupation." Ibn Barṭāl, whom she describes as a contemporary of al-Wansharīsī and the Portuguese incursions, lived well before both al-Wansharīsī and the Portuguese incursions. This is evident in Ibn Barṭāl's hope for the victory over the Christians of the Marīnid ruler, likely Abū al-Ḥasan 'Ali b. 'Uthmān II (r. 731–749/1331–1348), who made several raids against the Christians in Iberia until his forces were repelled in the early 1340s. The reference dates the *fatwā* to a period before the 15th-century Portuguese incursions in the Maghrib. The hope for the return of the town of Arzila (Aṣīla) to the Muslims which occurs in the *fatwā* is clearly the addition of a later copyist as neither the question nor the answer contain any reference to Christian rule in the area ('Abd al-'Azīz b. al-Ḥasan al-Zayyātī, *al-Jawāhir al-mukhtāra*. Bibliothèque Nationale du Royaume du Maroc, ms. 1698, 2: 44). The identity of this 8th/14th-century "Ibn Barṭāl" cannot be determined with certainty, but van Koningsveld and Wiegers have very plausibly identified him as Abū 'Abdallāh Muḥammad b. 'Alī b. Muḥammad Ibn Barṭāl. The latter is an 8th/14th century jurist who shared students with Ibn Rabī' (d. 719/1320), another jurist who wrote on the status of the Mudéjars. See van Koningsveld and Wiegers, "The Islamic Statute of the Mudéjars," 38. My thanks to Jessica Marglin for obtaining a copy of the above manuscript for me.

Some scholars have considered al-Wansharīsī's views so problematic that they attempt to exclude them from their analyses. Muhammad Khalid Masud, for example, excludes al-Wansharīsī's view from his article devoted to "the obligation to migrate" (*hijra*). Masud's exclusion of al-Wansharīsī is not an oversight. He is well aware of the *Asnā al-matājir* which he uses as a source from which to quote the views of other Mālikī jurists. On the basis of an incomplete analysis and an unusual reading of some of the sources that al-Wansharīsī quotes, he concludes that most Mālikīs believed that the obligation of *hijra* had been abrogated in its entirety after the conquest of Mecca.[84] He then claims that the concept was only revived in the eighteenth and nineteenth centuries by religious modernists in the Maghrib and the Sudan.[85]

A partial explanation for the radically different interpretations of al-Wansharīsī's *fatwās* among modern scholars is their discomfort with his message that Muslims are not permitted to live in Christian territory. I have come across only one scholar who gives unambiguous support to al-Wansharīsī's position. Francisco Vidal Castro writes that al-Wansharīsī did what he thought was necessary in order to protect his "Islamic" and "Arabic" culture from aggressive foreign incursions. Al-Wansharīsī's position, he says, should be fully understandable to anyone living in the present age of "nationalism" and "individualism."[86]

How then are al-Wansharīsī's *fatwās* to be interpreted? Peter Pormann, who notes their vastly differing interpretations, puts the problem thus: "War al-Wanšarīsī ein Hardliner ohne Herz und Verstand, ein grausamer Kasuistiker ohne jede Milde und Barmherzigkeit? Oder tat al-Wanšarīsī recht daran, die Muslime dazu aufzurufen, ihre Religion und Kultur zu bewahren?" Pormann does not take a position on the issue, merely noting that "es ist schwierig zu

84 Muhammad Khalid Masud, "The Obligation to Migrate: The Doctrine of *Hijra* in Islamic Law," in *Muslim Travellers: Pilgrimage, Migration, and the Religious Imagination*, ed. Dale F. Eickelman and James Piscatori (London: Routledge, 1990), 37.

85 Ibid., 46. One can only speculate regarding Masud's reasons for excluding al-Wansharīsī. It is possible that Masud's exclusion of al-Wansharīsī and his denial of a Mālikī tradition advocating *hijra* is caused by his alarm at the divisive potential of modern attempts to implement *hijra* and his reluctance to provide religious justification to outlawed groups, some of which he mentions in his article. For a modern example of one such group's use of al-Wansharīsī's *Asnā al-Matājir* in particular, see Aymān al-Ẓawāhirī, *Risāla fī tabri'at ummat al-qalam wa'l-ṣayf min manqaṣat tuhmat al-khawar wa'l-ḍuʿf* (n.p.: al-Saḥāb li'l-Intāj al-Iʿlāmī, n.d.), 146–48.

86 F. Vidal Castro, "Las obras de Aḥmad al-Wanšarīsī (m. 914/1508)," *Inventario analítico* 3 (1992), 81.

entscheiden."[87] I take Pormann's point one step further in that I believe that speculation regarding al-Wansharīsī's emotional state is not a productive area of research. Interesting though it might be to understand al-Wansharīsī's psychology, his writings on the subject of the Mudéjars are too brief to provide any firm insight into the matter. As we have seen from the secondary scholarship analyzed above, four main interpretations of his psychology are possible: (1) al-Wansharīsī had no sympathy for the human suffering of the Mudéjars; (2) his anger at the Christians overpowered his judgment; (3) he adopted an entirely rational approach in order to protect his culture from destruction; or (4) his obsession with Islamic law rendered him unable to countenance giving an opinion which did not conform exactly to a strict interpretation of its dictates. On the basis of al-Wansharīsī's few legal writings on the subject, there does not seem to be a reasonable way to arbitrate between these different explanations of his motivation. On the other hand, considerable insight can be gained by attempting to understand the nature of his legal argument and its relationship to the legal tradition in which he writes. As I have indicated, this is not an approach which has yet been pursued in any depth by scholars. This is because research into Mālikī legal literature is comparatively young and there are still many uncertainties regarding how the source material should be approached and interpreted.

My approach to understanding the legal position of the jurists regarding the Mudéjars is different from previous approaches not simply because it looks at a greater breadth of sources, but because it looks at a variety of genres of legal texts rather than *fatwā*s alone.[88] In addition, I occasionally extend my analysis beyond the realm of legal texts in order to place the law in the general context of the intellectual currents of the region. My claim is that by taking this wider view, one can better delineate the relationship between legal texts and

---

87 Peter E. Pormann, "Das Fatwa Die Herrlichsten Waren (*Asnā l-matāǧir*) des al-Wanšarīsī," *Der Islam* 80 (2003), 323 and 328.

88 Little has been written on the relationship between the various genres of Mālikī legal texts. For a preliminary examination of the subject, see María Arcas Campoy, "Algunas consideraciones sobre los tratados de jurisprudencia malikí de al-Andalus," *Miscelánea de Estudios Árabes y Hebraicos* 37 (1988), 13–21 and idem, "Valoración actual de la literatura jurídica de al-Andalus," in *Actas del II coloquio hispano-marroquí de ciencias históricas* (Madrid: Agencia Española de Cooperación Internacional, 1992), 31–49. On the genre of the *fatwā* in its Mālikī context, see Francisco Vidal Castro, "El muftí y la fetua en el derecho islámico. Notas para un estudio institucional," *Al-Andalus-Magreb* 6 (1998), 289–322 and David Powers, "Legal Consultation (*Futyā*) in Medieval Spain and North Africa," in *Islam and Public law*, ed. Chibli Mallat (London: Graham and Trotman, 1993), 105–6.

social reality, and better understand in what ways Islamic law developed in the course of responding to the crisis posed by the Reconquista.

The chapters of this book are organized by topic. Chapter One addresses the question of whether or not Mālikī law permits or prohibits Muslims from living under the rule of non-Muslims. In wrestling with this question, the jurists reflect upon the meaning and significance of the Qur'ānic command to perform *hijra* (migration) and upon the Prophet's migration from pagan Mecca to Yathrib, the city in which he founded the Islamic polity of Medina, which was the *hijra* par excellence. Based on this event, some claimed that Muslims were obligated to do as the Prophet had done, that is, leave non-Islamic for Islamic lands, even if this involved state-building and exile. The use of the concept of *hijra* in the legal tradition, however, was problematic given the belief of some jurists that it had been abrogated after Mecca had been conquered by the Muslims. This chapter will explore historical trends in the jurists' thought on living under non-Muslim rule and their changing interpretations of the meaning of the term *hijra*. Chapter Two deals with whether, according to Mālikī law, Muslim community leaders who live under non-Muslim rulers are legitimate holders of communal authority. I show that juristic thought on this issue underwent a major change at the beginning of the 8th/14th century. Whereas before this period, the jurists were tolerant of Muslim community leaders who lived under non-Muslim rule, after this period, they become less willing to tolerate them and more likely to demand their immigration to Islamic territory. I show that the jurists' new position was not based, as has been sometimes claimed, upon a rote enforcement of the legal tradition, but that it actually went against established legal opinion in order to deal with the new political reality wrought by the Reconquista, which had made significant territorial gains over the course of the 7th/13th century. Chapter Three traces changes in Mālikī thought on the legal protections for life and property that were granted to Muslims living in non-Muslim territory. I show that Mālikī thought underwent two major shifts of position on this issue. Mālik and his immediate Medinan circle offered little protection for the lives and property of Muslims who lived in non-Muslim territory. The Mālikīs of the Maghrib and al-Andalus were the product of a different political context. Living in a frontier society which was often interdependent with Christian lands, they were compelled to extend more rights to Muslims who found themselves living outside Islamic territory. However, the views of these Mālikīs changed towards the end of the Reconquista. In response to increasing tensions with Christendom, many Mālikīs sought to penalize Muslims who lived there and advocated for a return to the position of Mālik. These jurists wished to enforce greater separation between Christian and Muslim territories and saw Muslims who lived under

Christian rule as an economic and political threat. My final chapter deals with Islamic responses to French colonialism in the 19th-century Maghrib, which again raised the question of whether Muslims were permitted to live under the rule of non-Muslims. It shows how some 19th-century jurists drew upon Reconquista-era thought in formulating responses to colonialism and how others came to understand the colonial situation as being a new one requiring its own unique legal and moral solutions.

The Genre of the Sources

Many of the sources which I analyze fall into the legal genre of the *fatwā* and so it is worth considering how this genre is defined.[89] A *fatwā* is a response to a question (*istiftā*)[90] about what Islamic law mandates in a particular situation. Unlike a court decision, a *fatwā* does not include establishing the facts of a case. It accepts the facts as stated in the question as givens and determines which Islamic laws would then apply under such circumstances.[91] It often attempts to present a statement of the law which is not solely relevant to the situation at hand, but which also contains a broader legal principle which will hold in all like situations and which can therefore be referred to by later jurists as precedent.[92] The writer of a *fatwā*, who should be an expert in Islamic law, is called a *muftī*. A request for a *fatwā* can be made by any Muslim. A lay person might request a *fatwā* for personal clarification, a ruler might request a *fatwā* to support a decision that he regarded as being potentially controversial or

89 For a useful overview of the *fatwā* genre, see Alan Verskin, *Oppressed in the Land: Fatwās on Muslims Living under Non-Muslim Rule* (Princeton: Markus Wiener, 2013), 3 ff. For discussions of *fatwās* specific to the Mālikī legal context, see Muṣṭafā al-Ṣamadī, *Fiqh al-nawāzil 'inda al-Mālikiyya: tārīkh wa-manhaj* (Riyadh: Maktabat al-Rushd Nāshirūn, 2007); R. Daga Portillo, "Los nawazil y géneros relacionados en la literatura juridica: fetuas y masa'il," *Miscelanea de Estudios Árabes y Hebraicos* 40–1 (1991–2), 79–85; María Arcas Campoy, "Algunas consideraciones sobre los tratados de jurisprudencia malikí de al-Andalus," *Miscelánea de Estudios Árabes y Hebraicos* 37 (1988), 13–21; and idem, "Valoración actual de la literatura jurídica de al-Andalus," in *Actas del II Coloquio Hispano-Marroquí de Ciencias Históricas* (Madrid: Agencia Española de Cooperación Internacional, 1992), 31–49.

90 Literally, "request for a *fatwā*."

91 Louis Gardet, *La Cité Musulmane: vie sociale et politique*, 3rd ed. (Paris: Librairie Philosophique J. Vrin, 1969), 139.

92 Masud, Messick, Powers, *Islamic Legal Interpretation*, 18–19 and Harald Motzki, "Child Marriage in Seventeenth-Century Palestine," in *Islamic Legal Interpretation*, 132.

socially sensitive. However, it was more usual in the medieval period for *fatwās* to be solicited by *qāḍīs* and almost all the *fatwās* dealt with in this book are answers to *qāḍīs*' questions. A *fatwā* may be about any subject. *Fatwās* do not only address the legal ramifications of interpersonal disputes, that is, the issues which would normally be brought before a court of law, they also deal with all kinds of religious questions, even matters of theological speculation. The vast breadth of the genre is emphasized by Masud:

> The scope of *fatāwā* is wider than that of a regular *fiqh* book ... In scope, a *fatwā* is comparable to *ḥadīth*, which encompasses almost the same range of subjects as a *fatwā* does. It therefore shows that the jurisdiction of a *muftī* embraces almost all aspects of life. In this sense it accords with the conceptual system of *Sharīʿa*.[93]

The flexibility of the genre of the *fatwā* was an important factor in making it a convenient place for jurists to discuss points of legal development.

There is debate among contemporary scholars regarding what exactly the *muftī* does when he issues a *fatwā*. Some see the *muftī*'s activities as exclusively embodying an intellectual interaction with the texts of Islamic law; others see the role of the *muftī* as engaging more with society itself in order to fit Islamic law to the needs of his time. On the textual end of the spectrum is Louis Gardet who believes that the *muftī*'s function is to search through law books for precedents of which the *qāḍī* is ignorant. This is because the *muftī* is appointed to ensure that the law prescribed by the *qāḍī* is in accordance with tradition.[94] More recently, Kevin Reinhart has developed this idea in greater detail. He emphasizes that the activity of the *muftī* is closely analogous to the work of Western theologians. He says that the *Sharīʿa* "is not, in the legists' view, a law *legislated* but *discovered* ... The role of the legists is to produce a kind of practical metaphysics by which the transcendent norms of Revelation are brought to bear on the realities of society." For this reason, Reinhart remarks that, by the end of the 12th century, the rulings of the *muftīs* were regarded as being a part "of God's speech" which "existed coeternally with Him."[95] Reinhart

---

93 Muhammad Khalid Masud, Brinkley Messick and David S. Powers (eds.), *Islamic Legal Interpretation: Muftis and their Fatwas* (Cambridge: Harvard University Press, 1996), 20. The *fatwā* genre is thus much broader than the "*responsa prudentium*" of Roman law to which it is sometimes compared. See, for example, J. López Ortiz, "Fatwās Granadinas," 73.

94 Louis Gardet, *La Cité Musulmane*, 140.

95 A. Kevin Reinhart, "Transcendance and Social Practice: *Muftīs* and *Qāḍīs* as Religious Interpreters," *Annales Islamologiques* 27 (1993), 7, referring to Shihāb al-Dīn al-Qarāfī,

emphasizes that the *muftīs*' concern with this heavenly science of the law necessarily removes them from the circumstances of everyday life. He says that "*muftīs* represent a pure scholarship of Islamic indicants … There is a sense in which the detachment of the *muftī* from the world secures the applicability of his assessments to cases as they occur."[96] The community, Reinhart says, charges the *muftī* with the task of absorbing himself in Islamic law so that he can explain it to them in a form of which they can make use. The rulings of the *muftī* are "to be seen as a rectification of an uncertain fit between the circumstance and transcendent norms. His task is to connect the event with a rule grounded in Revelation, for not every event is found in Revelation's corpus."[97] This practical aspect of the activities of the *muftī*, Reinhart says, is not to be misconstrued as signifying the *muftī*'s involvement with society. It is the *qāḍī*, not the *muftī*, who handles all interactions with actual members of society. The *muftī* fulfils a strictly theological function:

> The *qāḍī* acts in history and makes history by determining effectively between two litigants or between society and the individual. He is necessary, but sullied. The *muftī* is the embodiment of the timeless *Sharīʿah* that unites because (in part) it is indeterminate. … By speculation, interpretation, and application of what always remains a metaphysical ideal, the legists seek to make the transcendent immanent in Muslim society.[98]

Reinhart's conception of the *muftī*'s role as being more focused on textual study than societal practice has been challenged by Norman Calder. Calder says that "when Reinhart summarily refers to 'the detached and speculative *muftī*' in contrast to 'the engaged and practical *qāḍī*,' he is insufficiently discriminating. To be detached and speculative is the function of the author-jurist, the *muftī* has to give up a measure of detachment and to abandon speculation in order to carry out his particular function."[99] Thus, for Calder, the *muftī* may be less involved with the affairs of the world than the *qāḍī*, but through his act of applying Islamic law to actual cases, he already has a much greater stake in it than the writer of legal manuals (the author-jurist) whose works more closely

---

Sharḥ tanqīḥ al-fuṣūl fī ikhtiṣār al-maḥṣūl fī al-uṣūl, ed. Ṭāhā ʿAbd al-Raʾūf Saʿd (Cairo: Maktabat al-Kulliyyāt al-Azhariyya, 1973), 67.

96 Ibid., 14.

97 Ibid., 15.

98 Ibid., 25.

99 Norman Calder, "Al-Nawawī's Typology of *Muftīs* and its Significance for a General Theory of Islamic Law," *Islamic Law and Society* 3 (1996), 164.

embody the theological speculation to which Reinhart refers. David Powers takes a similar view. He speaks of the "remarkable discursive vitality" displayed in *fatwās* which is achieved as a result of "manipulating established legal doctrine" to respond to "novel and unforeseen circumstances." The *fatwā* is not simply a detached investigation of the law, it is an exercise which is intimately connected with the contemporary needs to which the jurist must respond. Thus Powers writes:

> The issuance of a *fatwā* was a moment when the law was made real, when the principles and rules contained in the Qur'ān and *ḥadīth*, the legal concepts and doctrines set out in treatises on substantive law, and the rules of evidence and procedure, were brought to bear, with greater or lesser force and clarity, upon the facts of an actual dispute.[100]

Therefore, for Powers, the practical import of a *fatwā* precludes it from being understood simply as a consideration of Islamic legal texts entirely divorced from reality.

The *fatwā* genre has several important social and legal functions. The flexible nature of the *fatwā* made it the prime genre in which Islamic legal change occurred. David Powers explains the matter thus:

> With the crystallization of the major lines of Islamic legal doctrine ca. the tenth century A.D., the locus of legal development and of legal dynamism shifted from the level of the doctrinal lawbooks to that of *futyā*. In his role as mediator of the divine law to the masses, the *muftī* repeatedly was called upon to comment upon the lacunae that inevitably appeared in Islamic positive law, as it had been articulated in a particular place and time. The questions posed and the answers given constitute important evidence for the slow, almost imperceptible development of Islamic legal doctrine.[101]

The idea that the *fatwā* has the potential to change the law is not just the opinion of modern Western scholars of Islam but was also the opinion of many

100 David Powers, *Law, Society and Culture in the Maghrib, 1300–1500*, 231. Cf. Idem, "Four Cases Relating to Women and Divorce in al-Andalus and the Maghrib, 1100–1500," in *Dispensing Justice in Islam: Qadis and their Judgments*, ed. M. Masud, R. Peters and D. Powers (Leiden: Brill, 2006), 407.

101 David Powers, "Legal Consultation (*Futyā*) in Medieval Spain and North Africa," in *Islam and Public law*, ed. Chibli Mallat (London: Graham and Trotman, 1993), 105–6.

medieval Muslim jurists who acknowledge its sometimes radical potential to change tradition. Jalāl al-Dīn al-Suyūṭī (d. 911/1505), for example, dramatically remarks, "If everyone were a *muftī* there would be chaos."[102] Thus the *fatwā* was a natural place for jurists to write about the new aspects of Islamic law that they developed in response to the challenges of the Reconquista.

Fatwās also have an important educational function. *Fatwās* are usually only written regarding cases on which the position of the law is unclear. However, the state of clarity of the law is, of course, perspectival. A person who does not have a legal education or law books at his disposal might refer a relatively clear-cut legal question to the *muftī*. It is for this reason that some modern authors have understood *fatwās* to have a pedagogical function. Some have even described *fatwās*, not incorrectly, as being "un element de vulgarización del Derecho musulmán."[103] The educational dimension of this genre of legal texts will be particularly apparent in some of the later *fatwās* that I discuss in this book.

---

102 Quoted in E.M. Sartain, *Jalāl al-Dīn al-Suyūṭī: Biography and Background* (Cambridge: Cambridge University Press, 1975), 63.

103 Jose Manuel Perez-Prendes and Muñoz de Arraco, *Curso de historia del derecho español* (Madrid: Universidad Complutense de Madrid, 1983), 482, quoted in Juan Martos Quesada, "Características del muftí en al-Andalus: contribución al estudio de una institución jurídica hispanomusulmana," *Anaquel de estudios árabes* 7 (1996), 128. Cf. U. Heyd, "Some Aspects of the Ottoman *Fetva*," *Bulletin of the School of Oriental and African Studies* 31 (1969), 54.

CHAPTER 1

The Concept of *Hijra* (Migration) in Medieval Iberia and the Maghrib

During the late Almoravid period, a number of Mālikī jurists in Iberia and the Maghrib began to invoke the Qur'ānic concept of *hijra* (migration) in order to encourage Muslims to migrate from Christian to Islamic territory. This practice became widespread among Mālikī jurists during the Almohad period. In invoking *hijra*, these jurists were latecomers. *Hijra* had been practiced in the Maghrib before they sanctioned its use and there is evidence that familiarity with the concept was very widespread. It is easy to see why *hijra* had such broad appeal. The concept of *hijra* is central to Islamic collective memory. The Prophet Muḥammad's *hijra* from Mecca to Yathrib (Medina) where he founded an Islamic polity is the event which ushers in the Islamic calendar and the idea of *hijra* continued to have a profound religious and political impact on the course of Islamic history. This chapter explores why, despite this, *hijra* had long been absent from the Mālikī legal tradition and what eventually led some jurists to introduce the term into their writings. I further suggest that the jurists' emphasis or de-emphasis of *hijra* is closely tied to cycles of political power.

Hijra in the Early Islamic Period

In order to understand the complex attitude of the Mālikī jurists towards the concept of *hijra*, I will briefly consider its pre-Mālikī history. The Qur'ān frequently and forcefully emphasizes that *hijra* is a religious obligation of the utmost importance. It envisions a broad application of the doctrine, limiting it neither by time nor by place; rather, it says, "those who migrate in the way of God will find many a road to refuge and space in the land."[1] There are two separate but sometimes overlapping circumstances under which *hijra* should be made. First, *hijra* is obligatory from lands in which people are forced to commit wrongdoing (*ẓulm*). Those who do not make *hijra* under such circumstances are condemned to hell (*jahannam*). There, they will be held accountable even for the wrongdoing they committed under duress because they

1 Qur'ān 4:100.

© KONINKLIJKE BRILL NV, LEIDEN, 2015 | DOI 10.1163/9789004284531_003

could have avoided that duress through migration. Second, there are verses which do not mention the issue of duress and which simply describe *hijra* as an act of commitment to the community of believers. It mentions those who have performed *hijra* and have then "striven (*jāhadū*) with their possessions and persons in God's way."[2] Some such verses also connect *hijra* with a duty of fighting (*qitāl*) together with the believers.[3] Believers who do not perform this kind of *hijra* are not condemned to hell; however, the believing community has "no duty of guardianship" towards them.[4] Since they have not offered their political assistance to the Muslim community, that community is not under an obligation to help them. Thus both believers compelled by their communities to commit wrongdoing and believers who live outside the Muslim community are obligated to make *hijra*. The Qur'ān exempts from *hijra* only those "oppressed, be they men, women, or children, who cannot devise something (*ḥīla*) and are not guided to a way."[5] That is, those who are truly incapable of migrating.

The political impact of *hijra* in the early Islamic period was considerable. The Islamic garrison towns (*amṣār*), which were the central organs of Islamic settlement and expansion, were heavily dependent on migration to augment the early Muslim population and to weaken the migrants' places of origin. The importance of *hijra* for these towns was reflected in the fact that their residents were commonly referred to as *muhājirūn* and their military centers were known as *dūr al-hijra* (abodes of *hijra*).[6] This extensive use of *hijra* was, however, of limited duration. *Hijra* was a useful concept for a minority community with limited political power that was in the process of establishing itself. Once the balance of power shifted in favor of Muslims, the usefulness of *hijra* diminished for two main reasons. First, the power of an established community is not enhanced by destabilizing population transfers. Second, the principle of *hijra* involves a compromise of the ruler's authority by obligating his subjects to abandon him if they perceive him to be coercing them into wrongdoing. Indeed, the idea of religiously obligatory secession from

---

2 See, for example, Qur'ān 8: 72: *wa-jāhadū bi-amwālihim wa-anfusihim fī sabīl allāhi*. Cf. Qur'ān 8: 75, 9: 19–20 and 16: 110.

3 Qur'ān 3: 194. Cf. 8: 72, 8: 74–75 and 9: 19–20. Cf. M. Ebstein, "The Connection between *Hijra* and *Jihād* in Classical Islam," *Jamāʿa* 15 (2005–2006), 53–85.

4 Qur'ān 8: 72: *mā lakum min walāyatihim min shayʾin hattā yuhājirū*.

5 Qur'ān 4: 97–99.

6 See W. Madelung, "Has the *Hijra* Come to an End?", *Revue des études islamiques* 54 (1986), 232 ff; P. Crone, "The First Century Concept of *Hiǧra*," *Arabica* 61 (1994), 364 ff.; and P. Wheatley, *The Places Where Men Pray Together* (Chicago: University of Chicago Press, 2001), 267.

wrongdoing communities could and would be seized upon by minority Islamic opposition groups, like the Khārijites and Zaydīs, who sought divine justification for their actions.[7] When the early Muslim community was politically weak, the revolutionary energy of *hijra*, with its destabilizing effect on the *status quo*, could be enthusiastically embraced. However, with greater Muslim power, the disadvantages of *hijra* became quickly apparent and it ceased to be employed by the religious majority. Perhaps reflecting these concerns, a cautionary attitude to *hijra* is reflected in some *ḥadīths*.[8] Although some of these declare *hijra* to be a permanent religious obligation, others indicate that it was abrogated with the Muslim conquest of Mecca.[9]

In general, Sunnī jurists accepted the validity of the tradition abrogating *hijra*, although some still regarded *hijra* as legitimate under extreme circumstances of political weakness in which Muslims are not free to practice Islam.[10] This meant that, for the most part, they ceased to discuss the practice of *hijra* in any great detail. In keeping with this, the early legal works of the Mālikī jurists of al-Andalus and the Maghrib almost never mention the term.[11] Perhaps this is because they accepted the tradition abrogating *hijra*, or perhaps this is

7 On the *hijra* of the Khārijites, see Pierre Cuperly, *Introduction à l'étude de l'ibāḍisme et de sa théologie* (Algiers: Office des Publications Universitaires, 1984), 20 ff. On the *hijra* of the Zaydīs, see Riḍwān al-Sayyid, "al-Dār wa'l-hijra wa-aḥkāmuhumā 'inda Ibn al-Murtaḍā," *al-Ijtihād* 12 (1991), 213–40.

8 On the dating of these traditions, see Crone, "The First Century Concept," 368 ff. and M. Cook, *Early Muslim Dogma: A Source-Critical Study* (Cambridge: Cambridge University Press, 1981), 100 ff.

9 On the concept of abrogation, see John Burton, *The Sources of Islamic Law: Islamic Theories of Abrogation* (Edinburgh: Edinburgh University Press, 1990).

10 Khaled Abou El Fadl, "Islamic Law and Muslim Minorities: The Juristic Discourse on Muslim Minorities from the Second/Eighth to the Eleventh/Seventeenth Centuries," *Islamic Law and Society* 1 (1994), 144 ff.

11 One source cites the early Mālikī jurist, Saḥnūn b. Sa'īd (d. 240/854), as endorsing *hijra*: "*Hijra* will not cease so long as the unbelievers are fought, but *hijra* today is from the abode of the unbelievers to the abode of Islam. For example, one who converts in the abode of unbelief must migrate." The authenticity of this quotation, however, cannot be confirmed given that the work from which it was allegedly extracted, the *Kitāb Ibn Saḥnūn* by Muhammad Ibn Saḥnūn (d. 256/870), is no longer fully extant. Moreover, Saḥnūn himself studiously avoids the term *hijra* in all of his known writings and this alleged remark in favor of *hijra* is not referred to by subsequent Mālikī jurists. For the remark, see Ibn Abī Zayd al-Qayrāwanī, *al-Nawādir wa'l-ziyādāt 'alā mā fī al-mudawwana min ghayrihā min al-ummahāt*, ed. 'Abd al-Fattāḥ Muḥammad al-Ḥulw (Beirut: Dār al-Gharb al-Islāmī, 1999), 3: 20. On the *Kitāb Ibn Saḥnūn*, see Miklos Muranyi, *Materialien zur mālikitischen Rechtsliteratur* (Wiesbaden: Otto Harrassowitz, 1984), 79.

simply an example of the jurists using their personal authority to shape the law.[12] Regardless, it is not until the late Almoravid period that we find some jurists referencing *hijra* and only in the Almohad period that this practice becomes widespread. What prompted this change? No clue is to be found by looking at the legal texts themselves—the term simply emerges without explanation. For an insight into how this change occurred, one has to look outside Mālikī legal sources and indeed beyond the Sunnī tradition to the Shiʿites of the Maghrib—here, references to *hijra* abound.

Practicing *Hijra* in the Maghrib: Fāṭimids, Almoravids and Almohads

The tradition of *hijra* attained wide currency in the Maghrib with the 3rd/10th-century conquest of the region by the Fāṭimids, a Shiʿite Ismāʿīlī dynasty.[13] The concept of *hijra* was central to the military strategy of the Fāṭimids who, in emulation of the Prophet, expanded their political control through the establishment of migration centers known as "abodes of *hijra*" (*dūr al-hijra*).[14] The first Fāṭimid *dār al-hijra* in the Maghrib was founded at

12 On the phenomenon of jurists using their personal authority to diverge from Qurʾānic law, see J. Brockopp, "Competing Theories of Authority in Early Mālikī Texts," in *Studies in Islamic Legal Theory*, ed. B. Weiss (Leiden: Brill, 2001), 20 and J. Lowry, *Early Islamic Legal Theory* (Leiden: Brill, 2007), 207 ff. For a dissenting view, see H. Motzki, *The Origins of Islamic Jurisprudence*, tr. M. Katz (Leiden: Brill, 2002), 115–17 and 152–57.

13 It is possible that the precept of *hijra* was spread to the Maghrib even earlier by Khārijite missionaries who began to travel there as early as the eighth century, but no extant sources document this. By the time the successors of the Khārijites, known as the Ibāḍīs, came to prominence in the Maghrib, they espoused the view that *hijra* had been abrogated after the conquest of Mecca and therefore did not make use of the concept. On the rejection of *hijra* by the Maghribī Ibāḍīs, see ʿĀmir b. ʿAlī al-Shammākhī (d. 792/1389), *Uṣūl al-diyānāt*, in P. Cuperly, *Introduction à l'étude de l'ibāḍisme*, 337 and 176; Werner Schwartz, *Die Anfänge der Ibaditen in Nordafrika: der Beitrag einer islamischen Minderheit zur Ausbreitung des Islams* (Wiesbaden: Harrassowitz, 1983), 66; and A. de Calassanti-Motylinski, *L'Aqida populaire des Abadhites algériens* (Algiers: Fontana, 1905), 14 and 40. Ibn Sallām al-ʿIbāḍī (circa 3rd/9th century) reduces *hijra* to meaning only the shunning of evil and not physical migration, see his *Kitāb fīhi badʾ al-Islām wa-sharāʾiʿ al-dīn*, ed. W. Schwartz (Wiesbaden: Franz Steiner, 1986), 83.

14 Heinz Halm, *The Empire of the Mahdī*, tr. M. Bonner (Leiden: E.J. Brill, 1996), 47 ff.; M. Brett, *The Rise of the Fāṭimids* (Leiden: Brill, 2001), 89 and 142, and J. Lindsay, "Abu ʿAbd Allah's Mission among the Kutama," *International Journal of Middle East Studies* 24 (1992), 55 n. 34. Cf. Al-Qāḍī Nuʿmān, *Kitāb Iftitāḥ al-daʿwa*, ed. F. Dachraoui (Tunis, 1975), 48.

Tāzrūt by Abū ʿAbdallāh al-Shīʿī (d. 298/911). Once the settlement had grown in size, Abū ʿAbdallāh and his *muhājirūn* (migrants) declared war and eventually conquered most of the surrounding area. The Fāṭimids repeated this strategy in many areas of the Maghrib and it seems that it was through their efforts that *hijra* was introduced to the region as a living practice.[15]

The passage of *hijra* as a living practice from Fāṭimid Shiʿism to Sunnīsm can be sketched only tentatively because of the scant available sources. There is some evidence that it passed from the Fāṭimids to the Almoravids, the movement which eventually replaced them in the Maghrib and which succeeded in firmly entrenching both Sunnī Islam and the Mālikī legal school there. Accounts of the founding of the Almoravid movement suggest that it might have involved the practice of *hijra*. The founding narrative goes as follows. At some point during the early 430/1040s, the spiritual father of the Almoravids, ʿAbdallāh Ibn Yāsīn al-Jazūlī (d. 451/1059?),[16] went to live among the Ṣanhāja tribe in order to give them religious guidance.[17] The religious reforms that he proposed soon proved too strict for the tribe and they rebelled against him. In response, Ibn Yāsīn and his followers migrated in order to found a new community whose members came to be known as the Almoravids. After growing in strength, they launched a number of wars against their neighbors who did not share their new Islamic ideology.[18] Most modern scholars are in agreement that the concept of *hijra* was central to Ibn Yāsīn's community building activities because descriptions of his migration so closely resemble the Prophet's *hijra*.[19] While I agree with the scholarly consensus, it should be noted that the

15 Halm, *The Empire of the Mahdī*, 142, 164 and 397.

16 H. Norris, "New Evidence on the Life of ʿAbdullāh b. Yāsīn and the Origins of the Almoravid Movement," *Journal of African History* 12 (1971), 255–68.

17 Abū ʿImrān al-Fāsī of Qayrawān (d. 430/1039) had told his disciple Wājāj b. Zallū al-Lamṭī about the need of the Ṣanhāja Berbers for a teacher of religion and the latter appointed his disciple Ibn Yāsīn to the task. The Ṣanhāja Berbers were divided into many sub-tribes. Ibn Yāsīn was initially sent to the Juddāla, but his influence soon spread to the Lamtūna and the Massūfa. See Nehemia Levtzion, "ʿAbd Allāh b. Yāsīn and the Almoravids," in *Studies in West African Islamic History*, ed. J. Willis (London: Frank Cass, 1979), 1: 78 ff.

18 J. Hopkins and N. Levtzion, *Corpus of Early Arabic Sources for West African History* (Cambridge: Cambridge University Press, 1981), 243.

19 See, for example, Abdallah Laroui, *The History of the Maghrib* (Princeton: Princeton University Press, 1977), 160–61; N. Levtzion, "ʿAbd Allāh b. Yāsīn and the Almoravids," 1: 85 and 92; H. Norris, *Saharan Myth and Saga* (Oxford, Clarendon Press, 1972), 22; Fritz Meier, "Almoravids and Marabouts," in *Essays on Islamic Piety and Mysticism*, tr. John O'Kane (Leiden: Brill, 1999), 376–77; and Paulo de Moraes Farias, "The Almoravids: Some Questions Concerning the Character of the Movement During its Periods of Closest

involvement of *hijra* can be posited only tentatively since the extant sources which describe the migration do not refer to it by this term. If Ibn Yāsīn did indeed use it, it would have had resonance with his first recruits, the Ṣanhāja Berbers, as the latter had a long history as defenders of the Fāṭimid *dūr al-hijra*.[20]

If there are doubts regarding whether Ibn Yāsīn used the term *hijra*, there are none regarding its use by the Sunnī reformer, Muḥammad Ibn Tūmart (d. 524/1130), whose Almohad forces displaced the Almoravids. Ibn Tūmart's doctrine of *hijra* was likely inspired by the Fāṭimids, given that much of his thought can be seen as a Sunnī reformulation of Fāṭimid theology.[21] In his writings, Ibn Tūmart speaks of *hijra* as a divinely ordained act:

> *Hijra* from among the enemies of God to God and His Prophet is obligatory for all the servants of God. The duty of leaving homes and property for religion is never nullified for any reason. Rather, upholding God's commandment is obligatory and it must be done immediately and without delay. Consideration for upholding God's commandment takes precedence over consideration of bloodshed and loss of life and property—for corruption must be entirely repelled.[22]

Other sources also affirm the importance of *hijra* to Ibn Tūmart's vision. Ibn al-Qaṭṭān (c. 7th/13th century), for example, describes a book which used to be committed to memory by Ibn Tūmart's followers and which contains several discussions on the status of Ibn Tūmart as *mahdī* and the importance of his *hijra*:

> [The book] affirmed that the Mahdī [Ibn Tūmart] is the *imām* and that the imāmate was a necessary Islamic institution. It then went on to specify what duties of honor and obedience are owed to him. Among these duties is that of *hijra*. *Hijra* to the Mahdī is obligatory. Nothing can cancel this duty, not concern for family, children or

---

Contact with the Western Sudan," *Bulletin de l'Institut fondamental d'Afrique noire*, series B, 29 (1967), 812. For a dissenting view, see H. Fisher, "What's in a Name? The Almoravids of the Eleventh Century in the Western Sahara," *Journal of Religion in Africa* 22.4 (1992), 309.

20 Hady Idris, *La Berbérie orientale sous les Zīrīdes, Xe–XIIe siècles* (Paris: Adrien-Maisonneuve, 1962), 1: 241 and 283.

21 On this, see Maribel Fierro, "The Almohads and the Fatimids," in *Ismaili and Fatimid Studies* (Chicago: Middle East Documentation Center, 2010), 161–75.

22 Ibn Tūmart, *Kitāb Muḥammad ibn Tūmart mahdī al-muwaḥḥidīn*, ed. I. Goldziher (Algiers: P. Fontana, 1903), 252.

> property. On the contrary, anyone who is aware that he [the Mahdī] exists is obligated to migrate to him. One who does not do so commits unbelief (*yakfuru*).[23]

Ibn Tūmart's own *hijra*, like that of Ibn Yāsīn, was from a Muslim land which had been branded as one of unbelief, in this case the Almoravid-controlled Maghrib.[24] In 517/1123, this migration led him to the town of Tīnmallal in the Atlas Mountains, his "Medina," in which he established a society run according to his interpretation of the *Sharīʿa*. Once the society became strong, he used Tīnmallal as a base from which to conquer the territory of his neighbors and the Almohad dynasty was born.

Like the Fāṭimids before him, Ibn Tūmart was responsible for bringing the doctrine of *hijra* to the forefront of religious consciousness in the Maghrib.[25] It is noteworthy that although Ibn Tūmart's example of *hijra* was later to be imitated by many subsequent *mahdī* figures in the region,[26] once the Almohad movement achieved stability, it ceased to make use of the term. This is evident in a letter from the Almohad Caliph ʿAbd al-Waḥīd al-Rashīd (r. 630–40/1232–42) to the Muslims of Valencia, written after it had been annexed by the Christians. In the letter, al-Rashīd strongly urges these Muslims to migrate and pledges to give them protection, financial support and housing if they travel to his lands. However, he avoids all reference to the term *hijra* and, when he refers to Muslim migrants, he uses the neutral term *muntaqilūn*, which is a synonym for *hijra*, but which does not have its theological connotations.[27] Thus, notwithstanding the important place that *hijra* enjoyed in Almohad thought,

---

23 Ḥasan b. ʿAlī Ibn al-Qaṭṭān, *Naẓm al-jumān li-tartīb mā salafa min akhbār al-zamān*, ed. Maḥmūd ʿAlī Makkī (Beirut: Dār al-Gharb al-Islāmī, 1990), 81.

24 V. Lagardère, "Le Ǧihād Almohade: théorie et pratique," in *Los Almohades: problemas y perspectivas*, ed. P. Cressier et al. (Madrid: Consejo Superior de Investigaciones Científicas, 2005), 2: 163–87.

25 On relations between the Mālikīs and Almohads, see Maribel Fierro, "The Legal Policies of the Almohad Caliphs and Ibn Rushd's *Bidāyat al-Mujtahid*," *Journal of Islamic Studies* 10 (1999), 226–48.

26 Mercedes García-Arenal, *Messianism and Puritanical Reform: Mahdīs of the Muslim West*, tr. Martin Beagles (Leiden: Brill, 2006), 193 ff.

27 Muḥammad b. al-Murābiṭ, *Kitāb ẓawāhir al-fikar wa-jawāhir al-fiqar* (ms. Escorial (Arabic) no. 520, f. 115–16), edited in E. Molina López, "Dos importantes privilegios a los emigrados Andalusies en el Norte de Africa en el siglo XIII, contenidos en el *Kitāb ẓawāhir al-fikar* de Muḥammad b. al-Murābiṭ," in *Cuadernos de Historia del Islam* 9 (1978–79), 21 ff. On the reign of al-Rashīd, see A. Huici Miranda, "El reinado del califa almohade al-Rašīd, hijo del al-Ma'mūn," *Hespéris* 41 (1954), 9–45.

al-Rashīd, like many Muslim rulers before him, was reluctant to use a term which held the potential of negatively impacting the stability of his regime.

The Mālikī Jurists and the Concept of *Hijra*

The first affirmations by Mālikīs that the obligation of *hijra* was still in force occur in the works of the late-Almoravid period jurists, Ibn Rushd "the Grandfather" (d. 520/1126)[28] and Abū Bakr Ibn al-ʿArabī (d. 543/1148).[29] Their views on the subject do not, however, seem to have been widely adopted and it is not until the Almohad period that references to *hijra* begin to proliferate. I believe that its appearance can be seen as the product of two separate factors. First, the instability caused by the Christian annexation of Muslim areas during the Almoravid period forced the issue of migration to be contemplated as a defensive strategy,[30] whether or not the term *hijra* was used to describe

28 Ibn Rushd's statement in favor of *hijra* includes a way of reconciling *ḥadīth*s which affirm the continuing obligation of *hijra* with those that affirm its abrogation. First, he says that the Prophet's abrogation of *hijra* from Mecca means that those who perform *hijra* after this period can neither be a part of the group known as the *muhājirūn* nor can they attain the merit of that group. Second, he says that the abrogation of *hijra* means that those *muhājirūn* who left Mecca to join the Prophet in Medina are permitted to return there if they so desire. Thus, for Ibn Rushd, the abrogation of *hijra* was only intended to end the ban on living in Mecca. It was not intended to end the obligation of *hijra*, which he believes is established as an eternal obligation in Qur'ān 4: 97–98 and 8: 72. He says that this interpretation is confirmed by the consensus of the jurists who mandate *hijra* "until the Day of Resurrection" for anyone who converts to Islam in the abode of war. See Ibn Rushd, *Kitāb al-muqaddimāt al-mumahhidāt li-bayān ma-aqtaḍathu rusūm al-Mudawwana* (Beirut: Dār al-Gharb al-Islamī, 1988), 2: 151–53. However, despite this clear endorsement of *hijra*, in his commentary on the *ʿUtbiyya* where he discusses the same issue, he substitutes the word *kharaja* (leave) for *hājara* (migrate). See Ibn Rushd, *al-Bayān wa'l-taḥṣīl wa'l-sharḥ wa'l-tawjīh wa'l-taʿlīl fī masā'il al-mustakhraja*, M. Ḥajjī (Beirut: Dār al-Gharb al-Islamī, 1984), 4: 171. It is unclear why there is a discrepancy between these two works given that they were both written at almost the same time towards the end of Ibn Rushd's life. On the connection between these two works, see Muḥammad Ḥajjī, "al-Mustakhraja li'l-Utbī wa'l-bayān wa'l-taḥṣīl wa'l-muqaddimāt li-Ibn Rushd," in *Actas del II coloquio hispano-marroquí de ciencias históricas: 'historia, ciencia y sociedad'* (Madrid: Agencia Española de Cooperación Internacional, 1992), 43–48.

29 Lucini, M., "Ibn al-ʿArabī, Abu Bakr," in J. Lirola Delgado and J.M. Puerta Vílchez, *Diccionario de Autores y Obras Andalusíes* (Seville: Junta de Andalucía, Consejería de Cultura, 2002), 1: 457–68.

30 I have elaborated elsewhere on the defensive dimension of *hijra* during the Reconquista period. In brief, the Mudéjars were essential to the political and economic well-being of many Christian territories and encouraging their emigration weakened the Christian hold

it. Second, I suggest that the practice of *hijra* in the Maghrib had instilled a widespread belief that it was a part of the Islamic tradition. The fact that it had been excluded from Mālikī texts until this point became a problem given that it represented a visible disjunction between what was widely thought to be Islamic, on the one hand, and the content of the written legal tradition, on the other. The problem caused by this disjunction would only grow in the Almohad period because of the central place of *hijra* in that dynasty's foundation narrative. These factors forced the jurists to take a new interest in a term which their predecessors had deliberately sought to marginalize. How this change in the law occurred is important for what it can show us about the mechanisms by which the jurists developed new laws to deal with sensitive political issues.

The term *hijra* was introduced cautiously into legal texts. It was not generally placed directly into legal manuals (*matn/mutūn*), the convenient reference works used by judges and jurisconsults,[31] but was introduced in a limited

---

on these areas. On the Christian need to preserve Muslim communities in order to populate newly conquered lands, see Robert Burns, "Immigrants from Islam: The Crusaders' use of Muslims as Settlers in Thirteenth-Century Spain," *The American Historical Review* 80 (1975), 21–42. On the economic importance of the Mudéjars to the Christians, see John Boswell, *The Royal Treasure: Muslim Communities under the Crown of Aragon in the Fourteenth Century* (New Haven: Yale University Press, 1977), 471 and José-Enrique López de Coca Castañer, "Sobre la emigración mudéjar al reino de Granada," *Revista d'Història Medieval* 12 (2001), 243 ff. On the use and importance of Mudéjar guards and soldiers in Christian armies, see Ana Echevarría, *Knights on the Frontier: The Moorish Guard of the Kings of Castile (1410–1467)*, tr. M. Beagles (Leiden: Brill, 2009).

31 Thus, for example, none of the following major legal manuals deal with *hijra* as a religious obligation: Muḥammad b. Aḥmad al-ʿUtbī's (d. 255/869) supplement to the *Mudawwana, al-Mustakhraja min al-asmiʿa mimmā laysa fī al-Mudawwana* (generally referred to as *al-ʿUtbiyya*); Ibn Abī Zayd's *Risāla* (a major précis of Mālikī law); Yūsuf Ibn ʿAbd al-Barr (d. 463/1071), *al-Kāfī fī fiqh ahl al-madīna al-Mālikī* (Beirut: Dār al-Kutub al-ʿIlmiyya, 2002). Commentaries similarly omit reference to the term. For examples, see Sulaymān b. Khalaf al-Bājī (d. 474/1081), *al-Muntaqā: Sharḥ Muwaṭṭa' Mālik*, ed. Muḥammad ʿAṭā (Beirut: Dār al-Kutub al-ʿIlmiyya, 1999); Khalaf b. Muḥammad al-Barādhiʿī's (d. 400/1009) influential guide to the *Mudawwana, Tahdhīb masā'il al-Mudawwana* and Qāḍī ʿIyāḍ Ibn Mūsā's commentary to the same work *al-Tanbīhāt al-mustanbaṭa ʿalā al-kutub al-mudawwana wa'l-mukhtalaṭa*, ed. M al-Wathīq (Beirut: Dār Ibn Ḥazm, 2011). This trend continues in such later Egyptian handbooks of Mālikī law as Ibn al-Hājib's (d. 646/1249) *Jāmiʿ al-ummahāt*, ed. A. al-Akhḍarī (Damascus: al-Yamāma, 1998) and Khalīl b. Isḥāq al-Jundī's (d. 767/1365) *Mukhtaṣar Khalīl*, ed. Ṭ. al-Zāwī (Cairo: Dār Iḥyā' al-Kutub al-ʿArabiyya, 1980), which were broadly circulated in the Maghrib. Shihāb al-Dīn al-Qarāfī's (d. 684/1285) *al-Dhakhīra* also has no discussion of the issue. It does, however, quote the tradition "there is no *hijra* after the conquest, but only intention and *jihād*" without comment in a section devoted to establishing the mandatory nature of *jihād*. See al-Qarāfī, *al-Dhakhīra*, ed. M. Ḥajjī (Beirut: Dār al-Gharb al-Islāmī, 1994), 3: 385.

way to the genres of Qur'ānic commentary (*tafsīr*), legal manual commentary (*sharḥ*) and legal responsum (*fatwā*). This aversion to discussing *hijra* in legal manuals is evident in the work of Muḥammad b. Yūsuf al-Mawwāq (d. 897/1492),[32] the chief judge of Granada. The latter omits the term in his commentary on Khalīl's *Mukhtaṣar* (a legal manual), when describing the obligation to leave the abode of war, and instead uses the words "leave" (*kharaja*) and "flee" (*haraba*).[33] However, in one of his *fatwās*, al-Mawwāq uses the term *hijra* and affirms its continuing religious validity. *Hijra* is so important, he says, that it takes precedence over obedience to parents.[34] Explanations for the absence of *hijra* in legal manuals must necessarily be tentative. Perhaps *hijra* might have been excluded because, given the sensitive nature of the material, the jurists did not want it to become a legal concept of first resort. They preferred to deal with it either in works of commentary, or on a case-by-case basis in responsa, rather than expressing it in a manual as a general rule which carried the risk that it might become subject to broad application. The Qur'ānic commentary was particularly useful as a vehicle for expounding on *hijra* as the issue in this genre arose naturally and demanded to be addressed simply because it appeared in the Qur'ān.[35] Commentators were thus able to express its importance without laying down rules which would immediately be applied in practice.[36]

---

32 Muḥammad Makhlūf, *Shajarat al-nūr al-zakiyya fī ṭabaqāt al-Mālikiyya* (Beirut: Dār al-Kitāb al-ʿArabī, 197?), 1: 262 and C. Brockelmann, *Geschichte der arabischen Litteratur* (Leiden: Brill, 1996), Supplement 2: 37.

33 Muḥammad b. Yūsuf al-Mawwāq, *al-Tāj wa'l-iklīl li-mukhtaṣar Khalīl* (Tripoli: Maktabat al-Najāḥ, 1969), 3: 354.

34 Kathryn Miller, "Muslim Minorities and the Obligation to Emigrate to Islamic Territory: Two *Fatwās* from Fifteenth-Century Granada," *Islamic Law and Society* 7 (2000), English: 285, Arabic: 286.

35 The following Qur'ānic commentaries all consider *hijra* to have contemporary applications: Muḥammad b. ʿAbdallāh Ibn al-ʿArabī (d. 543/1148), *Aḥkām al-Qur'ān*, ed. ʿAlī al-Bajāwī (Cairo: ʿĪsā al-Bābī al-Ḥalabī, 1967), 1: 484–6 and 2: 888; Muḥammad b. Aḥmad al-Qurṭubī (d. 671/1273), *al-Jāmiʿ li-aḥkām al-Qur'ān* (Cairo: Dār al-Kātib al-ʿArabī, 1967) to Qur'ān 4: 97 ff.; Muḥammad b. Muḥammad Ibn ʿArafa, *Tafsīr Ibn ʿArafa*, ed. Jalāl al-Asyūṭī (Beirut: Dār al-Kutub al-ʿIlmiyya, 2008), 2: 48; and ʿAbd al-Raḥmān al-Thaʿālibī (d. 873/1468), *al-Jawāhir al-ḥisān fī tafsīr al-Qur'ān*, ed. ʿAmmār al-Ṭālibī (Algiers: al-Mu'assasa al-Waṭaniyya li'l-Kitāb, 1985), 1: 484. There were also commentators who make no mention of the contemporary application of *hijra*. See, for example, ʿAbd al-Ḥaqq b. Ghālib Ibn ʿAṭiyya (d. 541 or 546/1147 or 1151), *al-Muḥarrar al-wajīz fī tafsīr al-Kitāb al-ʿazīz* (Beirut: Dār al-Kutub al-ʿIlmiyya, 1995) on Qur'ān 4: 97 and 8: 72.

36 Another possible explanation for its absence is the relative rigidity of the legal manual genre as compared to the more flexible genre of the *fatwā*. Since the foundational Mālikī

I now turn to the use of *hijra* within *fatwā* literature. The earliest *fatwās* that deal with *hijra* date from after the Almohad period. It was during this period that the urgency of the situation of Muslims living under Christian rule became evident as jurists realized that Christian territorial gains would not be short-lived. Many of these jurists state that living in the abode of war is forbidden and that this is proven by the existence of the obligation of *hijra*. Jurists of this opinion include Muḥammad b. Yaḥyā Ibn Rabīʿ (d. 719/1319),[37] Ibn Miqlāsh (d. 794/1392),[38] Muḥammad b. ʿAlī al-Ḥaffār (d. 811/1408),[39] Abū al-Qāsim b. Aḥmad al-Burzulī (d. 841/1438),[40] ʿAbdallāh al-ʿAbdūsī (d. 847/1442 or 849/1445),[41] al-Mawwāq (d. 897/1492), and Aḥmad b. Yaḥyā al-Wansharīsī (d. 914/1508).[42] Many of these *fatwās* give the impression that the issue of *hijra* was widely discussed. Further evidence of the popularity of the *hijra* concept is found in a call for *hijra* on behalf of Yūsuf III, the ruler of Granada (r. 810–20/1408–17), which was intended for broad circulation among the Mudéjars.

---

texts, like Mālik's *Muwaṭṭa'* or Saḥnūn's *Mudawanna*, did not include discussions of *hijra*, this made it difficult for later manuals to include it. The rigidity of legal manuals, however, can only be a partial explanation given that it has been demonstrated that these manuals are sometimes susceptible to development and innovation. On this, see Wael Hallaq, "Murder in Cordoba: *Ijtihād, Iftā'* and the Evolution of Substantive Law in Medieval Islam," *Acta Orientalia* 55 (1994), 55–83.

37 Aḥmad b. ʿAlī Ibn Ḥajar al-ʿAsqalānī, *al-Durar al-kāmina fī aʿyān al-mi'a al-thāmina*, ed. Muḥammad Sayyid Jād al-Ḥaqq (Cairo: Dār al-Kutub al-Ḥadītha, 1967), 4: 793 and P.S. van Koningsveld and G.A. Wiegers, "The Islamic Statute of the Mudéjars in the Light of a New Source," *al-Qanṭara* 17 (1996), 20. Ibn Rabīʿ was a judge and *wazīr* who lived in Málaga.

38 Biblioteca Nacional de Madrid, ms. 4950, f. 226r ff., published in H. Buzineb, "Respuestas de jurisconsultos maghrebíes en torno a la inmigración de los musulmanes hispánicos," *Hesperis-Tamuda* 26–7 (1988), 62–6. The author's full name is Abū Zayd ʿAbd al-Raḥmān al-Ṣinhājī, he is usually known as Ibn Miqlāsh.

39 Aḥmad Bābā, *Kitāb nayl al-ibtihāj bi-taṭrīz al-Dībāj* (Cairo: ʿAbbās b. ʿAbd al-Salām ibn Shaqrūn, 1932), 282.

40 Al-Burzulī, *Fatāwā al-Burzulī: Jāmiʿ masā'il al-aḥkām limā nazala min al-qaḍāyā bi'l-muftiyyīn wa'l-ḥukkām*, ed. Muḥammad al-Ḥabīb al-Hayla (Beirut: Dār al-Gharb al-Islāmī, 2002), 2: 22–23. On al-Burzulī, see *E.I.*[2] 1: 879.

41 Anonymous, *al-Ḥadīqa al-mustaqilla al-naḍira fī al-fatāwā al-ṣādira ʿan ʿulamā' al-ḥadra*, ed. Jalāl ʿAlī Juhānī. (Beirut: Dār Ibn Ḥazm, 2003), 144–45 and al-Mahdī al-Wazzānī, *al-Nawāzil al-jadīda al-kubrā fī mā li-ahl Fās wa-ghayrihim min al-badw wa'l-qurā al-musammā bi'l-miʿyār al-jadīd al-jāmiʿ al-muʿrib ʿan fatāwā al-muta'akhkhirīn min ʿulamā' al-Maghrib* (Rabat: Wizārat al-Awqāf wa'l-Shu'ūn al-Islāmiyya li'l-Mamlaka al-Maghribiyya, 1996), 3: 35. On al-ʿAbdūsī, see Makhlūf, *Shajarat al-nūr*, 255.

42 On al-Wansharīsī, see Francisco Vidal Castro, "Aḥmad al-Wanšarīsī (m. 914/1508). Principales aspectos de su vida," *al-Qanṭara* 12 (1991), 315–52.

Yūsuf's intention was to rally the Mudéjars against the Christians by persuading them to migrate to his armies in Granada. He writes:

> Oh brethren, strive to make the *hijra* which … God has made obligatory for each Muslim—to flee (*yafirru*) with his property and children from injustice and unbelief in God … and in His Prophet. You already know … what is in the Holy Qur'ān regarding *hijra* and what the Prophet decreed and stipulated regarding it. By God, oh Muslims, there is no city like that of Granada and no place like the frontier fortress (*ribāṭ*) during the *jihād*.[43]

This is one of the few documents in which an appeal to *hijra* is made on a popular level. Given the fact that the population had been familiar with the concept since the time of the Fāṭimids, it is possible that others existed but are no longer extant.

Some jurists, while supporting the principle that Muslims should leave the abode of war, felt that the use of the term *hijra* was inappropriate and called the obligation by other names. Abū al-Ḥasan b. ʿUthmān al-Zawāwī of Bijāya (circa 9th/15 century)[44] is representative of this view.[45] He writes:

> The meaning of *hijra* is to leave one's homeland (*waṭan*) for a place in which the *Sharīʿa* of the Prophet is in force … This was an obligation for all those who converted to Islam before the conquest of Mecca. As for [what happens] after the conquest of Mecca, the Prophet said: "There is no *hijra* after the conquest, but there is *jihād* and intention (*niyya*)." However, the obligation of flight (*firār*) remains, either from a

43 J. Ribera and M. Asín, *Manuscritos árabes y aljamiados de la Biblioteca de la Junta* (Madrid: Centro de Estudios Históricos, 1912), 259–60. Referred to in L.P. Harvey, *Islamic Spain, 1250 to 1500* (Chicago: University of Chicago Press, 1990), 59–60. For a discussion of such political sermons with reference to the Muslim West, see Linda Jones, *The Power of Oratory in the Medieval Muslim World* (Cambridge: Cambridge University Press, 2012), 131–157.

44 ʿĀdil Nuwayhiḍ, *Muʿjam aʿlām al-Jazāʾir min ṣadr al-Islām ḥattā muntaṣaf al-qarn al-ʿishrīn* (Beirut: al-Maktab al-Tijārī li'l-Ṭibāʿa wa'l-Nashr wa'l-Tawzīʿ, 1971), 117 and Aḥmad Bābā, *Nayl al-Ibtihāj*, 206–7.

45 An earlier jurist, Muḥammad b. ʿAlī al-Māzarī (d. 536/1141), also discusses the importance of leaving the abode of war but avoids the term *hijra*, instead using the verb *kharaja* (to leave). Al-Wansharīsī's treatise, *Asnā al-Matājir*, cites an abbreviated version of this *fatwā*. Full versions are contained in al-Burzulī, *Fatāwā*, 4: 49–51, al-Wansharīsī, *al-Miʿyār al-muʿrib* 10: 107–9, and Abdel-Magid Turki, "Consultation juridique d'al-Imām al-Māzarī sur le cas des musulmans vivant en Sicile sous l'autorité des Normands," *Mélanges de l'Université Saint-Joseph* 50 (1984), 691–704.

> place in which one fears for one's religion … or from a place in which there is no one [i.e., no religious leadership] to advise one regarding religion. Flight from the lands of unbelief is necessary lest unbelief gain dominion over faith and [the believers] become subject to the laws of unbelief.[46]

Al-Zawāwī thus feels the need for a religious injunction which would command migration from the lands of unbelief, but he does not want this injunction to be grounded in the idea of *hijra*. He accepts that *hijra* has been abrogated in its entirety, but cites another obligation, which he calls "the obligation of flight (*firār*)" from the lands of unbelief, which fulfills the same function. Al-Zawāwī's statement underscores the ambivalent attitude of many jurists towards the concept of *hijra*. Even under circumstances in which the precept would eminently serve their needs, its problematic nature made them reluctant to employ it.

By the time al-Wansharīsī wrote his *fatwas* on the Mudéjars, there were already many references to *hijra* in Mālikī works. However, perhaps because the concept had not been included in Mālikī legal manuals, it had not been the subject of systematic treatment. Al-Wansharīsī therefore gives an expansive outline of what he thinks *hijra* means and how it is to be applied to the situation of his Muslim contemporaries in al-Andalus. *Hijra*, he says, is an obligation which will not be abrogated until the Day of Resurrection. The obligation of *hijra* is of comparable weight to the prohibition against eating carrion or pork, and even to that against murder.[47] Its importance is such that living in non-Muslim territory for even a single hour is prohibited.[48] Some have argued, al-Wansharīsī says, that *hijra* in the contemporary period is void, given that all lands are sinful and that a migration from one sinful land to another is thus bereft of any religious meaning. He refutes this objection by quoting Ibn al-ʿArabī (d. 543/1148), who says that *hijra* does not obligate one to move to a land which is free from sin, but to move to a land which is of a lesser degree of sin. Ibn al-ʿArabī sketches a hierarchy of sin as a guide to where *hijra* should be made. For example, since the presence of unbelief in a land is worse than the presence of injustice, a Muslim is obligated to make *hijra* from a land of unbelief in which justice prevails to a land of belief in which injustice prevails.[49]

---

46 Al-Wazzānī, *al-Nawāzil al-jadīda*, 3: 42.

47 *Al-Miʿyār al-muʿrib*, 2: 124. Al-Wansharīsī's *fatwās* on the Mudéjars are translated in full in the appendix.

48 Ibid., 2: 138.

49 Ibid., 2: 121. Al-Wansharīsī's source is Ibn al-ʿArabī, *ʿĀriḍat al-aḥwadhī li-sharḥ ṣaḥīḥ al-Tirmidhī* (Beirut: Dār al-Kitāb al-ʿArabī, 1992), 7: 88–89.

This hierarchy allows al-Wansharīsī to argue against those who refuse migration on the grounds that justice does not prevail in Muslim lands.

After quoting Ibn al-ʿArabī, al-Wansharīsī introduces the debate as to whether the obligation of *hijra* has been abrogated.[50] The resolution of this question was, of course, of great importance to Mālikī jurists who wished to introduce *hijra* into the legal tradition. He quotes two *ḥadīth*s as representative of the two opposing traditions on whether *hijra* had been abrogated. The first says: "*Hijra* will not cease until repentance does; and repentance will not cease until the sun rises in the West."[51] The second says: "There is no *hijra* after the conquest [of Mecca], but only *jihād* and intention (*niyya*); so if you are called [for *jihād*], offer yourself up."[52] How, al-Wansharīsī asks, can the two traditions, one of which declares that *hijra* is abrogated and the other that it can never be abrogated, be reconciled? In response, he quotes the resolution given by the Shāfiʿī scholar, Abū Sulaymān al-Khaṭṭābī (d. 386 or 388/996 or 998):[53]

> At the beginning of Islam, migration (*hijra*) was recommended but not obligatory in accordance with the words of the Sublime, may He be exalted, "One who migrates in the way of God will find much refuge and abundance in the earth" (Qurʾān 4:100). This verse was revealed when the harm caused to the Muslims in Mecca by the idolaters became severe. It was then, when the Prophet, may God bless him and grant him peace, left for Medina, that migration became obligatory for Muslims. They were ordered to migrate to where he was in order to be together with him, to help one another, to make common cause in times of difficulty, and to study and come to understand religious matters. The greatest fear in that time was caused by the Quraysh tribe, who were the people of Mecca. When they [the Muslims] conquered Mecca and subdued them [the Quraysh], [migration] retained its meaning, but its obligation was removed, although it still remained recommended and desirable. There are two kinds of migration: one which is obligatory but which has been

---

50 On this debate, see Crone, "The First-Century Concept," 354 ff.

51 *Al-Miʿyār al-muʿrib*, 2: 126. Al-Wansharīsī's source for this tradition is *Sunan Abī Dāwūd* (Cairo: al-Maktaba al-Tijāriyya al-Kubrā, 1935), 3: no. 2479. For other sources, see Crone, "The First-Century Concept," 372 n. 103.

52 See above.

53 A Shāfiʿī scholar born in Bust (Sijistān), see *GAL* 1: 165, *Supplement* 1: 275 and *EI*², 4: 1131.

> discontinued and one which remains [in effect], but is [only] recommended. This is how the two *ḥadīth*s are to be reconciled.[54]

According to al-Khaṭṭābī, when the Prophet declared that *hijra* was abrogated following the conquest of Mecca, he meant only that it was no longer obligatory, not that its performance was no longer praiseworthy. Al-Wansharīsī, however, rejects al-Khaṭṭābī's resolution of the contradiction and argues that *hijra* from the abode of war always has been and always will be obligatory. To support his opinion, he quotes Ibn al-ʿArabī's reconciliation of the two *ḥadīth*s. According to the latter, *hijra* was "an obligation in the days of the Prophet...and this *hijra* remains obligatory until the Day of Resurrection (*yawm al-qiyāma*)." As for the *hijra* which ceased with the conquest [of Mecca], it was that of heading towards the Prophet...wherever he might be."[55] For Ibn al-ʿArabī, therefore, the two traditions on *hijra* do not conflict, they merely refer to different sets of circumstances.[56] The *ḥadīth* which states that *hijra* ended with the conquest of Mecca refers to a specific historical *hijra* which can no longer be implemented since Mecca has been conquered. The *ḥadīth* stating the eternal obligation of *hijra* refers to the more general obligation of *hijra* which can always be implemented so long as there are Muslims who live in the abode of war. Thus, basing himself on Ibn al-ʿArabī, al-Wansharīsī concludes that *hijra* from the abode of war continues to be obligatory.

Having thus established that there are two kinds of *hijra*, only one of which has been abrogated, al-Wansharīsī proceeds to discuss how juristic works have dealt with whether *hijra* is obligatory from Christian lands. There is no precise precedent for this obligation in juristic works, he says, because it was only recent political events that compelled jurists to deal with this issue. He says, however, that their opinion can be inferred from their remarks on another case. In this other case, the jurists penalize those who convert to Islam in the

54 *Al-Miʿyār al-muʿrib*, 2: 126, quoting *Kitāb maʿālim al-sunan* in the margins of *Sunan Abī Dāwūd*, ed. ʿIzzat ʿUbayd al-Daʿās and ʿĀdil al-Sayyid (Homs: Muḥammad ʿAlī al-Sayyid, 1969), 3: 8.

55 Al-Wansharīsī, *al-Miʿyār al-muʿrib*, 2: 127. Cf. Ibn al-ʿArabī, *Aḥkām al-Qurʾān*, 1: 484–6 and 2: 888. Ibn al-ʿArabī deals with *hijra* in a number of places. In his Qurʾān commentary, he indicates that *hijra* from the abode of unbelief to the abode of Islam is a duty which continues until the Day of Resurrection and that the Prophet's abrogation of *hijra* applies only to the *hijra* of the Prophet's community to Medina, not to other kinds of *hijra*.

56 See also Ibn al-ʿArabī's explanation of this contradiction in his *Kitāb al-qabas fī sharḥ Muwaṭṭaʾ Mālik ibn Anas*, ed. Muḥammad Karīm (Beirut: Dār al-Gharb al-Islāmī, 1992), 2: 587–88.

abode of war but do not then move to the abode of Islam.[57] Al-Wansharīsī surmises that the jurists' rationale behind penalizing these converts was that the law mandated *hijra* from the abode of war for all Muslims. He is aware, however, that objections could be raised against this inference and he attempts to anticipate some of them. First, while the early Mālikī jurists do indeed say that such converts are obligated to leave the abode of war, they do not use the term *hijra* to describe this obligation.[58] However, apparently beginning with Ibn Rushd, some Mālikī jurists start to associate *hijra* with this obligation and al-Wansharīsī quotes them to this effect.[59] This strengthens his argument for the necessity of *hijra* from Christian lands by giving the concept of *hijra* a place in juristic discourse which it had not previously enjoyed. Second, al-Wansharīsī anticipates the objection that a law specifically directed towards converts to Islam in the abode of war should not automatically apply to Muslims-from-birth who live in Christian territory because their lands have been conquered. Since these individuals belong to different categories, the fact that one category is not mentioned might indicate that it was deliberately excluded from the obligation of *hijra*. Al-Wansharīsī dismisses this objection claiming that the jurists focused on converts not because they wished to restrict the application of these laws to them, but because the case of converts was the only case of Muslims living in the abode of war of which they had experience. Al-Wansharīsī is thus able to argue that earlier Mālikī jurists would have supported mandating *hijra* from the abode of war even though these jurists did not explicitly indicate this in their writings.

As we have seen, al-Wansharīsī's argument for the continuing validity of *hijra* was not without precedent in the works of previous Maghribī Mālikī jurists. His contribution to the discourse is principally that he has gathered the disparate discussions on the topic into a single and convenient reference work. With the early 16th-century Christian edicts calling for the expulsion of Iberian Muslims and their subsequent migration or conversion to Christianity, discussions of *hijra* among Mālikī jurists ceased almost completely. The small remaining communities of crypto-Muslims seldom came to the jurists' attention and determining the law concerning life under non-Muslim rule became one of only theoretical importance. Those jurists who do discuss the subject,

57 Al-Wansharīsī, *al-Miʿyār al-muʿrib*, 2: 124–25.

58 See, for example, *al-Mudawwana al-kubrā* (Beirut: Dār al-Kutub al-ʿIlmiyya, 1994), 1: 508 and 2: 567, and ʿAbd al-Wahhāb b. ʿAlī al-Baghdādī, *al-Ishrāf ʿalā nukat masāʾil al-khilāf*, ed. Mashhūr b. Ḥasan Āl Salmān (Riyadh: Dār Ibn al-Qayyim, 2008), 4: 427.

59 *Al-Miʿyār al-muʿrib*, 2: 124–5. Cf. 2: 439.

however, do not seem to have significantly altered the thinking of their legal school.[60] Writing at the beginning of the Morisco period,[61] Aḥmad b. Abī Jumʿa al-Wahrānī (d. 917/1511)[62] affirms the continuing obligation of *hijra*, despite evincing considerable sympathy for those Muslims who had outwardly converted to Christianity but who continued to practice Islam in secret. Another jurist, ʿAbd al-ʿAzīz b. al-Ḥasan al-Zayyātī (d. 1055/1645), fully endorses the obligation of *hijra* from Christian lands.[63] His interest in *hijra* was perhaps a product of his residence in Jumāra, an area subject to frequent incursions and occupation by the Portuguese.[64] Abū al-ʿAbbās Ḥamdūn al-Abbār (d. 1071/1660)[65] deals with the question of whether Muslims should make *hijra* from areas controlled by an unnamed group of Muslim sectarians who, one can surmise, are Ibāḍī Muslims. He does not deny the obligation of *hijra*, but counsels against it being applied too broadly. He says that wrongdoing is present in most lands and that attempting to flee from it is therefore, under most circumstances, futile. A better strategy is for people to spiritually distance themselves from the wrongdoers in their regions rather than employing the risky strategy of moving to another community.[66] It is not clear whether al-Abbār would have had the same attitude to Muslims who lived in Christian lands. What is clear is that, from the fall of Granada until the nineteenth century, regardless of their views on whether Muslims should leave lands in which

60 On this, see H. Buzineb, "Respuestas de jurisconsultos maghrebíes," 54–55.

61 Dates on the *fatwā* are either given as 909/1503 or 910/1504, see Devin Stewart, "The Identity of 'the Muftī of Oran', Abū l-ʿAbbās Aḥmad b. Abī Jumʿa al-Maghrāwī al-Wahrānī (d. 917/1511)," al-Qantara 27 (2006), 269 ff.

62 This *fatwā* is edited together with photographs of the original in L. Harvey, "Crypto-Islam in Sixteenth-Century Spain," in *Actas del Primer congreso de studios árabes e islámicos* (Madrid: Comité Permanente del CEAI, 1964), 163–78. There is much debate regarding its interpretation. See, for example, Leila Sabbagh, "La Religion des Moriscos entre deux fatwas," in *Les Morisques et leur temps* (Paris: Centre National de la Recherche Scientifique, 1983), 55 and Stewart, "The Identity of 'the Muftī of Oran,'" 265–301. The *fatwā* was translated into Aljamiado (Spanish in Arabic script) and continued to be copied for over a century.

63 Al-Wazzānī, *al-Nawāzil al-jadīda*, 3: 38–41.

64 Mohamed Mezzine, "Les Relations entre les places occupies et les localités de la region de Fès aux XVIéme et XVIIéme siècles, a partir de documents locaux inéedits: Les *Nawāzil*," in *Relaciones de la Península ibérica con el Magreb siglos XIII–XVI*, ed. Mercedes García-Arenal and María J. Viguera (Madrid: Instituto Hispano-Árabe de Cultura, 1988), 544.

65 Muḥammad b. al-Ṭayyib al-Qādirī, *Nashr al-mathānī li-ahl al-qarn al-ḥādī ʿashar wa'l-thānī*, ed. M. Ḥajjī and A. al-Tawfīq (Rabat: Maktabat al-Ṭālib, 1982), 2: 109.

66 Al-Wazzānī, *al-Nawāzil al-jadīda*, 3: 36–38.

there was wrongdoing, however defined, the Mālikī jurists were unwilling to regard the concept of *hijra* as having been abrogated in its entirety.

Egyptian Mālikīs and the Concept of *Hijra*

Many scholars have viewed the Mālikī law of the Reconquista-period as being rigid, dogmatic, and unable to adapt to changing environments and circumstances.[67] I think that this is belied by the Mālikī jurists of the Maghrib who independently decided to revive the Qur'ānic concept of *hijra* and give it a place in their legal system in response to the needs of communities which had been adversely affected by the Reconquista. That their adoption of *hijra* was not an inevitable development forced on them by their legal tradition is perhaps best demonstrated by looking at the discussions of *hijra* by the Mālikī jurists of Egypt. The latter shared most of the same foundational texts as their counterparts in the Maghrib, but drew very different conclusions regarding their application.

In contrast to the Mālikī jurists of the Maghrib, the views on *hijra* of the Egyptian Mālikīs were very similar to the jurists of the other Sunnī legal schools. Like the latter, they limited the application of *hijra* to a narrow range of circumstances to ensure that the revolutionary concept could never be carried out on a large scale. Like the Maghribī jurists, the Egyptian Mālikī jurists do not generally mention *hijra* in their legal manuals. The earliest work in which I have seen *hijra* referred to, albeit obliquely, is by Ibn al-Ḥājj (d. 737/1336).[68] He disagrees with those who think that there is an obligation to flee (*firār*)[69] lands in which corruption (*fasād*) is prevalent. Although he does not use the word *hijra*, it can be deduced from the form of his argument that he does not consider it to be applicable. Most places, he says, are a mixture of good and bad rule. A person will generally not know until he reaches another

67 Husayn Mu'nis, "Asnā al-matājir fī bayān aḥkām man ghalaba 'alā waṭanihi al-Naṣārā wa-lam yuhājir wa-mā yatarattabu 'alayhi min al-'uqūbāt wa'l-zawājir," *Revista del Instituto de Estudios Islámicos en Madrid* 5 (1957), 5 ff. For similar views, see E. Molina López, "Algunas consideraciones sobre los emigrados andalusíes," *Homenaje al Prof. Darío Cabanelas* (Granada: University of Granada, 1987), 1: 425–26 and A. García Sanjuán, *Till God Inherits the Earth* (Leiden: Brill, 2007), 29.

68 See Ibn al-Ḥājj, *al-Madkhal* (Beirut: Dār al-Kitāb al-'Arabī, 1972), 1: 297–98. On Muḥammad b. Muḥammad Ibn al-Ḥājj al-'Abdarī al-Fāsī, see *GAL*, 2: 83 and Suppl. 2: 95.

69 He also uses the word *haraba*, see ibid., 2: 295.

community whether it is any better than the one from which he came. Moreover, even if a community is established as being better, the dangers of traveling there must be taken into consideration before departing for it. Flight, he says, should only be resorted to in the most extreme of circumstances. Generally, a person should withdraw (*iʿtazala*) from a place of corruption by confining himself to his home (*li-yakūn ḥilsat baytihi*). In this manner, he says, such people emulate the Prophet who said, "How good are the hermitages as houses for my people." For Ibn al-Ḥājj, therefore, a person can continue to be righteous even though he lives in an iniquitous society, provided that he entirely cuts himself off from its affairs. Since Ibn al-Ḥājj bans travel to the abode of war, one can conclude that it is likely that he would have encouraged Muslims who live in Christian lands to migrate from them, but it is unlikely that he would have used the term *hijra* in order to do so.

Other Mālikī Egyptian jurists did not reject the applicability of *hijra* but limited it to a narrow range of circumstances. In a *fatwā* written in 916/1510, the chief Mālikī judge of Cairo, Yaḥyā Ibn Muḥyī al-Dīn, says that it is permissible for Muslims to live in those parts of Iberia that have been annexed by Christians. He says that a Muslim "is allowed to postpone *hijra* if he does not fear for his life and his property. Nay, he is even ordered to postpone it in order not to ruin his property and let himself fall into captivity, because that is not permitted."[70] He adds that community leaders who wish to migrate are obligated to postpone their migration if they believe that it will damage the Muslim minority communities which they serve.[71] It is thus only under the most extreme of circumstances that a person is obliged to make *hijra*. The modern editors of this *fatwā* are surprised by this jurist's view, perhaps because it is not in line with the views on *hijra* held by the Mālikī jurists of the Maghrib. They therefore suggest that the relatively permissive position which the judge chose to adopt was a testament to governmental interference which compelled him to contradict the true opinion of his legal school. The Mamlūk government of Egypt, these editors claim, did not want to prejudice its relations with Christian Spain and therefore put pressure on the judges to endorse Morisco quietism. Militating against this theory, however, is the fact that the rulings of this judge seem to be fully in accord with the general trend of Egyptian Mālikī opinion. For example, a contemporary Egyptian Mālikī jurist, ʿAlī b. Nāṣir al-Dīn al-Manūfī

70 P. van Koningsveld and G. Wiegers, "Islam in Spain during the Early Sixteenth Century: The Views of the Four Chief Judges in Cairo (Introduction, Translation, and Arabic Text)," in *Poetry, Politics and Polemics*, ed. O. Zwartjes et al. (Amsterdam: Rodopi, 1996), 133.

71 Ibid., 138.

al-Shādhilī (d. 939/1532),[72] in a commentary on Ibn Abī Zayd al-Qayrawānī's *Risāla*, incorporates respect for governmental treaties with Christian countries into his view of *hijra*. In so doing, while not abrogating *hijra*, he articulates a position which would limit the scope of its application. Before a truce (*ṣulḥ*) is concluded, he says, all Muslims are obligated to make *hijra* from the abode of war. Once a truce is concluded, Muslims are free to remain so long as their observance of Islam is not impaired.[73] Thus al-Manūfī comes to a conclusion very similar to that of the chief Mālikī judge of Cairo.

Even after the Morisco period, Egyptian Mālikī jurists continue to reiterate the position that so long as Muslims can practice their religion in the abode of war, they are under no obligation to make *hijra*. One such writer, Aḥmad b. Ghunaym al-Nafrāwī (d. 1126/1714), notes that Ibn Abī Zayd's *Risāla* does not discuss the issue of whether a person who converts to Islam in the abode of war is obligated to migrate. He explains that this is because, whereas before the conquest of Mecca, a Muslim was obligated to migrate from the abode of war to the abode of Islam, after the conquest the obligation of *hijra* was abrogated and *hijra* became obligatory only for those Muslims living in the abode of war who are unable to practice Islam.[74] Thus, by using an argument *ex silentio*, al-Nafrāwī is able to project this later view of *hijra* back into earlier sources. Another Egyptian jurist, ʿAlī al-ʿAdawī (d. 1189/1775), who wrote a super-commentary on the aforementioned work by al-Manūfī, disagrees with the latter's view that Muslims are obligated to make *hijra* from non-Muslim lands which have not concluded truces with the abode of Islam. *Hijra*, he says, was abrogated after the conquest of Mecca and because of this there is no obligation to leave the abode of war unless Islam cannot be practiced. Even if a Muslim who cannot practice Islam does not migrate, al-ʿAdawī says, he is still deemed to be a Muslim and not an unbeliever, but he is regarded as a disobedient Muslim.[75] In a similar vein, Aḥmad al-Ṣāwī (d. 1241/1825), writing regarding the French conquest of Egypt, says that a territory remains Muslim regardless of who rules it provided that the Muslims who live there are able to practice their religion. He does not mention the term *hijra* which would be of limited

72 *GAL* 2: 316, Supplement 2: 434.

73 ʿAlī b. Nāṣir al-Dīn al-Manūfī al-Shādhilī, *Kifāyat al-ṭālib al-rabbānī li-Risālat Ibn Abī Zayd al-Qayrawānī* (Cairo: Muṣṭafā al-Bābī al-Ḥalabī, 1938), 2: 4.

74 Aḥmad b. Ghunaym al-Nafrāwī, *Kitāb al-fawākih al-dawānī ʿalā Risālat Ibn Abī Zayd al-Qayrawānī* (Cairo: Maṭbaʿat al-Saʿāda, 1913), 2: 117.

75 ʿAlī b. Aḥmad al-Ṣaʿīdī al-ʿAdawī, *Ḥāshiya ʿalā kifāyat al-ṭālib al-rabbānī li-Risālat Ibn Abī Zayd al-Qayrawānī* (Cairo: Muṣṭafā al-Bābī al-Ḥalabī, 1938), 2: 4.

applicability when Muslim territory is so broadly defined.[76] Thus, for these jurists, *hijra* is not required from a territory merely because it is governed by non-Muslims and is applicable only under a very limited set of circumstances. Egyptian Mālikī views on *hijra* continued to limit its scope until foreign rule over Egypt led the jurist Muḥammad ʿIllaysh (d. 1299/1882) to reverse this position and bring the views of his compatriots closer to those of the Maghribīs. Until then, the Mālikīs of Egypt, unpressured by either the Islamic revolutionary movements which repeatedly visited the Maghrib or by the constant pressure of Christian neighbors, simply adopted a stance on *hijra* in line with those of the other Sunnī legal schools. By comparing the different positions on *hijra* held by the Egyptian and Maghribī Mālikīs, one can see that the legal tradition did not force the Maghribī jurists to adopt a specific opinion on the subject; rather, they adopted a position which they believed was appropriate to the needs of their communities.

This chapter has traced the development of the concept of *hijra* as a basis for a Muslim's obligation to leave the abode of war. Despite the centrality of the concept in early Islamic thinking, jurists felt relatively free to decide when it should be applied and when it should be deemphasized. When making these decisions, they referred to statements attributed to the Prophet as precedent but, because such statements were subject to a broad range of interpretations, this did not fetter their ability to develop creative legal solutions to contemporary problems. Invocations of the concept of *hijra* can be seen as almost cyclical in nature. *Hijra* appeared in early Islam when Muslims were a persecuted minority and then faded once Muslims came to possess political power. It became popular again during periods of instability in the Almoravid and Almohad periods, but was swept to the sidelines once the Almohad dynasty had gained sufficient political power. It rose to prominence again in response to Christian territorial gains during the Reconquista, and then faded from discussions during the following period when the borders between Christian and Muslim lands became more stable. It would again rise to prominence in the nineteenth century as a result of French incursions in the Maghrib and would then experience a demise in the late nineteenth century once French gains in the region achieved a semblance of permanence and migration became

76 Aḥmad b. Muḥammad al-Ṣāwī, *Bulghat al-sālik li-aqrab al-masālik ilā madhhab al-Imām Mālik ʿalā al-sharḥ al-ṣaghīr liʾl-quṭb al-shahīr Aḥmad b. Muḥammad b. Aḥmad al-Dardīr* (Cairo: Muṣṭafā al-Bābī al-Ḥalabī, 1952), 1: 361. On al-Ṣāwī, see G. Delanoue, *Moralistes et politiques musulmans dans l'Egypte du XIXe siècle (1798–1882)* (Cairo: Institut Français d'Archéologie Orientale du Caire, 1982), 188 ff.

impractical. The jurists felt free to develop laws which responded to these cycles of power and the legal system thus cannot be seen as impairing their ability to determine when and how to invoke the concept of *hijra* in response to the needs of their societies.

Another Source of Prohibition Against Living in Non-Muslim Territory

Hijra was not the only principle to which Mālikī jurists made recourse in order to ban living under non-Muslim rule—another principle was the prohibition against traveling to the abode of war for the purpose of trade and in this way becoming subject to non-Islamic laws.[77] Unlike the principle of *hijra*, this prohibition was referred to with greater frequency in legal manuals and therefore had the advantage of having a less ambiguous legal status.

The earliest compilation of law used by Mālikī jurists, the *Muwaṭṭa'*, a selection of traditions transmitted by Mālik b. Anas (d. 179/795),[78] does not deal with the issue of such travel. The opinions cited in the *Muwaṭṭa'* were developed in Medina, a region remote from the border with the abode of war.[79] The Medinan jurists operated on the assumption that the world of Islam was

77 The jurists rarely discuss travel to the abode of war for purposes other than trade and the ransoming of captives. Mālikī authorities permitted the latter, but not the former, see David de Santillana, *Istituzioni di diritto musulmano malichita con riguardo anche al sistema sciafiita* (Rome: Istituto per l'Oriente, 1938), 1: 71. I have come across two discussions of the permissibility of travel for purposes other than trade and the ransoming of captives, both of which occur in non-legal sources. The famous traveler, Muḥammad b. Aḥmad Ibn Jubayr (d. 614/1217), notes that while it is prohibited to live in the abode of war, it is permissible to pass through it on one's travels, see *Riḥla*, ed. W. Wright and M.J. de Goeje (Leiden: Brill, 1907), 307, quoted in F. Maíllo Salgado, "Del Islam residual mudéjar," in *España, al-Andalus, Sefarad: síntesis y nuevas perspectivas* (Salamanca: Universidad de Salamanca, 1988), 139. The mystic, Muḥyī al-Dīn Ibn al-ʿArabī (d. 638/1240), notes that pilgrimage to lands governed by Christians is prohibited. For this reason, he says, travel to crusader-controlled Jerusalem is prohibited, see Ibn al-ʿArabī, *al-Waṣāyā li-Ibn al-ʿArabī* (Cairo: Dār al-Ghad al-ʿArabī, 1988), 38–39.

78 *EI*,[2] 6: 262.

79 There has been much debate regarding where the *Muwaṭṭa'* was composed. At present, the general consensus seems to be that, regardless of where it was redacted, the opinions expressed in it represent the views of the Medinan school. For a convenient summary of the debate, see Christopher Melchert, "The Early History of Islamic Law," in *Method and Theory in the Study of Islamic Origins*, ed. Herbert Berg (Leiden: Brill, 2003), 307–309.

rapidly expanding and that dependence upon the non-Muslim world for resources was not a matter of necessity. They therefore did not deal extensively with the legal issues which could arise either from a Muslim defeat at the hands of the unbelievers, or from an environment which required some degree of economic dependence on the non-Muslim world.

Discussions regarding whether Muslims are permitted to travel to the abode of war seem to have begun among the Mālikī jurists with Saḥnūn b. Saʿīd (d. 240/854).[80] In formulating the laws regarding this situation, Saḥnūn was developing a new field of jurisprudence. Unlike the jurists of Medina, Saḥnūn lived on the periphery of the Islamic world in Qayrawān, located in modern-day Tunisia. His work, the *Mudawwana*,[81] reflects the political and economic environment of Qayrawān, which was heavily dependent on trade with the Christian world for its food supply and other commodities. Christian traders were thus frequent visitors to the city and it was not uncommon for the Muslims traders of Qayrawān to visit Christian lands. The relationship between these Muslim and Christian lands was not always cooperative. Raids, conquests, and re-conquests were a frequent feature of the relationship between the Aghlabid-controlled Maghrib, and Christian Sicily and southern Italy.[82]

In the *Mudawwana*, Saḥnūn deals with many of the legal issues that arise from Muslim-Christian interactions in his work. In a section on trading in the abode of war, he discusses a prohibition against Muslims traveling to the abode of war for the purpose of trade. He ascribes this prohibition to Mālik who, he says, had "a great abhorrence" of this activity because Muslims who travel to the abode of war necessarily become subject to the laws of unbelief.[83]

---

80 Makhlūf, *Shajarat al-nūr*, 1: 69–70 and *EI*², 8: 843–45.

81 The authorship of the *Mudawwana* has been the subject of considerable debate among modern scholars, a debate to which I cannot do justice in this chapter. I note only that the views in the sections of the *Mudawwana* with which I deal in this chapter seem specifically tailored to the problems facing Muslim traders in Qayrawān from Saḥnūn's own time to the time of al-Qābisī (d. 403/1012), whose students who were likely responsible for making the final recension of the work. For a discussion of the authorship of the *Mudawwana*, see Miklos Muranyi, *Beiträge zur Geschichte der Ḥadīṯ und Rechtsgelehrsamkeit der Mālikiyya in Nordafrika bis zum 5. JH. D. H.* (Wiesbaden: Harrassowitz, 1997), 35 ff.

82 Mohamed Talbi, *L'Émirat aghlabide (184–296/800–909)* (Paris: Adrien-Maisonneuve, 1966), 531 ff. On Aghlabid relations with Christian states, see ibid., 380 ff; and Barbara M. Kreutz, *Before the Normans: Southern Italy in the Ninth and Tenth Centuries* (Philadelphia: University of Pennsylvania Press, 1991), 18 ff.

83 *al-Mudawwana al-kubrā* (Beirut: Dār Sādir, 1975), 4: 270.

Saḥnūn's view was not immediately adopted by all Mālikī jurists. For example, Yūsuf Ibn ʿAbd al-Barr al-Qurtubī (d. 463/1071),[84] the *qāḍī* of Lisbon, says that although permanent residence in the abode of war is forbidden, as is marriage for one who resides there, there is no prohibition against residing there temporarily for the purpose of trade or in the hope of winning converts to Islam.[85] Nevertheless, Saḥnūn's position was widely accepted by his contemporaries and successors and achieved universal acceptance among the Mālikī jurists of the Maghrib within two centuries of his death.

One of the earliest jurists to follow Saḥnūn's view was Ibn Abī Zayd al-Qayrawānī (d. 386/996).[86] In his *Risāla*, he asserts that traveling for trade to the land of the enemy and to the Sudan[87] is forbidden.[88] This view quickly spread through a growing number of commentaries on the work. An Egyptian commentator on the *Risāla*, ʿAbd al-Wahhab al-Baghdādī (d. 422/1031),[89] in accepting the view, explains that Ibn Abī Zayd derives the prohibition on travel from the legal concept of *hijra* which prevents Muslims from living in non-Muslim territory lest non-Muslim laws be applied to them.[90] Another

---

84 Maribel Fierro, "Ibn ʿAbd al-Barr, Abū ʿUmar," in J. Lirola Delgado and J.M. Puerta Vílchez, *Diccionario de Autores y Obras Andalusíes* (Seville: Junta de Andalucía, Consejería de Cultura, 2002), 1: 287–292 and Brockelmann, *Geschichte der arabischen Litteratur*, 1: 367 ff. and *Supplement* 1: 628 ff.

85 Yūsuf b. ʿAbdallāh b. Muḥammad Ibn ʿAbd al-Barr al-Namarī al-Qurṭubī, *al-Kāfī fī fiqh ahl al-madīna al-Mālikī* (Beirut: Dār al-Kutub al-ʿIlmiyya, 2002), 210.

86 *EI*[2], 3: 695 and Makhlūf, *Shajarat al-nūr*, 1: 96.

87 In the ninth/fifteenth century, Aḥmad Ibn Zarrūq (d. 899/1493) qualifies this view on the Sudan by noting that a Muslim is permitted to travel to those areas of it which are controlled by Muslims, see Hopkins and Levtzion, *Corpus of Early Arabic Sources for West African History*, 383 and Aḥmad b. Aḥmad al-Zarrūq, *Sharḥ Risālat Ibn Abī Zayd al-Qayrawānī*, ed. Aḥmad Farīd al-Mazīdī (Beirut: Dār al-Kutub al-ʿIlmiyya, 2006), 2: 478.

88 Abū Muḥammad Ibn Abī Zayd al-Qayrawānī, *Risāla*, ed. Léon Bercher (Algiers: Jules Carbonel, 1949), 318. Al-Qayrawānī considers travel to the abode of war to be so distasteful that he regards the travel itself as a part of the punishment for this sin. The tradition regarding travel being a punishment is included in a number of major *ḥadīth* collections, see, for example, *Saḥīḥ al-Bukhārī*, ed. Ludolph Krehl (Leiden: Brill, 1862), 1: 19, 26, and 450 and *Saḥīḥ Muslim*, ed. Muḥammad Fu'ād ʿAbd al-Bāqī (Cairo: Dār Iḥyāʾ al-Kutub al-ʿArabiyya, 1955), 3: 1526, no. 1927.

89 Brockelmann, *Geschichte der arabischen Litteratur*, Supplement 1: 660. As his name implies, al-Baghdādī originally lived in that city before immigrating to Egypt.

90 Quoted in Qāsim b. ʿĪsā Ibn Nājī, *Sharḥ Ibn Nājī al-Tanūkhī ʿalā matn al-Risāla li'l-Imām Abī Muḥammad ʿAbdallāh ibn ʿAbd al-Raḥmān Ibn Abī Zayd al-Qayrawānī*, ed. Aḥmad Farīd al-Mazīdī (Beirut: Dār al-Kutub al-ʿIlmiyya, 2007), 2: 485. In support of this position, he quotes Qur'ān, 4: 100.

Egyptian jurist, Tāj al-Dīn al-Fākihānī (d. 731/1331 or 734/1334),[91] quoting the *Mudawwana*, makes a similar point and again refers to the danger of a Muslim becoming subject to the laws of unbelief.[92] Ibn Abī Zayd's reference to travel in the Sudan was clearly a matter of great relevance to his contemporaries in Qayrawān. In a *fatwā*, the great jurist, ʿAlī b. Muḥammad al-Qābisī (d. 403/1012),[93] says that the prohibition against travel to the abode of war makes it illegal to entrust money by way of a *qirāḍ*[94] to someone who intends to use the funds to travel to the Sudan.[95] From the *fatwā*, one can gather that, despite the disapproval of the jurists, such trips were nonetheless quite common.[96]

About a century after Ibn Abī Zayd, the Andalusī jurist, Muḥammad b. Aḥmad Ibn Rushd "the grandfather" (d. 520/1126), expanded on Saḥnūn's views in a commentary on the *Mudawwana*. Ibn Rushd lived in a time of military crisis. The fifth/eleventh century had seen the fall of Toledo to the Castillians (478/1085), of Sicily to the Normans (484/1091), and even the brief loss of the Maghribī port city al-Mahdiyya to the Genoese and Pisans (479/1087). Ibn Rushd thus looked favorably on Saḥnun's policy of isolation from non-Muslim powers and, like him, espoused the view that Muslims are banned from travelling to the abode of war for the purpose of trade because, in doing so, they become subject to non-Muslim laws. Supporting Saḥnun's contention, Ibn Rushd cites the principle that anyone who converts to Islam in the abode of war is required to migrate to the abode of Islam.[97] This principle, he says, applies not just to converts, but to all Muslims who find themselves in the abode of war. He writes:

---

91 Brockelmann, *Geschichte der arabischen Litteratur*, 2: 22 and *Supplement*, 2: 15.

92 Quoted in *Sharḥ Ibn Nājī*, 2: 485. Al-Fākihānī adds that Ibn Abī Zayd's statement that the act of traveling itself is a part of the punishment means that those who engage in it are not subject to further punitive measures. Ibn Nājī of Qayrawān (837/1433) registers his disagreement with this position, indicating that additional punitive measures are in order.

93 Kaḥḥala, *Muʿjam al-muʾallifīn*, 7: 194–5 and Makhlūf, *Shajarat al-nūr*, 1: 97.

94 A *qirāḍ* is defined as "a commercial arrangement in which an investor or group of investors entrusts capital or merchandise to an agent-manager who is to trade with it and then return it to the investor with the principal and a previously agreed-upon share of the profits," see *EI*[2], 5: 129.

95 al-Wansharīsī, *al-Miʿyār al-muʿrib*, 9: 78–9.

96 On the extent of this trade, see Said Ennahid, *Political Economy and Settlement Systems of Medieval Northern Morocco: An Archaeological-Historical Approach* (Oxford: Archaeopress, 2002), 30.

97 Muḥammad b. Aḥmad Ibn Rushd, *Kitāb al-muqaddimāt al-mumahhidāt*, 4: 285 and idem, *al-Bayān wa'l-taḥṣīl wa'l-sharḥ wa'l-tawjīh wa'l-taʿlīl fī masāʾil al-mustakhraja*, ed. Muḥammad Ḥajjī (Beirut: Dār al-Gharb al-Islāmī, 1984), 4: 171.

> The Qur'ān, the tradition, and the consensus of the community oblige someone who converts to Islam in the land of war to migrate and join the abode of Islam, and not remain among the polytheists and establish his residence among them, lest their laws be applied to him. This being the case, how is it permissible for anyone to enter their lands when their laws of trade and of other matters will be applied to him? As Mālik...said: "It is disliked for anyone to live in a land where the forbears (*salaf*) are disrespected;"[98] so how is it possible to live in a land where the Merciful One is not believed in and where idols are worshipped?[99]

Thus, on the basis of Mālik's dislike of living in a land where the forbears are disrespected, Ibn Rushd bans Muslim merchants from traveling to the abode of war, emphasizing that it is on the grounds that non-Islamic laws would be applied to them.

Saḥnun's position was also adopted by other contemporaries of Ibn Rushd. For example, Muḥammad b. 'Alī al-Māzarī (d. 536/1141),[100] a jurist of Sicilian ancestry who lived in al-Mahdiyya, responded to a question put by the Zīrid ruler to a number of jurists regarding whether Muslims could travel to Norman Sicily in order to obtain grain during a time of famine. Al-Māzarī answered in the negative because, like Ibn Rushd, he was concerned that those who travelled there would become subject to the laws of unbelief.[101] The question was so pressing that al-Māzarī sent to his teacher, the venerable 'Abd al-Ḥamid Ibn

98 I have been unable to find the source of this exact *ḥadīth*, but for a similar statement, see Abū Muḥammad 'Abdallāh Ibn Abī Zayd al-Qayrawānī, *Kitāb al-Jāmi' fī al-sunan wa'l-ādāb wa'l-māghāzī wa'l-tārīkh*, ed. Muḥammad Abū al-Ajfān and 'Uthmān al-Baṭṭīkh (Beirut: Mu'assasat al-Risāla, 1985), 156, referred to in Michael Cook, *Commanding Right and Forbidding Wrong* (Cambridge: Cambridge University Press, 2001), 362.

99 Muḥammad b. Aḥmad Ibn Rushd, *Kitāb al-muqaddimāt al-mumahhidāt*, 4: 286–87.

100 Kaḥḥāla, *Mu'jam al-mu'allifīn*, 11: 32 and *EI*,[2] 6: 943.

101 It is interesting to note that a number of disputes between traders conducting business in Christian Sicily came before al-Māzarī. He gives his ruling on their disputes and makes no reference to the overall legality of trade in this region. See, for example, al-Wansharīsī, *al-Mi'yār al-mu'rib*, 8: 181–2 and 207–8, referred to in Sarah Davis-Secord, "Muslims in Norman Sicily: The Evidence of Imām al-Māzarī's Fatwās," *Mediterranean Studies* 16 (2007), 60–61. I do not think that it is necessary to posit, as Davis-Secord does, that al-Māzarī changed his mind on this matter. He probably considered such actions to be wrong but felt that there should nonetheless be justice among sinners. This kind of reasoning is also apparent in his *fatwā* on the Muslim judges of Norman Sicily which I discuss in another chapter.

al-Ṣā'igh (d. 486/1093),[102] to ask for his confirmation of the ruling. The latter responded that travel to such lands was forbidden because of the monetary advantage that it gave to the unbelievers, who would use the money which they received from Muslims to fight against them.[103] 'Abdallāh Ibn Ṭalḥa al-Yāburī al-Ishbīlī (d. 538/1144)[104] offers an exception to this view. Travelling to the abode of war, he says, is not permissible lest a Muslim become subject to non-Muslim law or be humbled by unbelievers. However, if a Muslim travels to uninhabited parts of non-Muslim territory where there is no risk that this might happen, such travel is permissible. Thus he says that it is permissible to hunt, cultivate land, and pasture in such areas.[105]

Later jurists continued to affirm the ban on travel. Muḥammad b. Aḥmad Ibn Juzayy of Granada (d. 741/1340),[106] who died while fighting on behalf of the Marīnids to reconquer Iberia, includes a section on trade in non-Muslim territory in his legal work, *Qawānīn al-aḥkām*. In it, he reiterates the position taken by Ibn Rushd and al-Māzarī and adds that travel to non-Muslim territory is banned except in circumstances where it is necessary in order to ransom captives.[107] About a century later, Abū al-Qāsim b. Aḥmad b. Muḥammad al-Burzulī (d. 841/1438) of Tunis,[108] quoting al-Māzarī, makes a similar point, but says that merchants who travel to the abode of war out of necessity in order to procure food commit a less serious offence.[109] Thus, by the time al-Wansharīsī compiled his *fatwā*s on the question of whether Muslims could live under non-Muslim rule, there had already been several significant Mālikī legal discussions which banned Muslims from residing there on a temporary basis.

What was the reason for the jurists' objections to Muslims being subject to non-Muslim rule even temporarily? The Egyptian Mālikī jurist, Muḥammad Ibn al-Ḥājj (d. 737/1336), says that a Muslim may not travel to the land of unbelief

---

102 Makhlūf, *Shajarat al-nūr*, 1: 117.

103 al-Wansharīsī, *al-Mi'yār al-mu'rib*, 6: 317–318. Cf. al-Burzulī, *Fatāwā al-Burzulī*, 2: 45–6. The matter is briefly discussed in H.R. Idris, "Commerce maritime et *ḳirāḍ* en Berbérie orientale: d'après un recueil inédit de *fatwās* médiévales," *Journal of the Economic and Social History of the Orient* 4 (1961), 228. Al-Māzarī confirms this view in his *Sharḥ al-Talqīn* (Tunis National Library n. 12206), f. 168, quoted in Ibrāhīm b. Mūsā al-Shāṭibī, *Fatāwā al-Imām al-Shāṭibī*, ed. Muḥammad Abū al-Ajfān (Tunis: n.p., 1985), 146 n. 59.

104 Makhlūf, *Shajarat al-nūr*, 1: 379.

105 al-Wazzānī, *al-Mi'yār al-jadīd*, 3: 47–48.

106 Makhlūf, *Shajarat al-nūr*, 1: 213 and Kaḥḥāla, *Mu'jam al-mu'allifīn*, 9: 11.

107 Muḥammad b. Aḥmad Ibn Juzayy al-Gharnāṭī al-Mālikī, *Qawānīn al-aḥkām al-shar'iyya wa-masā'il al-furū' al-fiqhiyya* (Beirut: Dār al-'Ilm li'l-Malāyīn, 1968), 319.

108 See *EI*², 1: 879.

109 al-Burzūlī, *Fatāwā al-Burzulī*, 2: 45–46.

because it is an essential religious principle, enshrined in a *ḥadīth*, that "Islam is exalted and nothing is exalted above it."[110] Since the word of a Muslim who travels to the abode of war is inevitably subordinated to that of the unbelievers, travel to such lands is prohibited.[111] Some *fatwās* in al-Wansharīsī's *al-Miʿyār al-muʿrib* suggest that jurists objected to Muslims living under non-Muslim rule because they worried that under such circumstances they would be placed in a position in which they would be compelled to violate Islamic law. In a section of the *al-Miʿyār al-muʿrib* dealing with the laws of trade, it is mentioned that certain non-Islamic laws and conventions of trade force Muslim merchants to commit usury, albeit unwittingly. Al-Wansharīsī cites a ruling by al-Māzarī in which Muslim traders reported on how, whenever they arrive in Christian Sicily, they are forced by its officials to exchange their gold dinars for local currency. The procedure arranged by these officials was such that Muslim currency lost considerable value in the exchange. Since the Christian officials apparently received this additional money for no added value, some Muslim jurists declared that the exchange was forbidden as it constituted *ribā*, or the forbidden taking of interest.[112] Al-Māzarī suggests that, given the seriousness of becoming subject to this law, Muslims should avoid trading in Sicily even in the event that failing to procure such items would lead to starvation in the Maghrib.[113]

It should be noted that the jurists' discussions regarding Muslims being subjected to non-Muslim laws might have had another subtext. *Al-Miʿyār*

110 *Ṣaḥīḥ al-Bukhārī*, no. 1288. The *ḥadīth* is discussed in Y. Friedman, *Tolerance and Coercion in Islam: Interfaith Relations in the Muslim Tradition* (Cambridge: Cambridge University Press, 2003), 35 ff.

111 Muḥammad b. Muḥammad Ibn al-Ḥājj, *al-Madkhal* (Cairo: al-Maṭbaʿa al-Miṣriyya, 1929), 4: 53–54.

112 See al-Wansharīsī, *al-Miʿyār al-muʿrib*, 6: 319. It should be noted that, according to most Mālikīs, the taking of interest, even in the abode of war, is forbidden. See, for example, *al-Mudawwana al-kubrā* (Beirut: Dār Sādir, 1975), 4: 271 and Khalaf b. Abī al-Qāsim al-Azdī al-Barādhiʿī, *Tahdhīb masāʾil al-Mudawwana* (*al-Tahdhīb fī ikhtiṣār al-Mudawwana*), ed. Aḥmad Farīd al-Mazīdī (Beirut: Dār al-Kutub al-ʿIlmiyya, 2006), 2: 65. See, however, the dissenting view of Ibn Rushd, *al-Muqaddimāt al-mumahhidāt*, ed. Muḥammad Ḥajjī (Beirut: Dār al-Gharb al-Islāmī, 1988), 2: 10–11.

113 In another *fatwa*, al-Wansharīsī does allow for a potential loophole to the rule against temporarily placing oneself under non-Muslim authority. He says that, so long as the Muslim sultan is strong, a Muslim may travel on a Christian ship despite the fact that a Muslim is not normally permitted to place himself under the authority of Christians. This is because he sees the existence of the Muslim sultan as a guarantee against religious corruption. See al-Wansharīsī, *al-Miʿyār al-muʿrib*, 1: 436.

al-muʿrib contains many references to Muslims fleeing to non-Muslim lands in order to escape the jurisdiction of Muslim judges. Some relate that there were Maghribī husbands and fathers who left their families for years on end while they sojourned in Norman Sicily.[114] Such travel resulted in a limitation on the authority of the jurists because they had no extraterritorial power and therefore had no way to compel such individuals to take responsibility for their families and other financial obligations. Prohibiting travel to the abode of war was thus one way in which jurists sought to preserve their authority. Despite the prohibition against travel to the abode of war, many Muslim merchants continued to travel there. Although there was little that the jurists could do about it, they registered their disapproval in any way they could. It is reported, for example, that Saḥnūn refused to allow the building of a bridge to his house because he knew that it would be funded from trade with the Sudan, which he regarded as being a part of the abode of war.[115] Similarly, many jurists called for a ban on the use of ivory and other items commonly imported from the Sudan, although the ban seems to have been largely ignored.[116]

The ban on becoming subject to non-Muslim laws is thus one of the main legal principles from which many Mālikī jurists, including al-Wansharīsī, derived their ban against living in non-Muslim territory. It was a powerful argument as it was based upon several centuries of Mālikī legal precedent, beginning with Saḥnūn in the *Mudawwana*.[117] Once jurists could establish in this way that temporary residence in the abode of war was prohibited, they could argue that, *a fortiori*, permanent residence in the abode of war was also prohibited. They were thus able to argue, with considerable force, that their views on the largely unprecedented situation of Muslims living under non-Muslim rule were entirely consistent with Mālikī tradition.

---

114 Udovitch, "Muslims and Jews," 89, and al-Wansharīsī, *al-Miʿyār al-muʿrib*, 3: 311–14.

115 al-Qāḍī ʿIyāḍ, *Tarājim Aghlabiyya mustakhraja min madārik al-qāḍī ʿIyāḍ*, ed. Muḥammad al-Ṭālibī (Tūnis: al-Jāmiʿa al-Tūnisiyya, 1968), 126, cited in Hopkins and Levtzion, *Corpus of Early Arabic Sources for West African History*, 103.

116 Abū Bakr ʿAbdallāh b. Abī ʿAbdallāh al-Mālikī (d. 453/1061), *Kitāb riyāḍ al-nufūs fī ṭabaqāt ʿulamāʾ al-Qayrawān wa-Ifrīqiya*, ed. Ḥusayn Muʾnis (Cairo: Maktabat al-Nahḍa al-Miṣriyya, 1951), 1: 388.

117 The ban continued to be promulgated into the thirteenth/nineteenth century. For examples, see B. Lewis, "Legal and Historical Reflections on the Position of Muslim Populations under Non-Muslim Rule," 49; idem, *The Muslim Discovery of Europe* (London: Phoenix, 1994), 117–119 and 179–182; and Muḥammad al-Ṣaffār and Susan Gilson Miller (tr.), *Disorienting Encounters: Travels of a Moroccan Scholar in France in 1845–1846: The Voyage of Muhammad As-Saffar* (Berkeley: University of California Press, 1992), 221.

Conclusion

The earliest Mālikī texts lacked an explicit prohibition against Muslims living permanently in non-Muslim territory and the jurists therefore looked to the concept of *hijra* and the ban on temporary travel to the abode of war as support for this prohibition. Each of these concepts had both strengths and weaknesses. While the concept of *hijra* more closely implied a prohibition against living in Christian territory, it possessed an ambiguous legal status as a result of the attempts of previous religious authorities to exclude it from the Islamic tradition. The ban on temporary travel to the abode of war could be invoked on firmer legal ground, but it clearly lacked the resonance of the concept of *hijra*. In addition, the fact that it had been widely neglected by merchants for centuries must have further weakened its force. By invoking the two concepts together, however, the jurists no doubt felt that they had produced a strong legal case against those Mudéjars who wished to remain in their homes in Christian Iberia.

CHAPTER 2

The Status of the Mudéjar Religious Leadership According to Mālikī Law[1]

In the previous chapter, the legal permissibility of Muslim residence in non-Muslim territory was examined. Although the laws developed in response to this issue might appear to also embrace the case of the Mudéjar religious leadership (*ʿulamāʾ*),[2] their case was often dealt with separately for the following reason. The jurists agreed that Mudéjars who were truly unable to migrate were to be excused from the obligation. They differed in how they defined "unable to migrate," but, regardless of how they did so, the Mudéjar *ʿulamāʾ* only rarely fitted this category. This was because, since the *ʿulamāʾ* were usually drawn from social elites, they often possessed the political connections and financial resources necessary to emigrate which most other Mudéjars lacked. They were thus often able to migrate even under circumstances in which migration for other Muslims was impossible.[3] It would therefore seem that, given their ability to emigrate, they would have a corresponding obligation to do so. Some jurists felt, however, that a straight application of this law would have the effect of destroying Mudéjar communities. One petitioner for a *fatwā* on whether the Mudéjar *ʿulamāʾ* could remain puts the position thus:

> Are their religious scholars (*ahl al-ʿilm*) allowed to postpone an emigration (*hijra*) which they are able to make in order to preserve the beliefs and strengthen the religion of those Muslims who dwell in Christian lands who are unable to leave? [These scholars remain] because they fear

1 A version of this chapter was published as "The Evolution of the Mālikī Jurists' Attitudes to the Mudéjar Leadership," *Der Islam* 90 (2013), 44–64.

2 The sources use a wide variety of terms to designate these scholars and leaders including *qāḍī*, *faqīh*, *khaṭīb*, *ahl al-ʿilm*, etc. I have opted for the general term *ʿulamāʾ* because the Arabic terms and their European language (Castilian, Latin, etc.) equivalents fluctuate considerably. On this fluctuation, see L.P. Harvey, *Muslims in Spain, 1500 to 1614* (Chicago: University of Chicago Press, 2005), 89 and John Boswell, *The Royal Treasure: Muslim Communities under the Crown of Aragon in the Fourteenth Century* (New Haven: Yale University Press, 1977), 90.

3 Indeed, a common reward given to Mudéjar *ʿulamāʾ* by Christian rulers was the right to immigrate to Islamic lands. See Boswell, *The Royal Treasure*, 396–97.

© KONINKLIJKE BRILL NV, LEIDEN, 2015 | DOI 10.1163/9789004284531_004

> the beliefs [of these Muslims] will become corrupt and that ignorance (*jahl*) will reign upon their departure.[4]

This petitioner, and indeed many others, believed that without the guidance of the *ʿulamāʾ*, the Mudéjar communities would quickly abandon Islam. A decision to ban *ʿulamāʾ* from living in Christian Iberia was thus viewed as tantamount to a decision to destroy these Muslim communities.

Research on Christian Spain has confirmed the centrality of the*ʿulamāʾ* in the political, economic and religious lives of the Mudéjars.[5] With the fall of Muslim rule in the Iberian Peninsula, they emerged as leaders who were responsible for organizing most aspects of the communal lives of their coreligionists. John Boswell notes that it was generally the Mudéjar *qāḍī* (judge) who negotiated capitulation treaties with Christian rulers and ensured Muslim compliance with them. It was also generally the *qāḍī* who represented the Muslim community before the Christian authorities. At times, in addition to adjudicating legal disputes, the *qāḍī* was responsible for ensuring the safety of the *morería* or Muslim quarter, in some cases providing it with a police force from his own entourage.[6] Given the vast array of roles that the *ʿulamāʾ* occupied, it is clear why many thought that without them the Mudéjar communities would disintegrate. Without the *ʿulamāʾ*, the Mudéjars would have no one to care for their religious lives, no one to regulate their communities, and no

---

4 P.S. van Koningsveld and G.A. Wiegers, "Islam in Spain during the Early Sixteenth Century: The Views of the Four Chief Judges in Cairo (Introduction, Translation and Arabic text)," in *Poetry, Politics and Polemics: Cultural Transfer between the Iberian Peninsula and North Africa* (Amsterdam: Rodopi, 1996), 147.

5 Mark Meyerson, *The Muslims of Valencia in the Age of Fernando and Isabel* (Berkeley: University of California Press, 1991), 263. Cf. Míkel de Epalza, "Caracterización del exilio musulmán: La voz de Mudéjares y Moriscos," in *Destierros aragoneses* (Saragossa: Institución Fernando el Católico, 1988), 1: 222; Tuli Halperin Donghi, *Un conflict nacional: Moriscos y Cristianos viejos en Valencia* (Valencia: Institución Alfonso el Magnánimo, 1980), 107 ff; and Boswell, *The Royal Treasure*, 77.

6 Boswell, *The Royal Treasure*, 86. Their assumption of this role is not surprising given that, even under Muslim rule, the Iberian *ʿulamāʾ* enjoyed a broad range of power and, in times of political turmoil, there are frequent examples of *qāḍīs* becoming political rulers. See Maribel Fierro, "The *Qāḍī* as Ruler," in *Saber religioso y poder político en el Islam* (Madrid: Agencia Española de Cooperación Internacional, 1994), 71–116 and Robert Burns, *Medieval Colonialism: Postcrusade Exploitation of Islamic Valencia* (Princeton: Princeton University Press, 1975), 13. The pervasiveness of the ruling function of *qāḍīs* is perhaps indicated by the fact that the Romance term *alcalde*, derived from *qāḍī*, is usually used to designate, not a judge, but the mayor of a town. On this, see Émile Tyan, *Histoire de l'organisation judiciaire en pays d'Islam* (Paris: Annales de l'Université de Lyon, 1943), 2: 120–21.

one to serve as intermediaries between themselves and the Christian authorities. Without a religious community to give their lives structure, many thought that it was only a matter of time before they were converted to Christianity. Could such considerations, some jurists wondered, make it permissible for the *ʿulamāʾ* to delay their religious obligation of emigration?

Given the centrality of the *ʿulamāʾ* to Mudéjar religious life, some contemporary historians have regarded it as self-evident that they should have been granted special dispensation to delay their migration and have been shocked by the views of Mālikī jurists who have suggested otherwise. Some of these Mālikī jurists not only urged the Mudéjar *ʿulamāʾ* to migrate, even if the communities they led could not do so, but also declared them to be illegitimate holders of religious authority so long as they remained in Christian lands. Some historians have consequently characterized the jurists' writings as representing fanatical or anti-progressive trends within Islam which privilege Islamic precepts over humanitarian concerns.[7] By offering a chronological analysis of the jurists' works and coupling this with documentary evidence on the relationship between Mudéjar communities and their Christian rulers, I show that the jurists based their arguments mainly on pragmatic concerns pertaining to social welfare rather than on Islamic law or dogma. In the previous chapter, I showed how the jurists' thinking on *hijra* changed radically over the course of the Reconquista. In this chapter, I show how their thinking on the Mudéjar leadership underwent similar changes. Before the 14th-century, jurists seem to have been relatively unconcerned by the presence of Muslim communities in non-Muslim lands. Beginning in the 14th century, however, jurists generally recommend that Muslims migrate from such lands.

Juristic Thought Prior to the Fourteenth Century

When considering the problem posed by the Mudéjar *ʿulamāʾ*, the Mālikī jurists addressed the following questions. May a Muslim community appoint *ʿulamāʾ* to enforce Islamic law in a region which has no Muslim ruler? May a Muslim community accept the authority of *ʿulamāʾ* appointed by a non-Muslim ruler? Are the *ʿulamāʾ* who stay in non-Muslim territory, although they have the ability to emigrate, sinners? More generally, is the existence of *ʿulamāʾ* in non-Muslim territory an advantage for Islam as a whole because it prevents the assimilation of these communities or does it contain the threat of religious corruption and perhaps a political threat as well? Prior to the fourteenth

7 Please see my introduction.

century, jurists wrote relatively little about these issues because the phenomenon was not yet widespread. The first to grapple with the problem did so in response to the scattered Muslim communities living among practitioners of indigenous African religions. The Qayrawānī jurist, ʿAlī b. Muḥammad al-Qābisī (d. 403/1012),[8] is asked about whether the legal ruling of "a Muslim whom the [non-Muslim] king … appointed superintendent (*nāẓir*) of the Muslims, and whom the Muslims have accepted" can be regarded as legitimate. He answers in the affirmative:

> Because the place in which this matter occurred was one in which Muslims had settled and dwelt, they had no choice but to have someone to oversee their affairs and judge between them so that they would have authority to overpower someone who disobeys the laws. All this would be ordered by the one who conquered that place because it is not possible to escape from kings in power—especially from the power of unbelief and hostility. Hence, if the superintendent of the Muslims judges them according to Islamic law, his judgment is effective if it is in accordance with the law. It is binding on those who choose to come under his authority or remain under his supervision, whether they live there permanently or whether they are [merely] passing through [his area of jurisdiction].[9]

Al-Qābisī does not think that remaining in non-Muslim territory is an ideal course of action but he nonetheless permits Muslim community leaders to function there. He acknowledges that such leaders will be influenced by the non-Muslim authorities which appoint them but still grants them legitimacy on the grounds that the disorder caused by their absence is the greater evil. Al-Qābisī thus grants permission for Muslim community leaders to function in non-Muslim areas of the Sudan on the basis of his belief in the primacy of social welfare, an argument often used among jurists of the Mālikī legal school.[10]

In approximately the same period, Abū Jaʿfar b. Naṣr al-Dāwūdī (d. 402/1011) deals with whether *qāḍīs* have the authority to enforce the law among the Maṣmūda in the High Atlas where the petitioner alleges there was no Muslim political authority. It is difficult to establish with certainty what the petitioner means by a land with no Muslim political authority. It seems likely that he

8 Muḥammad Makhlūf, *Shajarat al-nūr* (Beirut: Dār al-Kitāb al-ʿArabī, 197?), 1: 97.

9 al-Wansharīsī, *al-Miʿyār al-muʿrib*, 10: 135.

10 On *maṣlaḥa* in Mālikī law, see ʿAbd al-Ḥayy Ḥasan al-ʿUmrānī, *al-Madhhab al-Mālikī wa-madā akhdhihi biʾl-maṣālīḥ al-mursala* (Rabat: al-Mamlaka al-Maghribiyya, Wizārat al-Awqāf waʾl-Shuʾūn al-Islāmiyya, 2003).

means a superficially Islamicized area which would not submit to a central authority. In any case, al-Dāwūdī says that "local trustworthy professional witnesses (*ʿudūl*) or people of knowledge (*ahl al-ʿilm*) can take over everything in place of the ruler" in "any land in which there is not a ruler or in which there is a ruler who neglects to impose the *ḥudūd* (a category of legal penalties) or who is unjust."[11] Al-Dāwūdī does not, as other jurists were later to do, exhort Muslims to leave these lands on the grounds that their activities, in the absence of a just Muslim ruler, are without any value. Rather, he enjoins these Muslims to appoint their own community leaders whose pronouncements would have the force of law.

Prior to the 14th century, jurists addressing the case of religious leaders living in Christendom seem to have followed a similar philosophy to those addressing the case of the Sudan or the High Atlas. The earliest response that I have located occurs in a *fatwā* by the jurist ʿUthmān b. Abī Bakr Ibn al-Ḍābiṭ (d. c. 442/1050).[12] Ibn al-Ḍābiṭ was asked whether a man can be given his inheritance in a case where the evidence that the testator is dead is provided by a Sicilian *qāḍī* appointed by the Christian ruler (al-Rūmī).[13] Can this *qāḍī*'s evidence be accepted, Ibn al-Ḍābiṭ wondered, given that he was appointed by a Christian ruler and therefore might not possess probity (*ʿadāla*)? Ibn al-Ḍābiṭ only accepted his evidence once witnesses from the Muslim town of Mahdiyya affirmed that the *qāḍī* possessed probity.[14] Thus, for Ibn al-Ḍābiṭ, although the rulings of *qāḍī*s appointed by Christian rulers are not to be uniformly discounted, they are to be subjected to close scrutiny before being accepted.

---

11 al-Wansharīsī, *al-Miʿyār al-muʿrib*, 10: 102. In the *fatwā* which follows this one, al-Dāwūdī makes the same point about lands in which both the sultan and properly-qualified *qāḍī*s are absent.

12 On ʿUthmān b. Abī Bakr Ibn al-Ḍābiṭ, see Makhlūf, *Shajarat al-nūr*, 1: 109 and Hady Idris, "Contribution à l'étude de la vie religieuse en Ifrīqiya Zīrīde (Xème–XIème siècles)," in *Mélanges Louis Massignon* (Damascus: Institut Français de Damas, 1957), 2: 357–9. Idris notes that Ibn al-Ḍābiṭ was known to have traveled to Christian lands on diplomatic missions.

13 Ibn al-Ḍābiṭ likely refers to a Christian ruler of eastern Sicily as not all of Sicily had yet fallen to the Christians. On this period of turmoil, see A. Metcalfe, *Muslims and Christians in Norman Sicily* (London: RoutledgeCurzon, 2003), 24 ff.; M. Gil, "Muslim Rule in Sicily," in *Jews in Islamic Countries in the Middle Ages* (Leiden: Brill, 2004), 545 and J. Gay, *L'Italie méridionale et l'Empire byzantin depuis l'avènement de Basile Ier jusqu'a la prise de Bari par les Normands (867–1071)* (Paris: Albert Fontemoing, 1904), 435.

14 Abū al-Qāsim b. Aḥmad al-Burzulī, *Fatāwā al-Burzulī*, ed. Muḥammad al-Ḥabīb al-Hayla (Beirut: Dār al-Gharb al-Islāmī, 2002), 4: 51 and al-Wansharīsī, *al-Miʿyār al-muʿrib*, 10: 113.

A more thorough examination of the issue is conducted by the Tunisian jurist of Sicilian origin, Muḥammad b. ʿAlī al-Māzarī (d. 536/1141). The latter wrote a *fatwā* concerning the *qāḍīs* of Sicily which possessed one of the first sizeable Muslim communities to have fallen under Christian rule.[15] Al-Māzarī was asked whether the pronouncements of *qāḍīs* and "professional witnesses" (*shuhūd ʿudūl*) who lived in Christian Sicily possessed probity and whether this was also the case if they had been directly appointed by Christian officials. He answers that, under most circumstances, they should be regarded as legitimate. Al-Māzarī bases his argument on the legal principle that one is obligated to think well of Muslims and that, as a result, the assumed default state of any Muslim is one of probity (*ʿadāla*),[16] unless there is firm evidence to the contrary.[17] Al-Māzarī then looks into the factors which might impugn such a *qāḍī*'s probity. If the *qāḍī* has not emigrated from non-Muslim territory, he says, this is not an automatic indication of his lack of probity because he might be one of those who is unable to emigrate and is therefore to be excused for not fulfilling this religious obligation. If, on the other hand, the *qāḍī* remains there of his own choice, a number of considerations must be taken into account in order to determine if his probity has been impugned. If he remains because of a wish to guide the people towards Islam, his probity is not impugned because his conduct is analogous to that of someone who travels to non-Muslim territory in order to ransom prisoners, an activity which is permitted by Mālik because its utility outweighs its harm.[18] Al-Māzarī's legal argument here may

15 al-Wansharīsī, *al-Miʿyār al-muʿrib*, 10: 107–9. Cf. *Fatāwā al-Burzulī*, 4: 49–51. On this *fatwā*, see Abdel-Magid Turki, "Consultation juridique d'al-Imām al-Māzarī sur le cas des musulmans vivant en Sicile sous l'autorité des Normands," *Mélanges de l'Université Saint-Joseph* 50 (1984), 691 ff. and idem, "Pour ou contre la légalité du sejour des musulmans au territoire reconquis par les Chrétiens: Justification doctrinale et réalité historique," in *Religionsgespräche im Mittelalter*, ed. B. Lewis and F. Niewöhner (Wiesbaden: Harrassowitz, 1992), 305–23.

16 Al-Māzarī refers to his own fuller discussion of *ʿadāla* in *Īḍāḥ al-maḥṣūl min Burhān al-uṣūl*, ed. ʿAmmār al-Ṭālibī (Beirut: Dār al-Gharb al-Islāmī, 2001), 460 ff. On the Mālikī application of this term to *qāḍīs*, see Alfonso Carmona, "Le Malékisme et les conditions requises pour l'exercice de la judicature," *Islamic Law and Society* 7 (2000), 137 ff. and 142 ff. and David Pelaez Portales, *El Proceso judicial en la España Musulmana* (*siglos viii–xii*) (Cordoba: Ediciones el Almendro, 2000), 223 ff.

17 This same point is made by Muḥammad b. Aḥmad Ibn Rushd "the Grandfather" (d. 520/1126) in a discussion of the case of whether the evidence of one prisoner in non-Muslim territory can be used regarding another. See al-Wansharīsī, *al-Miʿyār al-muʿrib*, 10: 157–58 and *Fatāwā Ibn Rushd*, ed. al-Mukhtār b. al-Ṭāhir al-Talīlī (Beirut: Dār al-Gharb al-Islāmī, 1987), 3: 1645.

18 David de Santillana, *Istituzioni di diritto musulmano malichita*, 1: 71.

seem weak. The analogy between temporary travel to non-Muslim territory for the purpose of ransoming prisoners and effectively permanent residence there in order to guide Muslim communities seems tenuous at best. Al-Māzarī, however, is forced to make this analogy because, as I have noted, the law regarding the ransoming of prisoners is the only instance other than that of *jihād* in which a Muslim's presence in non-Muslim territory is permitted by Mālikī law. Al-Māzarī concludes that it is only under circumstances in which the *qāḍī* remains in non-Muslim territory in deliberate violation of the prohibition against living there that he is to be regarded as illegitimate.

Al-Māzarī then deals with the issue of whether such a *qāḍī* can be considered legitimate if he is appointed to his position by non-Muslims. He says that, even under such circumstances, the *qāḍī* is to be regarded as legitimate so long as he is appointed in order to prevent public disorder. He argues that since appointing a *qāḍī* for such a purpose is a "rational obligation" (*wājib ʿaqlan*), by which he seems to mean a natural law[19] without which society itself would cease to function, the appointment is valid even though the involvement of non-Muslims would normally serve to invalidate it. He adds that if the *qāḍī*'s appointment is supported by the Muslims, this in itself gives him complete validation.

It is difficult to determine with certainty whether the views of these pre-14th-century jurists represent the dominant Mālikī legal opinion on this matter, but the fact that the jurists discussed above were among the most prominent of their time certainly lends weight to this contention. These jurists' arguments seem to rest not so much on legal precedent as on an appeal to benefit the social welfare of the Mudéjars.[20] They word their opinions with the utmost caution lest their rulings be interpreted as an unrestricted justification for living in non-Muslim territory. They argue that their rulings are justified only because the Muslim communities of non-Muslim territory cannot be relocated and that it is therefore important to give them the legal protection which would allow them to maintain their religious lives as best as they can. They clearly indicate that it is better for Muslims to live under Islamic law than outside of it and that, consequently, although living in non-Muslim territory is not

19 For a study of "natural law" in the Islamic tradition, see Anver Emon, *Islamic Natural Law Theories* (Oxford: Oxford University Press, 2010).

20 Al-Māzarī claims that earlier authorities supported his view. He says that, according to Ibn al-Mājishūn (d. 164/780) and Muṭarrif (d. 282/895), when a ruler is overthrown and the enemy appoints *qāḍīs*, the rulings of those *qāḍīs* are valid. Unfortunately, neither of these authors' works survive in their entirety and I have been unable to find confirmation of their views in other sources.

recommended, those who do so should still be protected by affording them the leadership of the *ʿulamāʾ*.

The Fall of the Almohads and the Emergence of New Attitudes Toward the Mudéjar *ʿUlamāʾ*

A shift in Mālikī opinion on the Mudéjar *ʿulamāʾ* occurred after the end of the Almohad period (668/1269). For reasons that they do not make clear, after this period, jurists are generally unwilling to accommodate the Mudéjar *ʿulamāʾ* and insist on their immediate migration to Muslim territory. This change is noted by the jurist, al-Mawwāq (d. 897/1492).[21] Quoting Ibn ʿArafa (d. 803/1401),[22] he says that whereas originally the legitimacy of a *qāḍī* was not prejudiced by the fact that he was appointed by a usurper of the rightful ruler—because the jurists feared that doing so would lead to the law being suspended (*taʿṭīl al-aḥkām*)—they changed their opinion in response to the situation of the Mudéjar *qāḍī*s, and made the legitimacy of a *qāḍī* dependent on the legitimacy of the ruler who appointed him.[23] Thus the earlier view which was based on concern for the welfare of Muslims who were left without the protection of the law was replaced by a view reflecting the tense political circumstances of the Reconquista. The balance of this chapter will examine some of these new views in their historical context.

The earliest representative of the new view seems to be Muḥammad b. Yaḥyā Ibn Rabīʿ (d. 719/1319), who regards the legal testimony of those who live

---

21 Makhlūf, *Shajarat al-nūr*, 1: 262.

22 Brockelmann, *Geschichte der arabischen Litteratur* (Leiden: E.J. Brill, 1949), Supplement 2: 347.

23 Muḥammad b. Yūsuf al-Mawwāq, *al-Tāj wa'l-iklīl li-Mukhtaṣar Khalīl* (Ṭarābulus: Maktabat al-Najāḥ, 1969), 6: 143. It is not at all clear whether this was the view of Ibn ʿArafa. In a *fatwā* by al-Wansharīsī, Ibn ʿArafa's statement regarding the legitimacy of the *qāḍī* appointed by a usurper is quoted separately from his ruling on the status of Mudéjar *qāḍī*s, giving the impression that he was the author of two contradictory statements. It may be that al-Mawwāq's comment that one of these statements applied to the situation before the Mudéjar period was al-Mawwāq's own interpretation. Al-Mawwāq's quotation of Ibn ʿArafa varies slightly in the printed editions, see al-Wansharīsī, *al-Miʿyār al-muʿrib*, 2: 133–34, 10: 66 and 109, and *Fatāwā al-Burzulī*, 4: 49. Further, in another *fatwā*, Ibn ʿArafa says that rulings of Mudéjar *qāḍī*s may be accepted providing one exercises the appropriate caution (*iḥtirāz*). He therefore accepts a document written by a *qāḍī* from non-Muslim territory because he knows him to be of good character. See al-Wansharīsī, *al-Miʿyār al-muʿrib*, 10: 66–67.

in non-Muslim territory as invalid.[24] Another jurist, Muḥammad Ibn Barṭāl, whose exact dates are unknown but who shared several students with Ibn Rabīʿ,[25] says that those students of religion (*ṭalaba*) and those muezzins who are content to live under the pact of protection (*dhimma*) of the Christians are evil (*su'*). He therefore says that it is forbidden to accept their evidence or leadership in prayer. It is the greatest sin (*wizr*) for them to live under Christian rule, he says, and they must do penitence after leaving these lands.[26] Ibn Barṭāl does not cite extensive textual proofs for his position and merely indicates that his *fatwā* is in harmony with the views of the Mālikī school.

One of the more detailed arguments for this new position on the Mudéjars is by the jurist, al-Mawwāq,[27] who attempts to justify this new view on the basis of earlier precedents. He quotes Ibn ʿAllāq (d. 806/1404),[28] who says that if non-Muslims rule over a region and appoint a *qāḍī*, his authority is not to be accepted.[29] In searching for even earlier views, however, al-Mawwāq encounters

---

24 P.S. van Koningsveld and G.A. Wiegers, "The Islamic Statute of the Mudéjars in the Light of a New Source," *al-Qanṭara* 17 (1996), 33. Ibn Rabīʿ was a judge and *wazīr* who lived in Málaga. On his life, see Aḥmad b. ʿAlī Ibn Ḥajar al-ʿAsqalānī, *al-Durar al-kāmina fī aʿyān al-mi'a al-thāmina*, ed. Muḥammad Sayyid Jād al-Ḥaqq (Cairo: Dār al-Kutub al-Ḥadītha, 1967), 4: 793.

25 Van Koningsveld and Wiegers have plausibly identified this jurist as Abū ʿAbdallāh Muḥammad b. ʿAlī b. Muḥammad Ibn Barṭāl, see "The Islamic Statute of the Mudéjars," 38. For references to this jurist, see Ibn al-Khaṭīb, *al-Iḥāṭa fī akhbār Gharnāṭa*, ed. Muḥammad ʿAbdallāh ʿInān (Cairo: Maktabat al-Khānjī, 1973), 4: 13 and 387. For my arguments in favor of this dating, see above, page 22.

26 His *fatāwā* are found in ʿAbd al-ʿAzīz b. al-Ḥasan al-Zayyātī (d. 1055/1645), *al-Jawāhir al-mukhtāra fī mā waqaftu ʿalayhi min al-nawāzil bi-jibāl ghumāra* (Bibliothèque Nationale du Royaume du Maroc, ms. 1698, 2: 40 ff.) and, in abbreviated form, in al-Mahdī al-Wazzānī, *al-Nawāzil al-ṣughrā* (Rabat: Wizārat al-Awqāf wa'l-Shu'ūn al-Islāmiyya li'l-Mamlaka al-Maghribiyya, 1992), 1: 419.

27 Makhlūf, *Shajarat al-nūr*, 1: 262.

28 On Abū ʿAbdallāh Muḥammad b. ʿAlī Ibn ʿAllāq, see Makhlūf, *Shajarat al-nūr*, 1: 247. Al-Wazzānī's *al-Miʿyār al-jadīd*, 3: 34 gives his name as Ibn ʿAllāl. If this is correct, the jurist to whom the text refers is no doubt Abū Mahdī ʿĪsā b. ʿAllāl al-Kutāmī al-Maṣmūdī al-Fāsī Ibn ʿAllāl (d. 823/1420), see Makhlūf, *Shajarat al-nūr*, 1: 251. Either of these jurists could plausibly have issued this *fatwā*.

29 al-Mawwāq, *al-Tāj wa'l-iklīl li-Mukhtaṣar Khalīl*, 6: 143. It is important to note that even relations between a Muslim ruler and the qāḍīs whom he appointed could be fraught. For studies of such power conflicts, see Hiroyuki Yanagihashi, "The Judicial Functions of the Sulṭān in Civil Cases According to the Mālikīs up to the Sixth/Twelfth Century," *Islamic Law and Society* 3 (1996), 41–74 and Alfonso Carmona, "Le Malékisme et les conditions requises pour l'exercice de la judicature," *Islamic Law and Society* 7 (2000), 122–58.

difficulties. He points to a series of biographical entries written by al-Qāḍī ʿIyāḍ (d. 544/1149) which deal with the opposition of certain Mālikī jurists to the (Shiʿite) Fāṭimids. Al-Mawwāq's claim is that the attitudes of these jurists to Muslims living under non-Sunnī Muslim rulers can be applied, by analogy, to those living under Christian rulers.

If we look at the biographies by ʿIyāḍ, we find that the jurists whom al-Mawwāq mentions are indeed praised by him for their harsh stance against the Fāṭimids. These jurists sometimes refer to the Fāṭimids as unbelievers and consequently prohibit social interactions with them.[30] With one exception, none of the biographical entries indicate either that the Sunnī *ʿulamāʾ* who live under Shiʿite rule should lose their legitimacy or that Muslims are obligated to emigrate from Shiʿite-controlled areas. The exception is an entry on al-Dāwūdī who, ʿIyāḍ says, deemed the Fāṭimids unbelievers and said that everyone, including the *ʿulamāʾ*, must leave their lands and are not excused from this obligation even if the large size of their families makes travel difficult. While leaving such lands might have been previously "recommended" by the jurists, al-Dāwūdī elevates this recommendation to a religious obligation.[31] ʿIyāḍ indicates that al-Dāwūdī's contemporaries justly found this view to be unacceptable. They said that it had no force as al-Dāwūdī had used his own reason (*idrāk*) to attain his conclusion rather than relying on the mainstream view (*mashhūr*) of his legal school.[32] Were the *ʿulamāʾ* who lived under Fāṭimid rule to leave these areas, al-Dāwūdī's opponents said, Muslims would have no one to guide them and would suffer great harm.[33] Thus there is little evidence for al-Mawwāq's claim that ʿIyāḍ's biographical work provides support for delegitimizing *ʿulamāʾ* who live under Christian rule.[34]

---

30 See, for example, the entries on Abū Muḥammad b. Isḥāq Ibn al-Tabbān (d. 371/981) and Abū Bakr Ismāʿīl Ibn ʿUdhra (d. c. 430s/1040s) in ʿIyāḍ b. Mūsā al-Yaḥṣūbī, *Tartīb al-madārik wa-taqrīb al-masālik li-maʿrifat aʿlām madhhab Mālik*, ed. Aḥmad Bukayr Maḥmūd (Beirut: Maktabat al-Ḥayāh, 1967), 4: 518–19 and 4: 719.

31 Thus Mālik mentioned that "it is disliked (*makrūh*) for anyone to live in a land where the forbears (*salaf*) are disrespected," but never insisted, like al-Dāwūdī, that leaving such lands was obligatory (*wājib*).

32 On this term, see Sherman Jackson, *Islamic Law and the State: The Constitutional Jurisprudence of Shihāb al-Dīn al-Qarāfī* (New York: Brill, 1996), 83 ff.

33 ʿIyāḍ b. Mūsā, *Tartīb al-madārik*, 4: 623.

34 Interestingly, al-Mawwāq notes the dissenting view of the Shāfiʿī school, as represented by ʿIzz al-Dīn b. ʿAbd al-Salām (d. 660/1262), who says that the legitimacy of a *qāḍī* living in non-Muslim territory is to be accepted provided that he acts in accordance with Islamic law and shuns corruption. If, however, he remains there for base motives and acts unjustly, he is to be regarded as an unbeliever.

Despite its lack of legal precedent, al-Mawwāq's attitude towards the Mudéjar *ʿulamāʾ* was shared by many of his contemporaries. ʿĪsā b. Aḥmad al-Māwāsī (d. 896/1491), for example, says that one cannot accept the testimony or leadership of those who live under a non-Muslim's pact of protection (*dhimma*) for they engage in activities which violate the precepts of religion. He does not, however, specify which precepts of religion he is referring to.[35] The eminent jurist al-Wansharīsī (d. 914/1508) wrote a sternly-worded *fatwā* regarding a Muslim community leader who remained in the Iberian town of Marbella, which had been annexed by the Christians in 1485. Al-Wansharīsī's petitioner informs him that this community leader is universally acknowledged as pious. He remained in Christian territory only in order to give his assistance to its remaining Muslims who would be powerless to survive without his leadership. The tone of the petitioner's question to al-Wansharīsī indicates that he felt considerable sympathy both for this man and for these Mudéjars. Al-Wansharīsī, however, did not give him the answer for which he was hoping. Despite the certain ruin which would face the Muslims of these areas, he says that the *ʿulamāʾ* who lead such communities are not permitted to remain there and rules that the man must emigrate immediately.[36]

Like al-Mawwāq, al-Wansharīsī has difficulty justifiying his views on the basis of earlier precedent. Consider the following examples. Al-Wansharīsī reports that an earlier jurist, Abū al-Walīd al-Bājī (d. 474/1081),[37] forbade accepting the rulings of "the Mudéjar *qāḍī*s (*quḍāt ahl al-dajn*), like the *qāḍī*s of Valencia, Tortosa, Pantelleria and Majorca."[38] Al-Wansharīsī claims that al-Bājī justified his ruling on the grounds that a *qāḍī*'s ruling can only be accepted if it is established that his appointment is legitimate. There are a number of problems, however, with al-Wansharīsī's quotation. First, all of the places that al-Bājī mentions in the passage attributed to him fell under Christian rule only after his death. Second, usage of the term *ahl al-dajn* only began several centuries after his death. One therefore cannot rely on this quotation of al-Bājī's views. At another point, al-Wansharīsī cites an anonymous Egyptian jurist who gives the same view as al-Bājī regarding the *qāḍī*s of Christian Pantelleria.[39]

35 Ibid., 1: 418.

36 al-Wansharīsī, *al-Miʿyār al-muʿrib*, 2: 137. This *fatwā* is translated in the appendix.

37 On al-Bājī, see Maribel Fierro, "Al-Bāŷī, Abū al-Walīd," in J. Lirola Delgado and J.M. Puerta Vílchez, *Diccionario de Autores y Obras Andalusíes* (Seville: Junta de Andalucía, Consejería de Cultura, 2002), 1: 118–123 and Brockelmann, *Geschichte der arabischen Litteratur*, 1: 419 and Supplement 1: 743.

38 al-Wazzānī, *al-Miʿyār al-jadīd*, 3: 29–30.

39 Ibid., 2: 134. Cf. *Fatāwā al-Burzulī*, 2: 22–23.

This jurist justifies his view on the grounds that this was the attitude taken by earlier Andalusī jurists regarding the *qāḍīs* who lived under the rule of "the apostate," 'Umar Ibn Ḥafṣūn.[40] He does not, however, identify who these Andalusī jurists were. As far as I can determine, it is only this non-Andalusī source of uncertain dating and authorship which attributes this view to any Andalusī jurists of this period. While it is possible that the Andalusī jurists did distrust Ibn Ḥafṣūn's *qāḍīs*, there is no evidence that a complete ban was ever placed on their rulings. This anonymous Egyptian jurist's determination of Andalusī jurists' views of these *qāḍīs*, however, was accepted by al-Wansharīsī who refers to it in a number of places.[41] One gathers that al-Wansharīsī's need to demonstrate that his opinion on the Mudéjar leaders was traditional drove him to make use of this dubious text because of the absence of earlier sources in support of his opinion.

A further item of early evidence that al-Wansharīsī musters in support of his view that the Mudéjar leaders are illegitimate also involves some difficulties. He cites a debate between 'Abdallāh Ibn Farrūkh (d. 175/791)[42] and 'Abdallāh Ibn Ghānim (d. 190/806)[43] regarding whether a *qāḍī* who lives under an unjust ruler is legitimate. Ibn Ghānim claimed that such a *qāḍī* is legitimate and Ibn Farrūkh disagreed. The debate was later forcefully resolved by the famous jurist, Saḥnūn b. Sa'īd (d. 240/854), who dramatically said, "The Persian, that is Ibn Farrūkh, is correct and the one who claims he is an Arab, Ibn Ghānim, errs."[44] That is to say, Saḥnūn ruled that a *qāḍī* appointed by an unjust ruler is illegitimate and he humiliated Ibn Ghānim for thinking otherwise. While one can see why such a story would have been of use to al-Wansharīsī, it involves a

40 Whether or not Ibn Ḥafṣūn was indeed an apostate is now much debated. For the classic study on the issue, see Pedro Chalmeta, "Precisiones acerca de Ibn Hafsun," in *Actas de las II Jornadas de Cultura Árabe e Islámica* (Madrid: Instituto Hispano-Arabe de Cultura, *1980*), 163–75. Cf. David Wasserstein, "Inventing Tradition and Constructing Identity: The Genealogy of 'Umar Ibn Ḥafṣūn between Christianity and Islam," *al-Qanṭara* 23 (2002), 294–95. On the figure of Ibn Ḥafṣūn in general, see Virgilio Martínez Enamorado, *'Umar Ibn Ḥafṣūn, de la rebeldía a la construcción de la Dawla. Estudios en torno al rebelde de al-Andalus* (*880–927*) (San José: Universidad de Costa Rica, 2011).

41 See, for example, al-Wansharīsī, *al-Mi'yār al-mu'rib*, 2: 134, 6: 95 and 10: 109.

42 'Iyāḍ b. Mūsā al-Yaḥṣūbī, *Tartīb al-madārik*, 1: 340.

43 'Abdallāh b. Muḥammad al-Mālikī, *Kitāb riyāḍ al-nufūs fī ṭabaqāt 'ulamā' al-Qayrawān wa-Ifrīqiya*, ed. Bashīr al-Bakkūsh (Beirut: Dār al-Gharb al-Islāmī, 1981–3), 1: 215 and 220–22.

44 al-Wansharīsī, *al-Mi'yār al-mu'rib*, 10: 109, quoting al-Mālikī, *Kitāb riyāḍ al-nufūs*, 1: 178–79. Cf. Abū Zayd 'Abd al-Raḥmān b. Muḥammad al-Dabbāgh, *Ma'ālim al-īmān fī ma'rifat ahl al-Qayrawān*, ed. Ibrāhīm Shabbūḥ (Cairo: Maktabat al-Khānjī, 1968), 245–46.

problematic use of the source material. The debate between these two jurists is not about a *qāḍī* who lives under Christian rule but about what a *qāḍī* is to do in order to avoid being ensnared by the inherently corrupting influence of *all* power and politics. The debate forms part of a larger discussion between Ibn Ghānim and Ibn Farrūkh.[45] Ibn Farrūkh is famous for his efforts at avoiding the attempts of rulers to appoint him as a *qāḍī*. It is reported that he only accepted an appointment after the ruler's agents threatened to throw him off a building. Ibn Farrūkh's objections to becoming a government-appointed official were widely respected by Mālikī scholars. However, despite their almost ritualized distrust of rulers, jurists continued to occupy important political positions in the Iberian Peninsula and in the Maghrib.[46] The apolitical ideal was respected, but most jurists nonetheless acknowledged the necessity of maintaining some relationship with the ruling authorities. It is in this context that Saḥnūn's ruling on the dispute between Ibn Farrūkh and Ibn Ghānim should be understood. It is a moral tale which exhorts Muslims to be cautious of embroiling themselves in political matters. Al-Wansharīsī's argument that Saḥnūn's ruling implies that jurists of this early period would have denied legitimacy to Muslim *qāḍīs* living under Christian rule should therefore not be regarded as an accurate reflection of their views. In the 2nd/8th century, the issue of Muslims living under Christian rule had not yet arisen on a large scale and, consequently, these jurists had not given it special consideration. Again, we see that the novelty of al-Wansharīsī's view makes it difficult for him to muster early precedents in support of his position.

Although, beginning in the fourteenth-century, jurists did not usually accept the rulings of Mudéjar *qāḍīs*, some seem to have indicated a willingness to do so if their remaining in Christian territory was not of their choice. Qāsim Ibn Nājī (d. 837/1433), for example, mentions that, when he was in Jerba, he was asked to accept the testimony of a *qāḍī* from Pantelleria but refused to do so on the ground that the *qāḍī* chose to live under Christian rule even though he was free to leave.[47] Ibn Nājī does not explicitly say that he would

45 This debate is discussed in N.J. Coulson, "Doctrine and Practice in Islamic Law: One Aspect of the Problem," *Bulletin of the School of Oriental and African Studies* 18 (1956), 211–26.

46 Ibid., 214. Cf. Manuela Marín, "*Inqibāḍ 'an al-sulṭān: 'Ulamā'* and Political Power in al-Andalus," in *Saber religioso y poder político en el Islam: actas del Simposio Internacional* (Granada, 15–18 octubre 1991) (Madrid: Agencia Española de Cooperación Internacional, 1994), 127–39.

47 Qāsim b. 'Īsā Ibn Nājī, *Sharḥ Ibn Nājī al-Tanūkhī 'alā matn al-Risāla*, ed. Aḥmad Farīd al-Mazyadī (Beirut: Dār al-Kutub al-'Ilmiyya, 2007), 2: 485.

have accepted the testimony of the *qāḍī* had he been unable to leave Christian territory, but this seems to be implied by his ruling. The issue of the ability of the Mudéjars to choose is also raised by ʿAbdallāh al-ʿAbdūsī (d. 847/1442 or 849/1445),[48] who deals both with whether the testimony of Mudéjars can be accepted and with whether their *qāḍīs*' rulings are legitimate.[49] He says that their testimony cannot be accepted because their refusal to emigrate (*hijra*) is a grave sin (*kabīra aẓīma*) which impugns their probity. However, he says, if their emigration poses a danger to their lives and those of their families, they are permitted to remain and their testimony is not impugned. If, however, they fear to emigrate only because they believe that in doing so they will lose their property, this is not in itself sufficient to cancel their obligation to do so. On the contrary, he says, under such circumstances they are obligated to hand over their property if the non-Muslims make this a condition of their emigration. Thus al-ʿAbdūsī's position is that the Mudéjars can only be deemed to have probity if they remain in non-Muslim territory because they fear that by leaving they will lose their lives. Regarding the Mudéjar *qāḍīs*, he says that they are to be regarded as legitimate provided that it is shown that they have been appointed by the Muslim community.[50] This is allowed, he says, because it is a principle of law that the community can act in place of the ruler if the latter is unable to act. Even if the Christian ruler appoints the *qāḍī*, he is regarded as legitimate if this appointment has the uncoerced approval of the Muslim community. If this happens, it is regarded as if it is their appointment and not

48 Makhlūf, *Shajarat al-nūr*, 255.

49 Anonymous, *al-Ḥadīqa al-mustaqilla al-naḍira fī al-fatāwā al-ṣādira ʿan ʿulamāʾ al-ḥaḍra*, ed. Jalāl ʿAlī Juhānī. (Beirut: Dār Ibn Ḥazm, 2003), 144–45 and al-Wazzānī, *al-Miʿyār al-jadīd*, 3: 35. Some have suggested that al-ʿAbdūsī's *fatwā* was deliberately excluded from al-Wansharīsī's anthology because of its conciliatory attitude towards the Mudéjars, see Gerard Wiegers, *Islamic Literature in Spanish and Aljamiado* (Leiden: Brill, 1994), 87 n. 77; Jean-Pierre Molénat, "Le Problème de la permanence des musulmans dans les territoires conquis par les chrétiens, du point de vue de la loi islamique," *Arabica* 48 (2001), 399 and Kathryn Miller, "Muslim Minorities and the Obligation to Emigrate to Islamic Territory: Two Fatwās from Fifteenth-Century Granada," *Islamic Law and Society* 7 (2000), 269. The *fatwā* is translated and discussed in Louis Mercier, *L'Ornement des âmes et la devise des habitants d'el Andalus* (Paris, P. Geuthner, 1939), 59–65.

50 A similar view to that of al-ʿAbdūsī was given in 916/1510 by the chief Mālikī *qāḍī* of Cairo, Yaḥyā b. Muḥyī al-Dīn al-Damīrī (d. 939/1532). The latter says that if a Mudéjar community needs a leader to guide them in religion, such a leader has an obligation towards them and must postpone his emigration. Once an obligation to remain is established, the legitimacy of these *qāḍīs* is in no way diminished, see van Koningsveld and Wiegers, "Islam in Spain," 148.

that of the Christian ruler. Thus al-ʿAbdūsī's position is very similar to that of al-Māzarī, who regarded *qāḍī*s who were appointed by Christians as legitimate provided that they also had the support of the Muslim community.

Many modern scholars have had difficulty coming to terms with the rulings of the post-14th-century jurists on the Mudéjar *ʿulamāʾ*. They see the Mudéjars as victims and therefore characterize the jurists' writings about them as lacking in empathy.[51] I think that such an approach fails to appreciate the difficult position in which the jurists found themselves. The 13th century was a major turning point in Muslim-Christian relations in the Iberian Peninsula. The Almohad dynasty, which had retaken several areas from Christian forces, went into decline and eventually fell. Christians made many gains eventually conquering the entire peninsula save for Granada. These gains continued and, by the first quarter of the fifteenth century, much of the Maghribī coast had been occupied.[52] The result of these gains was a period of great pessimism among Iberian scholars, many of whom seemed to have believed in the inevitability of the Christian conquest of the region. Statements are made to the effect that, even in the triumphal days of Iberia's early conquest, the Caliph, ʿUmar Ibn ʿAbd al-ʿAzīz (d. 101/720), had ordered Muslims to leave the region because it was so remote from Islamic lands and was surrounded by the sea and hostile powers.[53] Apocalyptic literature emerged which predicted that Andalusī Muslims would be defeated and forced into exile but that God would part the sea in order to allow them to pass into North Africa.[54] Scholars no longer believed that salvation for Iberia's Muslims could come from within the Peninsula. Instead, they placed their hopes on the Maghrib; either as a refuge or as the region most likely to be able to use its military might to reconquer Iberia.[55]

---

51 See, for example, Husayn Mu'nis, "*Asnā al-matājir fī bayān aḥkām man ghalaba ʿalā waṭanihi al-Naṣārā wa-lam yuhājir wa-mā yatarattabu ʿalayhi min al-ʿuqūbāt waʾl-zawājir*," *Revista del Instituto de Estudios Islámicos en Madrid* 5 (1957), 5 ff.; and F. Maíllo Salgado, "Consideraciones acerca de una *fatwā* de al-Wanšarīsī," *Studia Historica* 3 (1985), 185. Cf. Peter Pormann, "Das Fatwā Die Herrlichsten Waren (*Asnā l-matāǧir*) des al-Wanšarīsī," *Der Islam* 80 (2003), 323 ff.

52 Andrew Hess, *The Forgotten Frontier: A History of the Sixteenth-Century Ibero-African Frontier* (Chicago: University of Chicago Press, 1978), 6 ff.

53 Maribel Fierro, "Christian Success and Muslim Fear in Andalusī Writings during the Almoravid and Almohad Periods," in *Dhimmis and Others: Jews and Christians and the World of Classical Islam*, ed. U. Rubin and D. Wasserstein (Winona Lake: Eisenbrauns, 1997), 161.

54 Maribel Fierro and Saadia Faghia, "Un nuevo texto de tradiciones escatológicas sobre al-Andalus," *Sharq al-Andalus* 7 (1990), 108.

55 Fierro, "Christian Success and Muslim Fear," 178.

A concomitant of this pessimistic view of the fate of al-Andalus was an emphasis placed on the defense of remaining Muslim territory. The jurists were consequently wary of all activities which might serve to strengthen Christian powers, and this influenced how they viewed the Mudéjars.[56] As a growing body of recent scholarship has shown, Mudéjar soldiers played important roles in Christian armies both in pacifying local Muslim populations and in directly fighting against Islamic armies.[57] Research has also revealed that the Mudéjars played an important economic role in maintaining the stability of Christian territories. Indeed, they were so vital to the economy that Christian rulers did everything in their power to prevent their emigration. An exodus of Muslims would harm their ability to economically exploit the territories that they had conquered and secure them against re-conquest by Muslim armies. As Robert Burns writes,

> Though the crusaders, from the king down, had deployed fierce rhetoric about expelling all Muslims beyond the boundaries of the new kingdom, they had in fact gone to extraordinary lengths to retain in place every Islamic community and Muslim farmer or craftsman ... Even where the surrender treaties allowed Muslim emigration to Islamic lands the crusaders sometimes sought to evade the permission.[58]

Since Christian rulers could not find Christians in sufficient numbers to settle the territories which they had conquered, they relied on Muslims to do so. Their need was so great that they not only compelled many Muslims to remain in Christian Iberia, but many often actively sought Muslims to immigrate

56 This is clearly evident in their discussions of travel for trade to Christian territory which is banned by Mālikī authorities on such grounds. See al-Burzulī, *Fatāwā al-Burzulī*, 2: 45–46 and al-Wansharīsī, *al-Miʿyār al-muʿrib*, 6: 317–18. Cf. al-Māzarī, *Sharḥ al-Talqīn* (Tunis National Library n. 12206), f. 168, quoted in Ibrāhīm b. Mūsā al-Shāṭibī, *Fatāwā al-Imām al-Shāṭibī*, ed. Muḥammad Abū al-Ajfān (Tunis: n.p., 1985), 146 n. 59 and H.R. Idris, "Commerce maritime et *ḳirāḍ* en Berbérie orientale: d'après un recueil inédit de *fatwās* médiévales," *Journal of the Economic and Social History of the Orient* 4 (1961), 228.

57 Hussein Fancy, "Theologies of Violence: The Recruitment of Muslim Soldiers by The Crown of Aragon," *Past and Present* 221 (2013), 39–73 and Ana Echevarría, *Knights on the Frontier: The Moorish Guard of the Kings of Castile (1410–1467)*, tr. M. Beagles (Leiden: Brill, 2009).

58 Robert Burns, "Immigrants from Islam: The Crusaders' Use of Muslims as Settlers in Thirteenth-Century Spain," *The American Historical Review* 80 (1975), 21–22. Cf. José-Enrique López de Coca Castañer, "Sobre la emigración mudéjar al reino de Granada," *Revista d'Història Medieval* 12 (2001), 243 ff.

there.[59] Without Muslims to provide these areas with sufficient populations, Christian rulers would have had difficulty maintaining their control. The financial importance of the Mudéjars was emphasized in the documents which outlined the legal protections to which they were entitled. They were not to be harmed, these documents said, because they belonged to the Christian king and were an important source of revenue for him. As such, the Mudéjars were sometimes referred to as "royal treasures" (*thesauri regii*).[60]

Many of the *ʿulamāʾ*, as leaders of the Mudéjars, played an important role in reaping economic benefits from them. The courts of the Mudéjar *qāḍīs*, for example, were a source of significant revenue for the Christian ruler since fines paid to the court belonged to him.[61] Aside from these direct contributions to the royal coffers, the crown benefited from the *qāḍīs*' ability to maintain order in the Muslim community and to ensure that Muslims fulfilled their financial obligations.[62] While it is doubtful whether the jurists of Islamic lands who discussed the Mudéjars would have known the specifics of their financial roles, they were clearly aware of their general economic importance to the Christian conquerers. This in itself clearly justifies their desire to protect themselves from them. What comes across even more vividly than financial concerns in the jurists' works are their worries about the assimilation of the Mudéjars to Christianity and their consequent distrust of their Islamic institutions. While a growing body of revisionist scholarship on the Mudéjar community has sought to portray its leaders and religious life more positively, the jurists of the Maghrib, rightly or wrongly, did not take this view.[63] Al-Wansharīsī, for example, comments on the phenomenon of assimilation.[64] As a result of social and political pressures, Muslims living in Christian lands will gradually come to resemble Christians. They will dress in similar clothing, speak their languages to the exclusion of Arabic, eat forbidden foods, and participate in Christian festivals. Al-Wansharīsī cites the Mudéjars of Ávila as examples of this assimilation claiming that they have so completely lost their knowledge of Arabic that they are unable to pray.

59 Ibid., 24.

60 Chancery of the Archive of the Crown of Aragon, C 913: 33. Transcribed in Boswell, *The Royal Treasure*, 471.

61 Isabel O'Connor, "The Mudéjars and the Local Courts: Justice in Action," *Journal of Islamic Studies* 16 (2005), 339 and Boswell, *The Royal Treasure*, 111–12.

62 Mark Meyerson, *The Muslims of Valencia in the Age of Fernando and Isabel*, 110 and 164.

63 See, for example, Kathryn Miller, *Guardians of Islam: Religious Authority and Muslim Communities of Late Medieval Spain* (New York: Columbia University Press, 2008) and Mark Meyerson, *The Muslims of Valencia in the Age of Fernando and Isabel*.

64 al-Wansharīsī, *al-Miʿyār al-muʿrib*, 2: 140–41.

To a certain extent, al-Wansharīsī's views on the perils of Muslims and Christians mixing might seem to be the product of a society in which Muslims and non-Muslims were increasingly geographically separate. Al-Wansharīsī's Fez was itself representative of this trend. In his own life time, Fez's main religious minority, the Jews, had been evacuated to a special quarter.[65] In Iberia, the spatial separation of religious communities began even earlier. The event which precipitated it was King Alfonso I of Aragon's 1125 attack on the city of Granada. The attack was unsuccessful and, as a result, the Christians of al-Andalus who joined in this venture were either deported or fled.[66] Over the course of the next century, in order to avoid Almohad persecution, many of the remaining Christians migrated or converted to Islam.[67] The result was that, by the 13th century, al-Andalus had become a place with many fewer Christians.[68] These *de facto* conditions of separation between Muslims and Christians may well have led to these conditions being viewed as legal requirements and may have paved the way for ideologies requiring Muslims to leave Christian-controlled areas.

The fact that jurists may have wished to create a spatial separation between different religious communities should not lead one to believe that their worries of religious syncretism were unreal. Consider the following anecdote about a Muslim scholar living in Christian Sicily:

> There is the story of recent years concerning one of the learned doctors in Islamic law in the capital of their tyrant king. He is known as Ibn Zurʿa,

65 Susan Gilson Miller, Attilio Petruccioli and Mauro Bertagnin, "Inscribing Minority Space in the Islamic City: The Jewish Quarter of Fez (1438–1912)," *Journal of the Society of Architectural Historians* 60 (2001), 310–27.

66 On this event, see V. Lagardère, "Communautés mozarabes et pouvoir almoravide en 519h/1125 en al-Andalus," *Studia Islamica* 67 (1988), 99–119; D. Serrano, "Dos fetuas sobre la expulsion de mozárabes al Magreb en 1126," *Anaquel de Estudios Árabes* 2 (1991), 162–182 and R. Oswald, "Spanien unter den Almoraviden. Die *Fatāwā* des Ibn Rušd als Quellen zur Wirtschafts- und Sozialgeschichte," *Die Welt des Orients* 24 (1993), 127–145.

67 A. Bennison and M.A. Gallego, "Religious Minorities under the Almohads: An Introduction," *Journal of Medieval Iberian Studies* 2 (2010), 143–54 and Maribel Fierro, "A Muslim Land without Jews or Christians: Almohad Policies regarding the 'Protected People,'" in M. Tischler and A. Fidora, *Christlicher Norden—Muslimischer Süden. Ansprüche und Wirklichkeiten von Christen, Juden und Muslimen auf der Iberischen Halbinsel im Hoch- und Spätmittelalter* (Munich: Aschendorff Verlag, 2011), 231–47 and Jean Pierre Molénat, "Sur le rôle des almohades dans la fin du christianisme local au Maghreb et en Al-Andalus," *Al-Qanṭara* 18 (1997), 389–414.

68 See Maribel Fierro, "Christian Success and Muslim Fear," 158.

> and was so pressed by the demands of the officials that he declared his renunciation of Islam and plunged into the Christian religion. He diligently memorized the New Testament, studied the usages of the Rūm, and learnt their canon law, until he was accepted into the body of priests who give judgment on lawsuits between Christians. When a Muslim case arose, he would give judgment on that too, based on his previous knowledge of Islamic religious law; and thus recourse was made to his decisions under both codes... God protect us from the results of apostasy and false ways.[69]

Ibn Jubayr adds that, despite all of this, he had heard that this *qāḍī* still secretly remained a Muslim. One can easily see, however, why some might have viewed his rulings, and those of other *qāḍīs* who were placed in similar positions, with suspicion.

Scholars of the Mudéjars are divided as to whether these examples of assimilation and syncretism are typical or atypical. I do not take a position on this issue except to note that a sufficient number of cases exist to give the jurists' observations some basis in reality. Consider the following examples, uncovered by historians of Christian Iberia, of the corruption of Mudéjar Islamic institutions, including its judiciary, resulting from attempts by Christian rulers to control them. The most extreme examples of this occurred towards the end of the Reconquista where there were cases of Christian rulers appointing Christians to the post of *qāḍī*.[70] The issue that the jurists more frequently dealt with, however, was the influence that Christians wielded over Muslims who held positions of communal authority. The Christian kingdom needed, as

69 Muḥammad b. Aḥmad Ibn Jubayr (d. 614/1217), *The Travels of Ibn Jubayr*, ed. W. Wright and M.J. de Goeje (Leiden: Brill, 1907), 340–41. English translation: *The Travels of Ibn Jubayr*, tr. R. Broadhurst (London: Jonathan Cape, 1952), 357, referred to in Iḥsān 'Abbās, *al-'Arab fī Ṣiqilliyya* (Beirut: Dār al-Thaqāfa, 1975), 152. Cf. M. Brett, "Muslim Justice under Infidel Rule: The Normans in Ifriqiya 517–555 H/1123–1160 AD," *Cahiers de Tunisie* 43 (1991), 329.

70 Boswell, *The Royal Treasure*, 81 and 84. Catlos says that this phenomenon was rarer than is suggested by Boswell, see Brian Catlos, *The Victors and the Vanquished: Christians and Muslims of Catalonia and Aragon, 1050–1300* (Cambridge: Cambridge University Press, 2004), 159. The case of the Christian *qāḍī* is not dealt with in Islamic sources, perhaps because of its rarity and perhaps because the very idea of a Christian *qāḍī* was incoherent from the perspective of Islam and therefore did not merit discussion. The jurists would probably have simply regarded these individuals as Christian judges who interfered in internal Muslim affairs.

Leonard Harvey puts it, "loyal and tame Muslims to man its administration"[71] and sought to groom a class of courtiers and bureaucrats who would achieve this aim. In most cases, Mudéjars were appointed to these offices by Christian rulers as a reward for their loyalty, which was often a loyalty displayed during wars against other Muslims.[72] They then became salaried officials of the Christian crown and were thus bound to obey its orders.[73] Thus some scholars have argued that, in many cases, Mudéjar institutions were so bound to and transformed by Christian ones that they barely deserved the Islamic names that they still held.[74] Many felt that this close relationship with the Christian authorities had a negative impact on the Muslims who were appointed to these positions. Archival sources reveal frequent allegations of corruption against those Mudéjars who chose to accept appointments to these new offices.[75] One of the best researched examples is the political machinations of the de Bellvís family, a powerful Mudéjar family which produced many courtier-*qāḍīs*[76] who frequently aroused the ire of their coreligionists.[77] One can only speculate as to whether the jurists of the Maghrib might have been familiar with such scandals. If they were familiar with them, it would have corroborated their belief that corruption was often a concomitant of a close financial relationship with the Christian ruler.

Corruption, however, was not the only reason for the jurists' concern about the Mudéjar *qāḍīs*. Even if they were not corrupt, they usually could not avoid being weak leaders with only a limited ability to guide their communities. Without a Muslim ruler to guarantee the enforcement of their rulings, the Mudéjar *qāḍīs* were unable to prevent many Muslims from applying

71 L.P. Harvey, *Islamic Spain, 1250 to 1500*, 103.

72 Boswell, *The Royal Treasure*, 87 n. 85.

73 Robert Burns and Paul Chevedden, *Negotiating Cultures: Bilingual Surrender Treaties in Muslim-Crusader Spain under James the Conqueror* (Leiden: Brill, 1999), 238 and Robert Burns, *Medieval Colonialism*, 238–39.

74 Catlos, *The Victors and the Vanquished*, 219. Cf. Halperin-Donghi, *Un Conflict nacional*, 97.

75 Boswell, *The Royal Treasure*, 87. For examples of these officials' corruption, see Catlos, *The Victors and the Vanquished*, 216 ff.

76 Members of the Bellvís family held such Islamic titles as *faqi*, *çabiçala* (i.e., *ṣāḥib al-ṣalāt*, meaning *imām* or prayer leader), *qāḍī* and *amīn*, see Boswell, *The Royal Treasure*, 47.

77 Manuel Vicente Febrer Romaguera, "Los Bellvís. Una Dinastía Mudéjar de alcadíes generals de Valencia, Aragón y el principado de Cataluña," *Actas del III simposio internacional de Mudéjarismo* (Teruel: Instituto de Estudios Turolenses, 1986), 277–90. Cf. Boswell, *The Royal Treasure*, 46–47 and Asunción Blasco Martínez, "Notarios Mudéjares de Aragón (siglos xiv–xv)," *Aragón en la Edad Media* 10–11 (1993), 117 ff.

to Christian courts to resolve intra-Muslim disputes. Boswell summarizes the situation thus:

> Though a majority of Mudéjar communities enjoyed the right to try civil cases between Muslims, in Valencia they were able to exercise this right only about ten percent of the time, and in Catalonia only about fifty percent. In Aragon they did actually exercise the prerogative a majority of the time, but even here well over half the cases (about 60%) originally heard before Mudéjar officials were subsequently removed or appealed to Christian ones, making the over-all competence of Muslim courts in Aragon even more limited than those in Catalonia.[78]

Thus, even the best-intentioned *ʿulamāʾ* could well have been regarded as ultimately ineffectual and to have had a net-effect of easing the Mudéjars into Christianity by a slow process of assimilation.[79]

To conclude, it appears that, beginning in the 14th century, when Christian territorial gains began to achieve a sense of permanence, many jurists became more distrustful of the Mudéjar *ʿulamāʾ*. This should not be seen as a failure on the part of these jurists to empathize with their plight but should be seen as an important and pragmatic mode of defending those Muslims who still remained after these great political upheavals. The jurists may well have been able to appreciate the good intentions of many of the *ʿulamāʾ* who resided in Christian lands, but they no longer had the luxury of treating them as they had prior to the 14th century when much smaller numbers of them existed and the strength of Islamic lands was greater. Beginning in the 14th century, the strength which the Mudéjars gave to Christian lands became increasingly evident. However good the intentions of the Mudéjar *ʿulamāʾ*, their presence in such lands was still of great use to Christian powers. They brought order to the Muslim communities, facilitated the Christian ruler's collection of taxes, and made the prospect of their return to Islamic rule ever more remote. What has been seen as the jurists' harsh response to these *ʿulamāʾ* should instead be seen as an understandable and pragmatic response to very difficult political circumstances. It should also be recognized that this response was not an obvious one nor was it intellectually the path of least resistance. It did not require

78 Boswell, *The Royal Treasure*, 110.

79 It is possible that the jurists' concerns regarding the assimilation and conversion of the Mudéjars were shaped by what they knew of the process of Christian conversion to Islam. Much of the relevant scholarly literature on this subject is cited in Mayte Pénelas, "Some Remarks on Conversion to Islam in al-Andalus," *al-Qanṭara* 23 (2002), 193–200.

the rote application of Islamic dogma but instead required the jurists to search for an alternative to the attitudes of their forbears, an alternative which could still be authoritative even as it was innovative.

CHAPTER 3

Life, Family and Property in the Abode of War

We have now seen several examples of changes to Islamic law occurring as a result of the political and social pressures brought about by the Reconquista. This chapter focuses on such changes which occurred in the laws governing protection for the lives, family and property of Muslims who live in the abode of war.[1] I document two periods in which changes to these laws occurred. The first period is that of the early Mālikī jurists of the Maghrib and al-Andalus, and the second that of the Mālikī jurists of the late Reconquista-period. I suggest that the issue of granting rights to Muslims living in the abode of war had considerable political implications and that jurists took these into account in their formulations of the law. During the first period of change, the jurists modified Mālik's laws which had been formulated in the Islamic heartlands in order to make them more appropriate to the needs of al-Andalus which, because it was a frontier society, encountered the case of Muslims living under non-Muslim rule more frequently. During the late Reconquista period, for reasons which will be discussed, some jurists advocated a return to the position of Mālik.

The Views of Mālik b. Anas and His Early Disciples

When Mālik b. Anas (d. 179/796)[2] and his early disciples discuss the subject of Muslims living under non-Muslim rule, they generally focus on people who convert to Islam while living in the abode of war[3] rather than on people who are

1 There are few modern works that deal with legal discussions on Muslim rights to life and property in the abode of war. None of these studies focuses on Mālikī law in any depth. Khaled Abou El Fadl briefly touches on this issue in his "Islamic Law and Muslim Minorities," *Islamic Law and Society* 1 (1994)," 141–87. Longer general treatments of the subject are contained in Ismāʿīl Luṭfī Faṭṭānī, *Ikhtilāf al-dārayn wa-atharuhu fī aḥkām al-munākaḥāt wa'l-ʿāmalāt* (Cairo: Dār al-Salām li'l-Ṭibāʿa wa'l-Nashr wa'l-Tawzīʿ wa'l-Tarjama, 1990), 399 ff. and ʿAlī b. ʿAbdallāh b. Musfir Āl Shuwayl al-Ghāmidī, *al-Aḥkām al-fiqhiyya al-mutaʿalliqa bi'l-dākhil fī al-Islām* (Mecca: self-published, 2006), 368–79.

2 *EI*[2], 6: 262.

3 It is important to emphasize that, by the "Abode of War," the jurists mean an area over which Muslims have no political control. Different laws apply to those who convert in areas conquered by Muslims, whether by treaty (*arḍ al-ṣulḥ*) or by force (*arḍ al-ʿanwa*). On the laws pertaining to the property of converts in these areas, see Sulaymān b. Khalaf al-Bājī,

© KONINKLIJKE BRILL NV, LEIDEN, 2015 | DOI 10.1163/9789004284531_005

Muslims from birth but who live in the abode of war. The *Mudawwana* discusses the case of a resident of the abode of war who converts to Islam and then migrates to the abode of Islam but leaves his family and property in the abode of war. It quotes the view of ʿAbd al-Raḥmān Ibn al-Qāsim al-ʿUtaqī (d. 191/806)[4] who says that, during a raid on the abode of war, these can be taken as booty. Mālik notes that the same applies to a person who converts to Islam but does not migrate.[5] Thus, for Mālik and Ibn al-Qāsim, property and family rights are not protected in the abode of war.[6] This principle is exhibited in other opinions given by Ibn al-Qāsim. Consider the following case.[7] A Muslim man's slave woman who lives in the abode of war is taken from him by polytheists who sell her to another Muslim. The latter knows that she was formerly the property of the aforementioned Muslim man. The question that arises is whether he is obligated to return her to him. Ibn al-Qāsim says that she should be returned, but only at a price, on the grounds that, since the slave woman was located in the abode of war, her former master cannot be said to have legitimately owned her.[8] Ibn al-Qāsim makes a similar point

---

al-Muntaqā: Sharḥ Muwaṭṭaʾ Mālik, ed. Muḥammad ʿAbd al-Qādir Aḥmad ʿAṭā (Beirut: Dār al-Kutub al-ʿIlmiyya, 1999), 4: 438 ff. and 446 ff.; Abū Muḥammad ʿAbd al-Wahhāb b. ʿAlī b. Naṣr al-Baghdādī al-Mālikī, *al-Maʿūna ʿalā madhhab ʿālim al-Madīna*, ed. Ḥasan Muḥammad Ḥasan Ismāʿīl al-Shāfiʿī (Beirut: Dār al-Kutub al-ʿIlmiyya, 1998), 1: 410–11 and idem, *Kitāb al-talqīn fī al-fiqh al-Mālikī* (Rabat: al-Mamlaka al-Maghribiyya, Wizārat al-Awqāf wa'l-Shu'ūn al-Islāmiyya, 1993), 73.

4 *EI*², 3: 817.

5 *al-Mudawwana al-kubrā* (Beirut: Dār al-Kutub al-ʿIlmiyya, 1994), 1: 508. The same opinion is reported in Abū Muḥammad ʿAbd al-Wahhāb b. ʿAlī b. Naṣr al-Baghdādī al-Mālikī, *al-Ishrāf ʿalā nukat masāʾil al-khilāf*, ed. Abū ʿUbayda Mashhūr b. Ḥasan Āl Salmān (Riyadh: Dār Ibn al-Qayyim, 2008), 4: 427.

6 The fact that the man under discussion has migrated and still does not possess ownership rights for his family and property in the abode of war precludes the possibility that these rights are denied him because he is not a client of an Arab tribe. On early Islamic legal positions on clientage (*walāʾ*) and conversion, see Jamal Juda, "Die sozialen und wirtschaftlichen Aspekte der *Mawālī* in frühislamischer Zeit" (Ph.D. diss.: Universität Tübingen, 1983), 71 ff.

7 This passage is found in Muḥammad al-ʿUtbī (d. 254/868), *al-Mustakhraja min al-asmiʿa (al-ʿUtbiyya)* in Abū al-Walīd Ibn Rushd, *al-Bayān wa'l-taḥṣīl wa'l-sharḥ wa'l-tawjīh wa'l-taʿlīl fī masāʾil al-mustakhraja*, ed. Muḥammad Ḥajjī (Beirut: Dār al-Gharb al-Islamī, 1984), 2: 533.

8 In this same passage, Mālik's opinion is also solicited and he says that she should be returned. Ibn al-Qāsim says that Mālik really means that she should be returned, but only at a price. It is, of course, unclear whether Ibn al-Qāsim is correct in his interpretation of Mālik, but his interpretation is in broad harmony with Mālik's thinking on related issues. It is difficult to understand precisely what makes a person who captures a slave woman obliged to sell her back to her former owner if he still wants her. This obligation appears to be a moral one

in another case regarding non-Muslims from the abode of war who come to the abode of Islam with an *amān* (document of safe conduct) and then steal some Muslim slaves who they take back with them to the abode of war. Later, they return to the abode of Islam using a new *amān* and attempt to sell the same slaves. According to Ibn al-Qāsim, any such sale would be valid because the slaves' presence in the abode of war permanently cancels their previous ownership.[9]

The cases discussed above involve property located in the abode of war. Mālik and Ibn al-Qāsim, however, also address the case in which the property is located in the abode of Islam while the owner is located in the abode of war. This occurs in a discussion regarding the slaves of a non-Muslim owner who escape from the abode of war to the abode of Islam. Mālik says that their owner cannot reclaim them as property even if he subsequently converts to Islam and migrates to the abode of Islam.[10] The position is different, according to Ibn al-Qāsim, if the slave-owners who live in the abode of war had been Muslims at the time when their slaves fled. In this case, while they still lose their ownership rights so long as they live in the abode of war, these rights are restored as soon as they migrate to the abode of Islam.[11] No reasons are given for these laws and one can only speculate regarding their rationale. Since there are no further discussions of the subject, it is unclear whether these are special laws designed to offer some protection to converted slaves or whether they also apply to other kinds of property. If it is assumed that these laws regarding slaves also apply to all other kinds of property, the following principles can tentatively be suggested.[12] No property located in the abode of war can be owned by a Muslim regardless of whether he lives in the abode of war or the abode of Islam. Property located in the abode of Islam can be owned only by a Muslim who lives in that abode. If he lives in the abode of war, his right to exercise his ownership ceases so long as he remains there, but this right can be restored to him as soon as he migrates to the abode of Islam. If, however, a non-Muslim's property is transferred from the abode of war to the abode of Islam, and this person subsequently converts and migrates to the abode of Islam, he has no right to this property. Property rights thus seem to depend on both the

---

rather than a legal one since Ibn al-Qāsim is very clear that her presence in the abode of war cancels all property rights.

9 al-ʿUtbī, *al-Mustakhraja*, 3: 25.

10 *al-Mudawwana al-Kubrā*, 2: 567.

11 Ibid., 1: 511.

12 Ibn al-ʿArabī seems to subscribe to this interpretation of Mālik, see his *ʿĀriḍat al-Aḥwadhī*, 7: 106.

territorial and confessional status of the owner. It is possible that the law that no property located in the abode of war can be owned might have been formulated because it was difficult for such property to be feasibly regulated by the Islamic courts located in the abode of Islam. However, the law that provides for the confiscation of property in the abode of Islam from Muslims for the duration of their stay in the abode of war seems designed to punish those who sinfully choose not to live in the abode of Islam.

The Views of the Pre-Reconquista Era Mālikī Jurists

For the most part, the early Mālikī jurists of al-Andalus and the Maghrib did not agree with Mālik's view that the abode of war had the effect of cancelling the ownership rights of those Muslims who lived there. Muḥammad Ibn Saḥnūn (d. 256/870) says that the view of his father, Saḥnūn (d. 240/854), as well as that of Ashhab (d. 204/819),[13] is that the free-born children and property of a convert to Islam, whether or not he has migrated to the abode of Islam, belong to him, but that his non-Muslim wife can be taken as booty.[14] The law, he says, also applies to a Muslim from birth who leaves the abode of Islam for the abode of war, "gets married, acquires property, and has children" there.[15] These views are supported by other early Mālikī authorities. Ibn al-Mawwāz (d. 269/882)[16] states the following law:

> If a resident of the abode of war comes to us with a document of safe conduct (*amān*) and he converts and then participates in a raid with us on his [former] land, and his property, family, and children are taken as

13 His name is Abū ʿAmr Ashhab b. ʿAbd al-ʿAzīz b. Dāwūd al-Qaysī al-ʿĀmirī al-Jaʿdī, see Muḥammad b. Muḥammad Makhlūf, *Shajarat al- nūr* (Beirut: Dār al-Kitāb al-ʿArabī, 197?), 1: 59.

14 Ibn Abī Zayd al-Qayrawānī, *Kitāb al-nawādir wa'l-ziyādāt ʿalā mā fī al-mudawwana min ghayrihā min al-ummahāt*, ed. ʿAbd al-Fattāḥ Muḥammad al-Ḥulw (Beirut: Dār al-Gharb al-Islāmī, 1999), 3: 282. The text reads "wife," but it appears that it intends only a non-Muslim wife. Later, Ibn Abī Zayd quotes Saḥnūn to this effect, see ibid., 3: 283.

15 Ibid., 3: 282. Cf. Ana Fernández Félix, "Children on the Frontiers of Islam," in M. García Arenal (ed.), *Conversions islamiques. Identités religieuses en Islam méditerranéen* (Paris: Maisonneuve et Laros, 2002), 61–72.

16 On Muḥammad b. Ibrāhīm b. Rabāḥ Ibn al-Mawwāz al-Iskandarānī (d. 269/882) of Alexandria, see Fuat Sezgin, *Geschichte des arabischen Schrifttums* (GAS) (Leiden: Brill, 1967), 1: 474. His work, the *Kitāb Ibn al-Mawwāz*, was one of the main sources for Ibn Abī Zayd's *Kitāb al-nawādir wa'l-ziyādāt*.

> spoils; his property, slaves, animals and house furnishings belong to him. As for his wife and grown children, they are booty both for him and the army ...[17] As for his young children, they are free Muslims on account of his own Islam.[18]

Ibn al-Mawwāz differs from Saḥnūn only in drawing an explicit distinction between the young and adult children of such a convert. It is likely that Saḥnūn would also have accepted this distinction since a person ceases to exercise guardianship over his children once they have reached the age of maturity.[19] Like Saḥnūn, Ibn al-Mawwāz affirms that wives living in the abode of war can be taken as booty from Muslim men despite the fact that the abode of war does not have the general effect of cancelling all property ownership. This law was likely motivated by a concern, shared by all the major Sunnī legal schools,[20] that a non-Muslim wife who lives with her husband in the abode of war is in a position to lead him away from Islam, especially if that Muslim is a recent convert to Islam. It thus seems reasonable to assume that the law permitting a wife to be taken as booty is directed at addressing concerns of cultural assimilation rather than being based on territorial factors.[21]

One jurist of this period who disagrees with this new Mālikī position is Muḥammad b. Yaḥyā Ibn Zarb (d. 381/991).[22] Like Mālik, Ibn Zarb is of the

17 Ibn al-Mawwāz adds that if this Muslim's wife is taken as booty, "his marriage is annulled because of the shared ownership of his wife."

18 Ibn Abī Zayd al-Qayrawānī, *al-Nawādir wa'l-ziyādāt*, 3: 283.

19 Indeed, a similar distinction between adult and young children is made in *al-Mudawwana al-kubrā*, 1: 507. It is interesting to note that, for Mālik, the fact that a parent has converted to Islam appears to have no effect on the religious status of the children. Thus he rules that the twelve-year-old children of one such parent who refuse to embrace Islam should not be forced to do so. There is some disagreement on this issue, however, among the other Medinan jurists, see ibid., 2: 307–309. Cf. Yohanan Friedmann, *Tolerance and Coercion in Islam: Interfaith Relations in the Muslim Tradition* (Cambridge: Cambridge University Press, 2003), 115.

20 On the views of these schools on this matter, see ibid., 186.

21 Concerns about cultural assimilation and religious syncretism were commonplace even in al-Andalus where, although Muslims held the reigns of power, there were substantial Christian populations. See, for example, al-Wansharīsī, *al-Miʿyār al-muʿrib wa'l-jāmiʿ al-mughrib* (Rabat: Wizārat al-Awqāf wa'l-Shu'ūn al-Islāmiyya li'l-Mamlaka al-Maghribiyya, 1981), 2: 140 and Ibn Bassām, *al-Dhakhīra fī maḥāsin ahl al-Jazīra* (Beirut: Dar al-Thaqāfa, 1979), 1: 14, quoted in Hanna E. Kassis, "Muslim Revival in Spain in the Fifth/Eleventh Century," *Der Islam* 67 (1990), 83.

22 On Abū Bakr Muḥammad b. Yaḥyā Ibn Zarb al-Qurṭubī, see Makhlūf, *Shajarat al-nūr*, 1: 100.

opinion that the wives, children and property of those who convert in the abode of war but do not migrate to the abode of Islam can be taken as booty. He notes, however, another view according to which such a convert has a right to buy back this property and also has a right to keep his young children.[23] It appears that Ibn Zarb's view was not held by most of his contemporaries.

While the Mālikīs of al-Andalus and the Maghrib do not say why they decided to shift their position away from that of Mālik, it is likely that they did so in order to adapt to new political realities. Laws that accorded property rights to Muslims living in the abode of war would have eliminated the social instability caused by the seizure of the property of the many Muslims who, for one reason or another, found themselves living there as a result of frequently shifting borders.[24] Further, Muslim rulers may have hoped that if they treated populations of local Muslims living in the abode of war well, they could be relied on for support in their attempts to gain control over these areas. It was therefore strategically unwise to alienate them by permitting their families and property to be taken as booty. That Mālikī views were influenced by the Andalusī political climate is perhaps supported by the fact that they were usually shared by other non-Mālikī Andalusī jurists of this period including Ibn Ḥazm (456/1064),[25] a Shāfiʿī jurist who came to adhere to the Ẓāhirī legal school, and al-Awzāʿī (d. 157/774). The latter, whose legal school was popular in al-Andalus before it came to be dominated by the Mālikīs, presented a similar position: "If [a Muslim] is married in the abode of war, has children, and then the Muslims conquer that territory, his free children belong to him as does his property. His marriage, however, is annulled (*wa-yasquṭu nikāḥuhu*) and he must pay the price of his wife from the shares in booty (*al-maqāsim*). After that, if he wishes, he can [re]marry her."[26]

---

23 Muḥammad b. Yaḥyā Ibn Zarb, *Kitāb al-Khiṣāl*, ed. ʿAbd al-Ḥamīd al-ʿAlamī (Rabat: Wizārat al-Awqāf wa'l-Shu'ūn al-Islāmiyya, al-Mamlaka al-Maghribiyya, 2005), 98.

24 It is also noteworthy that their new position was in line with those of most Sunnī jurists. For a summary of the views of the major Sunnī schools on Muslim property rights in the abode of war by a former Ẓāhirī, see Abū Ḥayyān al-Gharnāṭī (d. 745/1344), *al-Baḥr al-Muḥīṭ* (Beirut: Dār Iḥyā al-Turāth al-ʿArabī, 1990), 3: 324. For a modern summary of these views, see ʿAlī b. ʿAbdallāh b. Musfir Āl Shuwayl al-Ghāmidī, *al-Aḥkām al-fiqhiyya al-mutaʿalliqa bi'l-dākhil fī al-Islām*, 368–79. For a detailed analysis of the views of the Ḥanafīs, see Baber Johansen, "Der *ʿIṣma*-Begriff im Ḥanafītischen Recht," in idem, *Contingency in a Sacred Law*, 238–62.

25 Abū Muḥammad ʿAlī b. Aḥmad b. Saʿīd Ibn Ḥazm, *al-Muḥallā*, ed. Aḥmad Muḥammad Shākir (Cairo: Idārat al-Ṭibāʿa al-Munīriyya, 1934), 7: 309–10.

26 Ibn Abī Zayd al-Qayrawānī, *Kitāb al-nawādir wa'l-ziyādāt*, 3: 282. Cf. Muḥammad b. Jarīr al-Ṭabarī, *Kitāb ikhtilāf al-fuqahā'*, ed. Joseph Schacht (Leiden: Brill, 1933), 48 and

The utility of the new Mālikī position notwithstanding, it is important to emphasize that how or if these laws were applied in practice cannot be determined since few *fatwās* or other documents that might provide corroborating information are extant. Some of the extant *fatwās* of the jurists do seem to reflect the law as expressed in the law books. For example, Yaḥyā b. Yaḥyā al-Laythī (d. 234/848),[27] the famous transmitter of Mālik's *Muwaṭṭa'*, reports in a *fatwā* that he asked Ibn Nāfi' (d. 186/802–3)[28] about a Muslim from Barcelona who, a year after its conquest by the Christians, had still not migrated and who made raids on the Muslims who came to his land, killing, enslaving or robbing them. Ibn Nāfi' responds that this man's status is equivalent to that of a Muslim bandit (*muḥārib*)[29] who operates in the abode of Islam. Therefore, he says, he must be judged by the ruler according to the established laws that apply to bandits. According to these laws, while the ruler can force the bandit to provide compensation for the property he has taken or destroyed and can also punish him with death or exile, the law does not provide for the arbitrary confiscation of his property.[30] Moreover, Ibn Nāfi' says that if it is determined that he raided the Muslims because he was ordered to do so and feared for his life if he refused, he is neither to be killed nor otherwise punished.[31] Ibn Nāfi''s

---

Abū Yūsuf Ya'qūb b. Ibrāhīm al-Anṣārī, *al-radd 'alā siyar al-Awzā'ī* (Cairo: Maktabat Dār al-Hidāya, n.d.), 107 and 127.

27 *GAL*, Supplement, 1: 297.

28 On 'Abdallāh Ibn Nāfi' al-Ṣā'igh al-Makhzūmī (d. 186/802–3), see 'Iyāḍ b. Mūsā al-Yaḥṣubī, *Tartīb al-madārik wa-taqrīb al-masālik li-ma'rifat a'lām madhhab Mālik*, ed. Aḥmad Bukayr Maḥmūd (Beirut: Maktabat al-Ḥayāh, 1967), 2: 357 and Makhlūf, *Shajarat al-nūr*, 1: 55. It appears that Ibn Nāfi' responded to this question in the year preceding his death in Medina.

29 On the Mālikī position on the *muḥārib*, see Khaled Abou El Fadl, *Rebellion and Violence in Islamic Law* (Cambridge: Cambridge University Press, 2001), 135 ff.

30 Ibid., 255 ff.

31 I have consulted the following versions of this text: al-'Utbī, *al-Mustakhraja*, 3: 41–2; Ibn Abī Zayd al-Qayrawānī, *al-Nawādir wa'l-ziyādāt*, 3: 352; idem, *Der heilige Krieg (ǧihād) aus der Sicht der Mālikitischen Rechtsschule*, ed. Mathias von Bredow (Beirut: Franz Steiner Verlag, 1994), 445; and al-Wansharīsī, *al-Mi'yār al-mu'rib*, 2: 129–30. There are substantial differences between these versions. Most significantly, the versions in *al-Nawādir* and *al-Mustakhraja* say that the bandit remained a Muslim only so that he could seek protection from the Muslims in the event that they captured him (von Bredow: *iqāmatuhu hunāka 'alā al-islām ta'awwudh^{an} mi-mā yukhāfu min al-qatl idhā ẓufira bihi*). In contrast, al-Wansharīsī's text says that he raided the Muslims because he feared for his life if they captured him (*fa-aghāra 'alā al-muslimīn ta'awwadh^{an} mi-mā yukhāfu min al-qatl in ẓufira bihu*). I prefer al-Wansharīsī's reading because Ibn Nāfi''s response is directed towards someone who makes raids out of fear, not someone who remains a Muslim out of fear.

position is thus no different from that of Saḥnūn. Like the latter, he indicates that there are no special punishments that apply to a Muslim who chooses to remain under non-Muslim rule that would require him to forfeit his property. Rather, such a Muslim is to be punished solely for his crime of attacking Muslims just as anyone else would be punished for this kind of activity regardless of where he lives.

Other *fatwās* do not seem to fully confirm the position of Saḥnūn and his contemporaries, to wit, that the property rights of Muslims who live in the abode of war are not attenuated. One such *fatwā*,[32] written by the jurists of the Cordoban *shūrā*,[33] deals with the problem of property ownership in the abode of war. In this case, the abode of war is the territory of ʿUmar Ibn Ḥafṣūn (305/918),[34] the famous neo-Muslim (*muwallad*)[35] ruler of the province of Reíyo (Málaga) in al-Andalus who, beginning in 267/880, rebelled against the Umayyad ruler of Cordoba. Many generations of Mālikī jurists have heaped opprobrium on Ibn Ḥafṣūn, claiming that he was an apostate (*murtadd*),

---

32 Abū al-Aṣbagh ʿĪsā Ibn Sahl, *Dīwān al-aḥkām al-kubrā: al-Nawāzil wa'l-aʿlām li-Ibn Sahl*, ed. Rashīd al-Naʿīmī (Riyadh: Rashīd al-Naʿīmī, 1997), 2: 811–13. A more carefully edited version of this *fatwā* is found in *Wathā'iq fī aḥkām qaḍā' ahl al-dhimma fī al-Andalus: Mustakhraja min makhṭūṭ al-Aḥkām al-kubrā li'l-Qāḍī Abī al-Aṣbagh ʿĪsā Ibn Sahl*, ed. Muḥammad ʿAbd al-Wahhāb Khallāf (Cairo: Markaz al-ʿArabī, 1980), 83–5. A problematic translation of this *fatwā* appears in Rocío Daga Portillo, "Organización jurídica y social en la España musulmana" (Ph.D. dissertation, Universidad de Granada, 1990), 203–206. The *fatwā* has been analyzed on the basis of this translation by Virgilio Martínez Enamorado, "'Donde rigen las normas de Satán': Ibn Antuluh, Ibn Hafsun y el asunto de la propiedad sobre una esclava," in *Espacio, Tiempo y Forma. Serie III. Historia Medieval*, 23 (2010), 97–112.

33 The following jurists are said to have authored this *fatwā*: Abū Ṣāliḥ Ayyūb b. Sulaymān (d. 301/913), Muḥammad b. Ghālib (d. 295/907), ʿUbaydallāh b. Yaḥyā (d. 297/909), Muḥammad b. ʿUmar Ibn Lubāba (d. 314/926), Muḥammad b. Walīd (d. 309/921), Yaḥyā b. ʿAbd al-ʿAzīz (d. 295/907), Saʿd b. Muʿādh b. ʿUthmān (d. 308/920) and Aḥmad b. Yaḥyā (d. 297/909). On these jurists and the institution of the Cordoban *shūrā*, see Manuela Marín, "Šūrà et al-Šūrà dans al-Andalus," *Studia Islamica* 62 (1985), 25–51.

34 Abū al-Qāsim b. Aḥmad al-Balawī al-Burzulī, *Fatāwā al-Burzulī*, ed. Muḥammad al-Ḥabīb al-Hayla (Beirut: Dār al-Gharb al-Islāmī, 2002), 3: 90 and 4: 49, and al-Wansharīsī, *al-Miʿyār al-muʿrib*, 6: 95.

35 On the various interpretations of this term, see Maribel Fierro, "*Mawālī* and *muwalladūn* in al-Andalus," in *Patronate and Patronage in Early and Classical Islam*, ed. M. Bernards and J. Nawas (Leiden: Brill, 2005), 220 ff.

either because he had converted to Christianity[36] or, depending on the source, because of his close relationship with the Fāṭimids.[37] The precise historical context of the *fatwā* issued by the *shūrā* is not entirely clear because of its brevity and because it is written on the assumption that its audience, the Umayyad ruler,[38] was already familiar with the circumstances with which it dealt. It was written in response to a judge's question, originally directed to the ruler, but referred by the latter to his *shūrā*, about Ibn Abtala,[39] a Muslim living in a fortress in Bobastro (*Bubāshtar*), a territory controlled by Ibn Ḥafṣūn. The judge said that Ibn Abtala claimed that his Christian slave woman had been seized by and then married off to someone by Ibn Ḥafṣūn. This woman had then been awarded back to Ibn Abtala by an Umayyad military commander (*qā'id*). The judge deemed this award illegitimate as he felt that Ibn Abtala could not prove his original ownership of the woman and therefore had set her free on condition that she provide a surety (*ḥamīl*) while Ibn Abtala was given an opportunity to prove his ownership claim. The *shūrā* supports this judge's ruling although its leader, Abū Ṣāliḥ Ayyūb b. Sulaymān al-Maʿāfirī (d. 301/913),[40] added that providing a surety is unnecessary. The *shūrā* gives the following reasoning for its decision: Since Ibn Ḥafṣūn is an apostate, the lands that he controls have the status of the abode of war; and ownership in the abode of war does not have the same force as in the abode of Islam because of the laws

36 The truth of this claim is much debated, see David Wasserstein, "Inventing Tradition and Constructing Identity: The Genealogy of 'Umar Ibn Ḥafṣūn between Christianity and Islam," *al-Qanṭara* 23 (2002), 294–95.

37 Heinz Halm, *The Empire of the Mahdi: The Rise of the Fatimids*, tr. Michael Bonner (Leiden: Brill, 1996), 280.

38 I.e., 'Abdallāh b. Muḥammad (r. 275–300/888–912), see *EI*², 1: 49.

39 Different manuscripts give different variations of this name: *'btlh, 'ytlh*, and *'thylh*. I have chosen the vocalization Abtala only for the sake of convenience. Maribel Fierro has tentatively suggested that Ibn Abtala might be the Umayyad commander referred to by al-Tujībī in Ibn al-Quṭiyya's history: "When Ibn Ḥafṣūn had surrendered Bobastro, Hāshim commanded the building of a post (*dār*) on the summit of the mountain, where he had installed the 'Arīf al-Tujībī. Ibn Ḥafṣūn's uncle amassed a group of young men and added them to his nephew's men and together they forced al-Tujībī off the mountain. He took captive al-Tujībī's concubine, who was known as al-Tujībīya and who later became the mother of his son, Abū Sulaymān." See Muḥammad b. 'Umar Ibn al-Qūṭiyya (d. 367/977), *Tārīkh iftitāḥ al-Andalus*, ed. P. de Gayangos, E. Saavedra and F. Codera (Madrid: Revista de Archivos, 1926), 93–4; English: *Early Islamic Spain: The History of Ibn al-Qūṭīya*, ed. David James (London: Routledge, 2009), 121.

40 On Abū Ṣāliḥ Ayyūb b. Sulaymān al-Qurṭubī al-Maʿāfirī, see Makhlūf, *Shajarat al-nūr*, 1: 85.

of Satan (*aḥkām al-shayṭān*) that prevail there.[41] Although the *shūrā* does not specify what it means by this limitation on property rights, it clearly does not intend to entirely deny the possibility of ownership in the abode of war. It does, however, attenuate the force of ownership in the abode of war by stipulating that slaves residing there who claim that they are free have a right to which they are not normally entitled[42]—they can demand that their owners provide testimonial evidence (*bayyina*)[43] to show that they were legitimately enslaved and, if they fail to do so, they are to be set free.[44] The *shūrā* adds that the slave woman's word that she was once enslaved to Ibn Abtala cannot be accepted as evidence, thus increasing the owner's burden of proof. If Ibn Abtala can provide such proof, which the *shūrā* seems to regard as doubtful, the slave woman must be returned to him. Thus, unlike Mālik, the *shūrā* stops short of entirely denying the possibility of ownership in the abode of war. In its *fatwā*, the *shūrā* does not refer to Mālikī thinking on the issue of ownership in the abode of war but does indicate that it has frequently dealt with this issue in other *fatwā*s that were prepared for the Umayyad ruler.[45] One can infer that the *shūrā* seems to agree, at least partially, with the new Mālikī view according to which Muslims have some right to own and acquire property in the abode of war. It is not clear what made them attenuate this right by requiring higher burdens of proof to establish the ownership of slaves. One cannot discount the possibility that they did so as a result of pressure from the ruler to which they were frequently subject.[46]

---

41 *Wa-man malaka hunāka mamlūk^an lam yustaḥkam lahu imtilāk^an kamā yustaḥkam li-man malaka fī mawḍiʿ al-ṭāʿa.*

42 On the burden of proof in cases in which slaves claim to have been wrongly enslaved, see al-Wansharīsī, *al-Miʿyār al-muʿrib*, 9: 238–39.

43 On the definition of *bayyina*, see David de Santillana, *Istituzioni di diritto musulmano malichita con riguardo anche al sistema sciafiita* (Rome: Istituto per l'Oriente, 1938), 2: 593–94 and ʿAbd al-Wahhāb b. ʿAlī al-Baghdādī, *al-Maʿūna ʿalā madhhab ʿālim al-Madīna*, 2: 444.

44 It is likely that it is to this *fatwā* that Ibn Zarb and Ibn ʿAttāb (d. 462/1069) refer as precedent for their rulings that a *bayyina* is required in cases in which slaves claim that they are free because they were enslaved during periods in which many free people were enslaved. See al-Wansharīsī, *al-Miʿyār al-muʿrib*, 9: 219–20 and Ibn Sahl, *Dīwān al-aḥkām al-kubrā*, 1: 360–61. On Muḥammad b. ʿAbdallāh Ibn ʿAttāb, see Makhlūf, *Shajarat al-nūr*, 1: 119.

45 The issue of free people being taken as slaves in the territory of Ibn Ḥafṣūn was frequently raised by the jurists. See Francisco Vidal Castro, "Sobre la compraventa de hombres libres en los dominios de Ibn Ḥafṣūn," in *Homenaje al Profesor Jacinto Bosch Vilá* (Granada: Universidad de Granada, 1991), 1: 417–28.

46 The shūrā's *fatwā* was requested by and addressed to the caliph who was fighting an intense war against Ibn Ḥafṣūn. It is thus very likely that the jurists' were forced to take this war into consideration when giving their *fatwā*. For another example of jurists taking

In another *fatwā*,[47] the aforementioned leader of the *shūrā* council, Abū Ṣāliḥ, similarly affirms the law that the abode of war does not automatically cancel all ownership of property. In the case that he discusses, the property owner is located in the abode of Islam while the property is located in the abode of war. The *fatwā* concerns a Christian slave who escaped from his Muslim master in the abode of Islam and fled to the abode of war, where he became a merchant and then, after some time, returned to the town in the abode of Islam where he had formerly been a slave. Is his original owner, Abū Ṣāliḥ's petitioner asks, permitted to repossess him as a slave and take his property? Abū Ṣāliḥ answers that the owner cannot repossess him if there is a treaty (*ʿahd*) between the Christians and the Muslims. If, however, there is no treaty, he can take him because he is still, in fact, his slave. Thus, like the *shūrā* discussed above, and Saḥnūn and the early Mālikīs, Abū Ṣāliḥ affirms that property to which an owner has clear title remains his even in the abode of war. He adds, however, an exception to this general rule. Muslims lose ownership of property that is removed to an area outside of the abode of Islam which is protected by a treaty. This exception is perhaps introduced because the need of the Muslim ruler to maintain his treaties trumps that of his subjects to maintain ownership of their property. A Muslim ruler who wished to maintain smooth relations with Christian rulers with whom he had made treaties, especially a weak ruler like ʿAbdallāh,[48] would have welcomed Abū Ṣāliḥ's opinion. Such an opinion would have ensured that individual property claims could not come into conflict with the property provisions of a treaty. Thus Abū Ṣāliḥ's view can be seen as a pragmatic approach to what could well have been a frequently occurring problem.

Mālikī Law During the Reconquista

In the legal manuals, the new Mālikī view that accorded some protection to the property of Muslims living in the abode of war seems to have continued largely unmodified into the 6th/12th century, with the exception that, over time, most jurists no longer deemed it legitimate to take the wives of Muslims

into account the ruler's relations with Christendom, see *al-Miʿyār al-muʿrib*, 2:158–66, discussed in David Powers, "Legal Consultation (*Futyā*) in Medieval Spain and North Africa," in *Islam and Public Law*, ed. Chibli Mallat (London: Graham & Trotman, 1993), 93.

47 al-Wansharīsī, *al-Miʿyār al-muʿrib*, 9:236.

48 Janina Safran, *The Second Umayyad Caliphate: The Articulation of Caliphal Legitimacy in al-Andalus* (Cambridge: Harvard Middle Eastern Monographs, 2000), 146.

living in the abode of war as booty.[49] Post-6th/12th-century discussions also contain more extended inquires into the inviolability of the lives of Muslims located in the abode of war. The most detailed treatment of these issues is by Ibn al-ʿArabī (d. 543/1148) who dealt with them in his *ʿĀriḍat al-Aḥwadhī*, his *Aḥkām al-Qurʾān* and, apparently, at greatest length in his no longer extant work *al-Inṣāf fī masāʾil al-khilāf*.[50]

Most *ḥadīths*, Ibn al-ʿArabī argues, indicate that the life, property, and family of a Muslim are protected by virtue of his Islam regardless of where he lives. The Prophet said, "I have been ordered to fight people until they say there is no god but God and if they say it, they have gained protection (*ʿuṣimū*) from me for their lives and property except for what is due from it."[51] Similarly, the Prophet said: "Whosoever accepts Islam while owning something, it remains his,"[52] and "a Muslim's property is not permitted (*ḥalāl*) [to another] unless he consents [to give it]".[53] For Ibn al-ʿArabī, the implication of these statements is that the mere acceptance of Islam is sufficient to guarantee both life and property—the issue of where a person lives, whether in the abode of Islam or the abode of war, has no bearing on the matter. Whatever a Muslim owns remains his unless he freely chooses to relinquish it.[54] Thus, according to Ibn al-ʿArabī, the teaching of the Prophet is that the lives and property of those Muslims who live in the abode of war are protected.

---

49 The exceptions are the Egyptian Mālikīs who continue to follow the earlier Mālikī position, see Jalāl al-Dīn ʿAbdallāh b. Najm Ibn Shās (d. 616/1219), *ʿIqd al-jawāhir al-thamīna fī madhhab ʿālim al-Madīna*, ed. Muḥammad Abū al-Ajfān and ʿAbd al-Ḥafīẓ Manṣūr (Beirut: Dār al-Gharb al-Islāmī, 1995), 1: 476; Jamāl al-Dīn b. ʿUmar Ibn al-Ḥājib (d. 646/1249), *Jāmiʿ al-ummahāt* (Damascus: al-Yamāma, 1998), 254, and Shihāb al-Dīn Aḥmad b. Idrīs al-Qarāfī, *al-Dhakhīra*, ed. Muḥammad Ḥajjī (Beirut: Dār al-Gharb al-Islāmī, 1994), 3: 439–40.

50 On *al-Inṣāf*, see Joseph Drory, *Ibn al-ʿArabi mi-Sevilya* (Ramat-Gan: Bar-Ilan University, 1993), 46–48.

51 See, for example, *Ṣaḥīḥ al-Bukhārī*, ed. Muṣṭafā Baghā (Beirut: Dār Ibn Kathīr, 1993), 6: 2682.

52 See, for example, Aḥmad b. al-Ḥusayn al-Bayhaqī, *Sunan al-Kubrā* (Hyderabad: Maṭbaʿat Majlis Dāʾirat al-Maʿārif al-Niẓāmiyya, 1925), 9: 113.

53 See, for example, al-Bayhaqī, *al-Sunan al-Kubrā*, 6: 97 and 8: 182 and *Musnad al-Imām Aḥmad* (Beirut: Dār iḥyāʾ al-turāth al-ʿArabī, 1993), 5: 72.

54 Ibn al-ʿArabī, *ʿĀriḍat al-aḥwadhī bi-sharḥ ṣaḥīḥ al-Tirmidhī*, ed. Jamal Marʿashlī (Dār al-Kutub al-ʿIlmiyya, 1997), 7: 106. These *ḥadīths* are quoted and explained in another work by Ibn al-ʿArabī which is quoted in *Fatāwā al-Burzulī*, 2: 22–23 and al-Wansharīsī, *al-Miʿyār al-muʿrib*, 2: 117 and 438–39. It is possible that these are quotations from his lost work, *al-Inṣāf*.

However, while indicating his support for this position, Ibn al-ʿArabī gives a very detailed analysis of Mālik's opposing views. The uniqueness of his analysis is that it rests on his belief that Ḥanafī law expands at length on what Mālik expressed in only a few terse statements on the subject. Ḥanafī law, he explains, was more expansive on the subject than Mālikī law because Ḥanafī jurists had greater exposure to the problems of shifting borders through their experiences in Khurāsān.[55]

Ibn al-ʿArabī explains that, according to the Ḥanafīs,[56] a Muslim's life is always protected, but the type of protection afforded varies depending on whether he lives in the abode of Islam or the abode of war. The strongest type of protection, which the Ḥanafīs call "effective protection" (*ʿiṣma qawīma* or *muqawwima*),[57] can be offered only to someone living in the abode of Islam. It protects a person by ensuring that, if he is killed, his relatives are entitled to collect the blood-wit (*diya*) from those responsible. It protects his property in that, if it is stolen, the thief must make restitution to him. As Ibn al-ʿArabī understands Abū Ḥanīfa, this protection cannot be afforded in the abode of war because, as the latter says, protection can only come through "fortresses and citadels."[58] In other words, whether or not someone can receive protection depends on practical considerations—one cannot collect blood money or force thieves to compensate their victims for the goods that they have stolen unless the Muslim ruler has sufficient power to ensure the enforcement of these laws. Any claims to be able to do so without the necessary physical force are empty ones. Ibn al-ʿArabī adds, however, that for the Ḥanafīs, there is another kind of protection which is afforded to all Muslims regardless of where they live. This he terms "moral protection" (*al-ʿāṣim al-muʾaththim*). This protection simply means that it is a sin to kill anyone who is entitled to it. A Muslim who lives in the abode of war has this protection but does not have "effective protection," which means that if he is killed, expiation to God (*kaffāra*) must be made for his life, but the blood-wit (*diya*) does not have to be paid. In Islamic law, the *kaffāra* does not take the form of a payment to the family of the deceased. Instead, it takes the form of some act of expiation on the part of the murderer, for example, the freeing a slave or performance of

55 al-Wansharīsī, *al-Miʿyār al-muʿrib*, 2: 128 and Muḥammad b. ʿAbdallāh Ibn al-ʿArabī, *Aḥkām al-Qurʾān*, ed. ʿAlī Muḥammad al-Bajāwī (Cairo: ʿĪsā al-Bābī al-Ḥalabī, 1967), 1: 477.

56 The Ḥanafī concept of *ʿiṣma* is studied in detail in Baber Johansen, "Der *ʿIṣma*-Begriff im Ḥanafitischen Recht," 238–62.

57 Ibn al-ʿArabī, *Aḥkām al-Qurʾān*, 1: 477. The term "*al-ʿāṣim al-muqawwim*" is used in al-Wansharīsī, *al-Miʿyār al-muʿrib*, 2: 128.

58 al-Wansharīsī, *al-Miʿyār al-muʿrib*, 2: 128.

fasting.[59] Thus the family of the deceased gains no material benefit from the *kaffāra* but only the satisfaction of knowing that the murderer is being held to account by a higher power.

In his *ʿĀriḍat al-aḥwadhī*,[60] Ibn al-ʿArabī says that Mālik and the Ḥanafīs agree that the life of a Muslim living in the abode of war is protected (*ḥuqina damuhu*).[61] In his *Aḥkām al-Qurʾān*, however, Ibn al-ʿArabī adds that, according to Mālik, if the blood of such a Muslim is shed, neither *diya* nor *kaffāra* is due. He says that, according to Mālik, since migration (*hijra*) is an obligation for all Muslims, someone who converts but does not migrate is considered as if he has no Islam and therefore neither *diya* nor *kaffāra* is due for his life. *Diya* and *kaffāra*, however, are due for someone who has no obligation to make *hijra* because he is unable to do so.[62] If Ibn al-ʿArabī's description of Mālik's view is correct, it is harsher than that of the Ḥanafīs who require *kaffāra* under all circumstances. I have, however, been unable to locate sources that support this understanding of Mālik's views. In the sources that I have examined, I have not found a passage in which Mālik discusses the *diya* and *kaffāra* due for the lives of Muslims living in the abode of war. Ibn ʿAbd al-Barr (d. 463/1070) does attribute such a discussion to Mālik and his companions, but his description of their views is diametrically opposed to that of Ibn al-ʿArabī. According to Ibn ʿAbd al-Barr, Mālik said that if such Muslims are killed and the killer does not know that they are Muslims, both *kaffāra* and *diya* must be paid. If the killer does know, he pays with his life.[63]

Ibn al-ʿArabī's analysis of Mālik's views was so compelling that it was later used by al-Wansharīsī to justify a return to this position. Ibn al-ʿArabī, however, firmly rejects Mālik's conclusions:

> The view of our companions [the Mālikīs] that Islam gives inviolability to life but not to children or property, and the view of the Ḥanafīs that protection and inviolability can only be bestowed through fortresses is incorrect. This is because they are based on a concept of *de facto*

---

59 On this concept, see "Kaffāra," in *al-Mawsūʿa al-fiqhiyya* (Kuwait City: Dawlat al-Kuwayt, Wizārat al-Awqāf wa'l-Shu'ūn al-Islāmiyya, 1987), 37–106.

60 Ibn al-ʿArabī, *ʿĀriḍat al-aḥwadhī*, 7: 106.

61 This expression is used in ʿAbd al-Wahhāb al-Baghdādī, *al-Ishrāf ʿalā nukat masāʾil al-khilāf*, 4: 427.

62 Ibn al-ʿArabī, *Aḥkām al-Qurʾān*, 1: 477.

63 Yūsuf b. ʿAbdallāh b. Muḥammad Ibn ʿAbd al-Barr al-Qurṭubī, *Kitāb al-kāfī fī fiqh ahl al-Madīna al-Mālikī*, ed. Muḥammad al-Mūrītānī (Riyadh: Maktabat al-Riyāḍ al-Ḥadītha, 1980), 1: 470.

> immunity[64] which can be achieved [even] by the unbeliever and by the bandit (*muḥārib*), but which is not acknowledged by the Law [to have value]—but surely the discussion should proceed according to what the Law acknowledges?! Can you not see that Muslim bandits and unbelievers can secure themselves in fortresses, but that it is [still] permissible to take their lives and property—in the case of [an unbeliever] under all circumstances, and in the case of [a bandit] provided that he stubbornly perseveres [in his activities].[65]

For Ibn al-ʿArabī, the law as expounded by the Mālikīs and the Ḥanafīs brings about a situation in which the actions of the powerful are sanctioned without regard to the demands of justice. The law is flouted in that no regard is paid to the principle that taking property that is in someone's legitimate safekeeping (*ḥirz*) is not permissible. The fact that this principle has been broken by someone who is beyond the reach of Muslim authority does not mean that it falls away. It means only that, for the time being, human enforcement of the principle is impossible. On these grounds, Ibn al-ʿArabī rejects the views of Mālik and the Ḥanafīs.

Most Mālikī authorities writing after Ibn al-ʿArabī tend to agree with his position. For example, like Ibn al-ʿArabī, Abū al-Walīd Muḥammad b. Aḥmad Ibn Rushd "the Grandson" (595/1198),[66] says that Muslims living in the abode of war have rights not just to their property but also to their wives and children. Ibn Rushd describes the opinion of Mālik in a way that is at odds with Mālik's position in the sources that I have examined. In those sources, Mālik says that the property, children, and wives of Muslims living in the abode of war may all be taken as booty. According to Ibn Rushd, however, Mālik held that while the property of a convert to Islam who does not migrate is forfeited as booty, this person retains his right to his wives and children. It is unclear what led him to this analysis of Mālik.[67] In any case, he concludes that the view that he ascribes to Mālik is to be rejected on the grounds that it is not in accordance with the

64 Literally, tangible immunity (*al-ʿiṣma al-ḥissiyya*).

65 Ibn al-ʿArabī, *Aḥkām al-Qurʾān*, 1: 477 and al-Wansharīsī, *al-Miʿyār al-muʿrib*, 2: 129.

66 On this jurist and philosopher, known in the West as Averroes, see *EI*², 3: 909.

67 It is possible that Ibn Rushd is deliberately misrepresenting the views of Mālik. It is also possible that this confusing passage is the result of a corruption in the manuscript upon which this edition is based. Maribel Fierro remarks that "in the existing editions and manuscripts [of the *Bidāyat al-mujtahid*] there are serious errors and inconsistencies," M. Fierro, "The Legal Policies of the Almohad Caliphs and Ibn Rushd's *Bidāyat al-Mujtahid*," *Journal of Islamic Studies* 10 (1999), 244.

conclusions of analogical reasoning (*qiyās*). Instead, he suggests that the correct legal position is encapsulated in a *ḥadīth*[68] which states that the people of the abode of war are to be fought only until they pronounce the declaration of God's unity, at which point their right to their lives, families and property becomes inviolable.[69]

The position of Ibn al-ʿArabī and Ibn Rushd "the Grandson" seems to be reflected in brief a reference to this subject in the *fatwā* literature of the period. Abū ʿAbdallāh Ibn al-Ḥājj (d. 529/1134)[70] held that the property of Muslims living in the abode of war may not be taken as booty because, citing a *ḥadīth*,[71] property owned by Muslims may not be taken except with the consent of its owners.[72] He also cites al-Laythī's opinion that a Muslim who remains in the abode of war is still entitled to his property. Although Ibn al-Ḥājj did not deal with the issue in great detail, it appears that he was reluctant to punish Muslims for living in the abode of war by denying them the right to security for their lives, families and property.

It is possible that Ibn Rushd the Grandfather (d. 520/1126)[73] was an exception to this position of tolerance for Muslims in the abode of war. In one of his legal commentaries, he refutes the view ascribed to Ibn Nāfiʿ, discussed above, according to which no special punishment is given to a Muslim bandit for living in the abode of war. Ibn Rushd says that this position contradicts the views of Mālik who denies the rights of such individuals to property, and he refutes Ibn Nāfiʿ on these grounds.[74] Ibn Rushd's view, however, is given in the context of a passage dealing with bandits. Although he gives general support to Mālik's opinion, he may well have granted some exception to Muslims peacefully living in the abode of war.

As late as the first half of the ninth/fifteenth century, the opinion that the Mudéjars had the right to own property seems to have prevailed. An exchange of

68 *Ṣaḥīḥ al-Bukhārī*, 6: 2682.

69 Ibn Rushd, *Bidāyat al-mujtahid* (Beirut: Dār al-Maʿrifa, 1982), 1: 400.

70 Rachid El Hour, "Ibn al-Ḥaŷŷ al-Tuŷībī, Abū ʿAbd Allāh," in *Biblioteca de al-Andalus* (Almería: Fundación Ibn Tufayl de Estudios Árabes, 2004–2012), 3: 351–54 and Makhlūf, *Shajarat al-nūr*, 1: 132.

71 al-Bayhaqī, *al-Sunan al-kubrā*, 6: 97 and 8: 182 and *Musnad al-Imām Aḥmad*, 5: 72.

72 al-Wansharīsī, *al-Miʿyār al-muʿrib*, 2: 142.

73 Kaḥḥāla, *Muʿjam al-muʾallifīn*, 8: 228.

74 Ibn Rushd, *al-Bayān waʾl-taḥṣīl*, 3: 41–42. Ibn Rushd cites Abū Isḥāq Ibrāhīm b. Ḥasan al-Tūnisī's (d. 447 or 449 / 1056 or 1058) clarification of Mālik's view, but it is not clear whether the latter subscribed to this opinion or merely explained its meaning. On al-Tūnisī, see Ibn Farḥūn, *al-Dībāj al-mudhahhab fī maʿrifat aʿyān ʿulamāʾ al-madhhab* (Cairo: n.p., 1932), 88 ff.

fatwās preserved by al-Wansharīsī regarding the property of the inhabitants of Galera (*Ghalīra*), a Granadan town that fell under the control of John II of Castille in 1436, provides a glimpse into the historical factors that would eventually cause this opinion to be rejected.[75] The *fatwās* were written in response to a question from the Muslims of the nearby Muslim-ruled town of Baza (*Basṭa*), who asked whether they were permitted to purchase property from Christians that had been seized from Muslims. Two jurists respond to their questions.[76] Abū Yaḥyā Ibn ʿĀṣim (d. after 857/1453)[77] argues that such property cannot be purchased because Muslim property can only change ownership with the owner's free consent. Thus Ibn ʿĀṣim's position is firmly in line with the views of Saḥnūn, who sought to protect the property rights of Muslims living in the abode of war. Ibn ʿĀṣim does note, however, that there is no legal precedent on this issue which, he says, is because it was only recently that Muslim lands began to fall under the control of non-Muslims.[78] He thus indicates that there is some judicial uncertainty on this matter.

Although agreeing with Ibn ʿĀṣim that, in general, the property rights of Muslims living in the abode of war are protected, Muḥammad b. Muḥammad al-Saraqusṭī (d. 865/1461)[79] argues that an exception to this rule can be justified under a limited set of circumstances. His argument runs thus. If there is a treaty (*ʿahd*) in effect between the Christian and Muslim rulers regarding the town of Galera, then the property of its Muslims cannot be purchased by other Muslims from the Christians who had seized it. This is because, under a treaty, property transfer must be in accordance with the laws of trade; only during wartime may property be legitimately seized as booty. If, however, the treaty has been broken by the tyrant (*ṭāghiya*), and a state of war is in effect, there is no problem with purchasing this property because such a purchase is regarded as equivalent to a *jihād* for booty.[80] Thus, according to al-Saraqusṭī, once Muslim property has been seized by the non-Muslim inhabitants of the

---

75 Rachel Arié, *L'Espagne musulmane au temps des Nasrides (1232–1492)* (Paris: Éditions de Boccard, 1973), 419. Cf. J. López Ortiz, "Fatwās Granadinas de los siglos XIV y XV," *al-Andalus* 6 (1941), 91–93.

76 On the frequent interchanges between these two jurists, see Muḥammad b. Muḥammad Ibn ʿĀṣim al-Gharnāṭī, *Jannat al-riḍā fī al-taslīm li-mā qaddara Allāhu wa-qaḍā*, ed. Ṣalāḥ Jarrār (Amman: Dār al-Bashīr, 1989), 1: 48.

77 On Abū Yaḥyā Muḥammad b. Abū Bakr Muḥammad Ibn ʿĀṣim, see Makhlūf, *Shajarat al-nūr*, 1: 248–49.

78 al-Wansharīsī, *al-Miʿyār al-muʿrib*, 2: 151.

79 On Abū ʿAbdallāh Muḥammad b. Muḥammad al-Anṣārī al-Saraqusṭī, see Makhlūf, *Shajarat al-nūr*, 1: 260.

80 al-Wansharīsī, *al-Miʿyār al-muʿrib*, 2: 142–43.

abode of war under circumstances in which there is no treaty in effect, there is a transfer of ownership even if this transfer is not made with the consent of the property's former owners. In support of this contention, he cites the *fatwā* of Ibn al-Qāsim, discussed above, which says that slaves stolen from the abode of Islam, brought to the abode of war, and then brought back to the abode of Islam, may be purchased by Muslims because the trip to the abode of war cancels their former ownership.[81]

Al-Saraqusṭī emphasizes that his sanctioning of the purchase of Muslim property in Galera applies only to a situation in which no treaty is in place and in which the property in question is no longer in Muslim hands as a result of having been seized by non-Muslims. He does not mean that Muslims in the abode of Islam are free to seize the property of Muslims living in the abode of war on the grounds that they are inferior Muslims. He points out that, even if a Muslim heretic is killed, his family still inherits his property. Moreover, if an apostate returns to Islam, his property still belongs to him.[82] It is only if he is killed before he repents that his property becomes booty (*fay'*) for the Muslims.[83] Since, according to al-Saraqusṭī, Muslims who live in the abode of war are not considered apostates merely for living there, there are no Islamic grounds for seizing their property merely because they violate the law requiring their migration. An exception to this rule, for al-Saraqusṭī, is the case of converts to Islam who continue to live in the abode of war after their conversion. He explains that whereas Muslims from birth who live in the abode of war have an inalienable right to their property in the event of a Muslim raid on their lands, the property of converts who live there can be taken as booty.[84] Al-Saraqusṭī does not give a reason for discriminating against converts but merely asks, rhetorically, how one can compare Muslims from birth with those who have converted to Islam later in life.[85] His position against converts might, however, have been for the purpose of paying deference to Mālik's position on

81 al-ʿUtbī, *al-Mustakhraja*, 3: 25.

82 On the terms *zandaqa* and *ridda* in al-Andalus, see Maribel Fierro, "Accusations of 'Zandaqa' in al-Andalus," *Quaderni di Studi Arabi* 5–6 (1987–8), 251 ff. and her fuller study of the issue, *La heterodoxia en al-Andalus durante el período omeya* (Madrid: Instituto Hispano-Arabe de Cultura, 1987), 2 ff.

83 al-Wansharīsī, *al-Miʿyār al-muʿrib*, 2: 146–47.

84 Ibid., 2: 142–43.

85 Ibid., 2: 143. On the treatment of converts as inferior members of society in al-Andalus, see Ana Fernández Félix, "Cristianos y conversos al Islam en al-Andalus bajo los Omeyas: Una aproximación al proceso de islamización a través de una fuente legal andalusí del s. III/I," in *Visigodos y omeyas* (Madrid: Consejo Superior de Investigaciones Científicas, Instituto de Historia, Departamento de Historia Antigua y Arqueología, 2000), 426.

those who convert to Islam in the abode of war but do not migrate. Since such converts were few in number during this period, his concession to Mālik would have had a very limited impact.

Although clearly drawing on the Mālikī legal tradition, al-Saraqusṭī's view is very different from those of his predecessors. Al-Saraqusṭī agrees with Mālik that one may seize the property of converts to Islam who have not migrated to the abode of Islam, but does not want this law to be extended to Muslims from birth. Like Abū Ṣāliḥ, he draws a distinction between non-Muslim lands that have concluded treaties with Muslim rulers and those that have not. Al-Saraqusṭī, however, uses this distinction to draw a conclusion almost entirely opposed to that of Abū Ṣāliḥ. If Muslims live under a Christian ruler who has entered into a treaty with a Muslim ruler, they retain legal ownership of their property even if it is seized by Christians. If, on the other hand, Muslims live under a Christian ruler who has not signed a treaty with a Muslim ruler, they lose legal ownership of their property in the event that it is seized by Christians. Al-Saraqusṭī's view thus seems to cause the very disruption of a Muslim ruler's treaties with Christian lands which, I suggested, Abū Ṣāliḥ wanted to avoid. Whereas, when a treaty was in force, Abū Ṣāliḥ compelled Muslims to accept Christian ownership of property that Christians had illegally taken from them,[86] al-Saraqusṭī instructs Muslims to disregard such Christian claims of ownership. One can only speculate regarding why al-Saraqusṭī chose to adopt this idiosyncratic position in what can be seen as a valiant, if unusual, attempt to grapple with the problems faced by the increasing numbers of Muslims living under Christian rule. It is possible that he was motivated to do so by a desire to help the Muslims of Baza. Perhaps he thought that there was little prospect that the Christians who had seized the property of the Galeran Muslims would return it to them and simply wanted the Muslims of Baza to derive what benefit they could from it through being able to purchase it. He accomplished his goal by weakening the right of Muslims to own property in the abode of war. He was not prepared, however, to entirely eliminate this right by advocating a return to the position of Mālik.

The difficulty experienced by the jurists in determining the law with respect to the lives and property of Muslims who live in the abode of war is reflected in al-Wansharīsī's *fatwās* on Muslims living under non-Muslim rule. In a *fatwā*[87]

---

86 See above, page 93.

87 al-Wazzānī, *al-Miʿyār al-jadīd*, 3: 29. Cf. ʿAbd al-ʿAzīz b. al-Ḥasan b. Yūsuf al-Jumārī al-Zayyātī, *al-Jawāhir al-mukhtāra mimmā waqafat ʿalayhi min al-nawāzil bi-jabal jumāra* (BGR. no. 1694), 2: 45–46, referred to in Mohamed Mezzine, "Les Relations entre les places occupées et les localités de la région de Fès aux XVIème et XVIIème siècles, à

regarding some Bedouin who live under non-Muslim rule, al-Wansharīsī tentatively remarks that there is a judicial consensus that the security of their persons and property is incomplete (*lam takmul ḥurmatuhu*). He does not, however, explain the extent to which this is the case and what rights these Bedouin might still possess.

This lack of clarity, which seems to be intentional, is retained in al-Wansharīsī's *Asnā al-matājir*, his major *fatwā* on the status of the Mudéjars. Although al-Wansharīsī states in this *fatwā* that he intends it to be the definitive reference on the subject, he does not give his own views on the status of Mudéjar lives and property but instead presents the disputes among the jurists, not limiting himself to those of the Mālikī school. Thus, for example, he notes that while Mālik and the Mālikīs forbade the killing of Muslims who live in the abode of war, he quotes the views of Abū Ḥanīfa who said that while such killing is a sin, it does not necessitate the payment of the blood-wit (*diya*).[88] Regarding the question of property rights, al-Wansharīsī portrays the Mālikī school as being split between those who accept Mālik's denial of property rights to Muslims who live in the abode of war and those who accord such rights to them.[89] He does not indicate which of these views he believes to be correct but instead urges that a judicial "determination of preponderance (*tarjīḥ*)"[90] be made.[91] He closes this discussion by citing the opinion of "one of the authoritative jurists" (*muḥaqqiqūn*) which, he says, is an attempt to

---

partir de documents locaux inédits: Les *Nawāzil*," in *Relaciones de la Península Ibérica con el Magreb siglos XIII–XVI*, ed. Mercedes García-Arenal and María J. Viguera (Madrid: Instituto Hispano-Árabe de Cultura, 1988), 551.

88 Al-Wansharīsī indicates that, at least with respect to accidental killing, exegetes of the Qur'ān (whom he does not name) have supported the position of not paying the *diya*, see al-Wansharīsī, *al-Miʿyār al-muʿrib*, 2: 128. For an example of an exegete who supported this position, see al-Qurṭubī, *al-Jāmiʿ li-aḥkām al-Qur'ān* (Cairo: Dār al-Kātib al-ʿArabī, 1967), on Qur'ān, 4: 92.

89 In an earlier work, al-Wansharīsī attributes to Ibn al-Qāsim the view that a Muslim who remains in the abode of war has a right to his property if he is born a Muslim but not if he is a convert to Islam, see al-Wansharīsī, *ʿUddat al-burūq fī jamʿ mā fī al-madhhab min al-jumūʿ wa'l-furūq* (Beirut: Dār al-Gharb al-Islāmī, 1990), 216. As is clear from my discussion of Ibn al-Qāsim's views, this is an imprecise summary of the latter's position. On al-Wansharīsī's *ʿUddat al-burūq*, see F. Vidal Castro, "Las obras de Aḥmad al-Wanšarīsī (m. 914/1508)," *Inventario analítico* 3 (1992), 100–102.

90 On the concept of *tarjīḥ*, see Bernard Weiss, *The Search for God's Law* (Salt Lake City: University of Utah Press, 1992), 730 and Birgit Krawietz, "The Weighing of Conflicting Indicators in Islamic Law," in *Law, Christianity and Modernism in Islamic Society*, ed. Urbain Vermeulen and J.M.F. van Reeth (Leuven: Peeters, 1998), 71–74.

91 al-Wansharīsī, *al-Miʿyār al-muʿrib*, 2: 130.

reconcile these differences. Although he does not explicitly indicate his approval of this opinion, he does designate this author as an "authoritative jurist," and since this opinion is the last one that he cites on the subject, one may assume that it possessed some merit in his eyes. According to this opinion, how the Mudéjars are to be treated is dependent on how they choose to relate to the Muslims of the abode of Islam. If they fight against the Muslims together with their Christian rulers, then it is best to take their lives; but if, on the other hand, they help their Christian rulers by providing them with their property, then it is best to take their property. In other words, according to this jurist, Muslims who live in the abode of war are punished, not for having chosen to live there, but for whatever crimes they commit against Muslims living in the abode of Islam. The sole exception to this rule concerns their children, who must be taken away from them in order to remove them from the religious corruption that would certainly befall them in such lands.[92] However, although al-Wansharīsī seems to give preference to the view of this "authoritative" jurist, the fact that he cites a broad range of opinion in the *fatwā* gives the impression that jurists should be given considerable flexibility when dealing with such sensitive and ill-defined issues.

Other jurists of al-Wansharīsī's era, no doubt responding to greater Christian control over the Iberian Peninsula, thought that a harsher stand against the Mudéjars was necessary. The pragmatic nature of their position is evident when one considers how essential Mudéjars were to the political and economic well-being of many Christian territories.[93] These jurists therefore advocated a return to the views of Mālik which nullified Muslim ownership of property in the abode of war. Ibn Sarrāj (d. 848/1444), for example, was asked whether rent must be paid for land rented from a mosque that had subsequently been conquered by the enemy. Ibn Sarrāj answers that no rent is due because once the enemy has conquered this territory it becomes a part of the abode of war and the mosque's ownership of the land ceases.[94] He thus appears to endorse Mālik's view that there is no property ownership in the abode of war. ʿAbdallāh b. ʿAbd al-Wāḥid al-Waryājilī (d. 894/1488)[95] was asked whether it is permissible to shed the blood, enslave the women, and take the property of Muslims who

92 Ibid.

93 For further details on this phenomenon, please see the previous chapter.

94 Abū al-Qāsim Ibn Sarrāj al-Andalusī, *Fatāwā Qāḍī al-Jamāʿa Abī al-Qāsim Ibn Sarrāj al-Andalusī*, ed. Muḥammad Abū al-Ajfān (Abu Dhabi: al-Majmaʿ al-Thaqāfī, 2000), 164.

95 Maklūf, *Shajarat al-nūr*, 1: 266 and Muḥammad b. ʿAskar al-Ḥasanī al-Shafshāwanī, *Dawḥat al-nāshir li-maḥāsin man kāna bi'l-Maghrib min mashāyikh al-qarn al-ʿāshir*, ed. Muḥammad Ḥajjī (Casablanca: Markaz al-Turāth al-Thaqāfī al-Maghribī, 2003), 34–37.

live under the laws of unbelievers in the abode of war and who will not migrate to neighboring Muslim lands. He responds that killing them and taking their wealth is obligatory according to the laws of booty and that it is permissible for their women to be enslaved.[96]

This return to the earlier position of Mālik regarding property was not universally held. Some jurists, like ʿĪsā b. Aḥmad al-Māwāsī (d. 896/1491),[97] disagree with the principle of punishing Muslims merely for living in the abode of war by, for example, expropriating their property. Al-Māwāsī says that such Muslims may be punished only if they fight on behalf of unbelievers against Muslims. He does not, however, specify what such a punishment might involve.[98] In a similar vein, Ibn Zakrī (d. 900/1494)[99] rules that a certain group of Muslims who have love for and cooperate militarily with some Christians must be killed. He gives no general principle that Muslims living in the abode of war must be killed; rather, his ruling is directed against those who pose a danger to the abode of Islam.[100] His view thus seems to be in line with that of the "authoritative jurists" mentioned by al-Wansharīsī.[101] A similar ruling was issued by Muḥammad b. ʿAbd al-Karīm al-Maghīlī (d. 909 or 910 / 1503–4 or 1505–6)[102] in a *fatwā* written for the Middle Niger ruler Askiyā al-Ḥājj Muḥammad (r. 898–935 / 1493–1529).[103] The latter asked whether Muslims who live among communities of bandits (*muḥāribūn*) may be killed and their property expropriated. In his response, al-Maghīlī divides such Muslims into two categories: those who live there by choice (*ikhtiyār^an^*) and aid the bandits and those who do not live there by choice and give no aid to the bandits. Those in the first category may be killed during a raid and their property may

96 Laḥsan al-Yūbī, *al-Fatāwā al-fiqhiyya fī ahamm al-qaḍāyā min ʿahd al-Saʿdīyīn ilā mā qabla al-ḥimāya* (Rabat: al-Mamlaka al-Maghribiyya, Wizārat al-Awqāf wa'l-Shu'ūn al-Islāmiyya, 1998), 209, quoting *Nawāzil al-Tasūlī* (al-Khizāna al-Ḥasanīya bi'l-Ribāṭ, no. 798), 2: 235.

97 Aḥmad Bābā al-Tunbuktī, *Kitāb nayl al-ibtihāj bi-taṭrīz al-Dībāj* (Fez: al-Maṭbaʿa al-Jadīda, 1899), 194.

98 al-Wazzānī, *al-Nawāzil al-ṣughrā*, 1: 418.

99 See *EI*², 12: 402.

100 Ibid., 1: 419. Cf. Idrīs Karam, *al-ʿAlāqāt al-ijtimāʿiyya min khilāl al-nawāzil al-fiqhiyya bi'l-Maghrib* (Rabat: Éditions IDGL, 2005), 119.

101 For a sixteenth-century view that echoes the views of Saḥnūn and Ibn al-Qāsim, see Muḥammad b. Muḥammad al-Ḥaṭṭāb, *Mawāhib al-Jalīl* (Cairo: Maṭbaʿat al-Saʿāda, 1911), 3: 364.

102 *EI*², 5: 1165.

103 *EI*², 7: 393.

be expropriated.[104] Those in the second category may not be killed and their property may not be seized. If they are killed accidentally, those who kill them are not to be held responsible. If their property is seized, it must be returned. Thus al-Maghīlī is clear that no special punishments are to be applied to Muslims merely for living in the abode of war. The stipulation that those who kill them accidentally are not obligated to pay the blood-wit to their families appears to be a concession to those who go to fight the bandits rather than a punishment to those Muslims who unwillingly live in such territory.

To conclude, Mālikī opinion on the rights of Muslims living in the abode of war experienced two main turning points: one in the 3rd/9th century and the other in the 9th/15th century. The first change occurred when the early jurists of al-Andalus and the Maghrib rejected Mālik's opinion that curtailed the family and property rights of Muslims located in the abode of war. They likely took this position because the close geographical proximity and shifting borders between Muslim and Christian lands made Mālik's laws impractical. Their opinion prevailed largely unchallenged until the beginning of the 9th/15th century when Muslims were on the verge of losing all of their territories in al-Andalus. At this point, some jurists recommended a return to the position of Mālik because they thought that a greater separation between Muslims and Christians was desirable.

---

104 See Muḥammad b. ʿAbd al-Karīm al-Maghīlī, *Ajwibat al-Maghīlī ʿan asʾilat al-Amīn al-Ḥājj Muḥammad Askiyā*, ed. and tr. John O. Hunwick (London: Oxford University Press, 1985), Arabic: 38, English: 88.

CHAPTER 4

European Rule in the 19th-Century Maghrib and the Reception of Reconquista-Era Law

The French in the Maghrib, ʿAbd al-Qādir, and the Response of the Jurists

After the completion of the Reconquista, the issue of living under Christian rule was seldom discussed in the Islamic West. Other than a small number of *fatwās* on the fate of the Moriscos, the crypto-Muslims who remained in the Iberian Peninsula, and others dealing with European incursions on the Moroccan coast, the issue seems to have largely been largely ignored. This is because, by the end of the Reconquista, most Muslims of the Islamic West lived under Islamic rule and the issue of Christian rule became a largely theoretical matter. It was only with the invasion of the Maghrib by the French in 1830 that living under Christian rule came to be extensively discussed again by Mālikī jurists. Throughout the nineteenth century, most Mālikī jurists believed that Islamic law did not permit Muslims to live under Christian rule. As will be seen, however, many were prepared to grant a special dispensation to live under Christian rule in circumstances in which Muslims had little other alternative.

The revival of discussions in the Maghrib about the permissibility of living under Christian rule was precipitated by the 1830 surrender of the Ottoman Dey of Algiers to the French. Even once Algiers was conquered, French control was limited and did not extend to many parts of the country, including its Western border with Morocco. The result was that this area was left effectively without a ruler. While the Moroccan Sultan ʿAbd al-Raḥmān b. Hishām (d. 1276/1859),[1] was to briefly extend his dominion to fill this void in immediately neighboring territories, French pressure soon forced him to withdraw. The power vacuum was then filled by a tribal leader, ʿAbd al-Qādir b. Muḥyī Dīn al-Jazāʾirī (d. 1300/1883), who took power in 1248/1832 and established a capital in the town of Mascara from which he coordinated his resistance movement.[2]

---

1 *EI*², 1: 84.

2 For accounts of these events, see Bennison, *Jihad and Its Interpretations in Pre-Colonial Morocco*, 48–57; al-Jazāʾirī, *Tuḥfat al-zāʾir*, 147–61; al-Nāṣirī, *Kitāb al-istiqṣā*, 9: 26 ff; Jean-Louis Miège, *Le Maroc et l'Europe (1830–1894)* (Paris: Presses Universitaires de France, 1961), 2: 157 ff.; as well as Sultan ʿAbd al-Raḥmān's letters reproduced and translated in Hamet,

© KONINKLIJKE BRILL NV, LEIDEN, 2015 | DOI 10.1163/9789004284531_006

The success of ʿAbd al-Qādir's resistance depended upon immigration to his encampments and upon his ability to deal harshly with Muslims who provided stability to the French by choosing to peacefully live under their rule. He was thus very interested in the concept of *hijra*, upon which he wrote a treatise, and he was also interested in obtaining Islamic justification for taking punitive military action against Muslims who lived under French rule. To this end, he sent several requests for *fatwā*s to juristic authorities in order to build support for his view.

In 1252/1837, ʿAbd al-Qādir sent Sultan ʿAbd al-Raḥmān a request for a *fatwā* from the jurists of Fez. In it, he speaks of "the great calamity and distress in the land of Algiers which has become a slaughterhouse for the unbelievers" to kill the Muslims. In Algiers, he says, "the unbelieving enemy attempts to reign over and enslave the Muslims, sometimes by means of the sword and sometimes by means of the entanglements of politics." He asks what is to be done about "Muslims who mingle with the unbelievers, cooperate with them and bring them cattle, the most excellent of horses and such like," and who moreover willingly provide them with military intelligence against the Muslims. Is it is permissible, he asks, to kill them and expropriate their wealth, especially given that they cannot be punished for their actions except in battle?[3] It is clear that he hopes for a positive response to these questions.[4]

Sultan ʿAbd al-Raḥmān was reluctant to associate himself with ʿAbd al-Qādir's plan of action. He referred ʿAbd al-Qādir's questions to ʿAlī b. ʿAbd al-Salām al-Tasūlī (d. 1258/1842),[5] who provided a long and detailed response.[6]

Le Gouvernement marocain et la conquête d'Alger, 19–121. On the nature of ʿAbd al-Qādir's state, see Pessah Shinar, "ʿAbd al-Qādir and ʿAbd al-Krīm: Religious Influences on their Thought and Action," *Asian and African Studies* 1 (1965), 143 ff.

3 al-Jazāʾirī, *Tuḥfat al-zāʾir*, 316–17. An abbreviated and slightly different version of this text also appears in ʿAlī b. ʿAbd al-Salām al-Tasūlī, *Ajwibat al-Tasūlī ʿan masāʾil al-Amīr ʿAbd al-Qādir fī al-jihād*, ed. ʿAbd al-Laṭīf Aḥmad al-Shaykh Muḥammad Ṣāliḥ (Beirut: Dār al-Gharb al-Islāmī, 1996), 102–104.

4 ʿAbd al-Qādir's attitude to such Muslims had already been established by his father, Muḥyī al-Dīn, who ordered war to be waged against any tribe giving supplies to the French. He said that any Muslim caught delivering such supplies was to have his right hand, nose and ears amputated, see Danziger, *Abd al-Qadir and the Algerians*, 62.

5 On al-Tasūlī's biography, see *Shajarat al-nūr*, 1: 397 and al-Ḥasan al-Yūbī, "al-Faqīh ʿAlī b. ʿAbd al-Salām al-Tasūlī wa-nawāziluhu," in *al-Nawāzil al-fiqhiyya wa-atharuhā fī al-fatwā wa'l-ijtihād* (Casablanca: Jāmiʿat al-Ḥasan al-Thānī, Kullīyat al-Ādāb wa'l-ʿUlūm al-Insāniyya, 2001), 227–44.

6 al-Tasūlī, *Ajwibat al-Tasūlī*, 36 ff. Al-Tasūlī also produced an abbreviated version of this responsa (*mukhtaṣar*) which can be found in al-Wazzānī, *al-Miʿyār al-jadīd*, 10: 297 ff.

Al-Tasūlī notes that there is a debate among the jurists regarding how Muslims who live in non-Muslim territory are to be treated. All agree, he says, basing himself on al-Wansharīsī's *Asnā al-matājir* and on some of the sources that it quotes, that *hijra* from the abode of unbelief is obligatory unless a Muslim is truly unable to perform it. He gives the example of a person who is very sick or so physically weak that it is impossible for him to travel.[7] *Hijra*, he says, is an obligation which is of the same weight as such important obligations as prayer and fasting in Ramaḍān.[8] The rationale behind *hijra*, he says, is to separate Muslims from non-Muslims. Thus Muslims, even when living in Islamic territory, are enjoined not to live close to non-Muslims or to be their travelling companions. Absolutely prohibited, however, is for Muslims to place themselves in a situation in which they become subject to the laws of the unbelievers. This prohibition is so strict, he says, that Muslims are not even permitted to go to the abode of war temporarily for the purpose of trade.[9] Although living in the abode of war is not to be tolerated, he indicates that all jurists nevertheless agree that the lives of such Muslims are not automatically forfeit because of where they choose to live. At the very most, some jurists say that their property can be confiscated. Al-Tasūlī, however, believes that the exigencies of his era call for such individuals to be treated more harshly than they were in the past. Thus he attempts to show that by the mere fact of living in non-Muslim territory, such Muslims are also necessarily guilty of the illicit activity of giving assistance to their non-Muslim rulers:

> It is evident that everyone who stays in their abode necessarily pays the *jizya* tax to them and therefore is a perpetual helper to them … This favors

---

7 Ibid., 301–310.

8 Ibid., 118. This view regarding the importance of *hijra* and the impermissibility of living under non-Muslim rule was almost universal in the Maghrib during this period. For examples of other jurists who held this view, see Aḥmad b. al-Ma'mūn al-Balghaythī (d. 1348/1929), *Kitāb ḥusn al-naẓra fī aḥkām al-hijra* (Cairo: Maṭba'at 'Abd al-Raḥmān, 1970). This work was written in 1330/1911, shortly before the beginning of the French protectorate. See also, Muḥammad b. al-Madanī Gannūn, "Risāla fī al-hijra min arḍ al-'adūw," in *al-Tasliya wa'l-salwān li-man ibtilā bi'l-idhāya wa'l-buhtān* (Fez: lithograph, 1301/1884), 122 ff., referred to in Muḥammad al-Manūnī, *al-Maṣādir al-'Arabiyya li-tārīkh al-Maghrib* (Rabat: al-Mamlaka al-Maghribiyya, Jāmi'at Muḥammad al-Khāmis, Kullīyat al-Ādāb wa'l-'Ulūm al-Insāniyya, 1983), 2: 137. In his treatise, Gannūn emphasizes the absolute necessity of migration from lands ruled by Christians. On this author, see Kaḥḥala, *Mu'jam*, 12: 10. For a discussion about the prevalence of thinking on *hijra* in the nineteenth-century Maghrib, see Laroui, *Les Origines sociales et culturelles du nationalisme marocain*, 320.

9 Ibid., 305.

> permitting the expropriation of their wealth in accordance with the doctrine of Mālik... [Moreover], according to [Aḥmad b. Muḥammad] Ibn Zakrī (d. 900/1494):[10] "They may be killed in a battle against the unbelievers when they help them, even if they do this [only] with their property."[11]

Thus al-Tasūlī establishes that it may be assumed that Muslims living in non-Muslim territory are always in a position of helping the enemy because of the taxes that they pay and may therefore, according to the view of Ibn Zakrī, be killed with the sanction of the law. In another place in his treatise, he summarizes the import of this view: "Even if they are not favorably disposed towards the unbelievers, do not collude with them, and do not inform on the Muslims for them, or do anything else like that, but on the contrary distance themselves from their troops, they may still be killed as rebels."[12] When these Muslim residents of non-Muslim territory are not being fought, they are to be completely ostracized and their testimony in court is not to be accepted.[13] Al-Tasūlī emphasizes, however, that any actions taken against these Muslims have to be performed under the supervision of the sultan. ʿAbd al-Qādir, as the sultan's deputy, is not himself authorized to take action against them without the sultan's prior approval.

A different approach from that of al-Tasūlī was taken by ʿAbd al-Hādī al-ʿAlawī (d. 1271/1855),[14] another jurist of Fez who, in 1256/1840, responded to a similar set of questions from ʿAbd al-Qādir.[15] ʿAbd al-Qādir's main question to this jurist was whether Muslims who live under French rule, giving the French material support and fighting on their behalf, are to be considered apostates. He emotionally describes Muslim soldiers who wear France's *Médaille d'Honneur* which is awarded to them, he says, for having successfully killed many Muslims. If it is determined that such Muslims are apostates, he asks whether they can be immediately killed or whether they must first be given an

10 See *EI*², s.v. "Muḥammad b. Zakrī".

11 al-Tasūlī, *Ajwibat al-Tasūlī*, 310. This *fatwā* is recorded in al-Wazzānī, *al-Nawāzil al-ṣughrā al-musammā al-minaḥ al-sāmiya fī al-nawāzil al-fiqhiyya* (Rabat: al-Mamlaka al-Maghribiyya, Wizārat al-Awqāf wa'l-Shu'ūn al-Islāmiyya, 1992), 1: 419.

12 Ibid., 210. Al-Tasūlī also warns against those Muslims who trade with the enemy and thus strengthen their position, see ibid., 143 ff.

13 Ibid., 274.

14 Abū ʿAbdallāh Muḥammad b. Jaʿfar b. Idrīs al-Kattānī, *Salwat al-anfās wa-muḥādathat al-akyās bi-man uqbira min al-ʿulamāʾ wa'l-ṣulaḥāʾ bi-Fās*, ed. ʿAbdallāh al-Kāmil al-Kattānī, *et al.* (Rabat: Dār al-Thaqāfa, 2004), 1: 123–24.

15 The *fatwā* is contained in al-Wazzānī, *al-Miʿyār al-jadīd*, 10: 291–97 and idem, *al-Nawāzil al-ṣughrā*, 1: 414–17.

opportunity to repent. He further asks whether their goods may be confiscated and whether their wives and children may be killed or enslaved. If they are not deemed apostates, he asks whether their property may still be confiscated.

Al-ʿAlawī grants more protection to Muslims living under the French than al-Tasūlī. He is not moved by ʿAbd al-Qādir's plea to consider those Muslims who fight for the French as apostates. He cites Abū Ḥāmid al-Ghazālī's *Fayṣal al-tafriqa bayna al-Islām wa'l-zandaqa* (*The Criterion for Distinguishing Islam from Heresy*) to indicate how cautious jurists historically have been before allowing the charge of heresy to be brought against individuals who assert that they are Muslims. As an example of this, he says that even Ibāḍī Muslims, although they do not practice normative Islam, cannot be automatically categorized as unbelievers. He therefore counsels ʿAbd al-Qādir not to use the term "unbeliever" with reckless abandon.

Many people, al-ʿAlawī says, incorrectly use the Qur'ānic verse, "Whoever of you takes them [the unbelievers] as friends, is one of them,"[16] as a justification for designating Muslims who fight for the French as "unbelievers." This, he says, involves a mistaken understanding of the meaning of the verse. Quoting the respected Qur'ānic commentary of Muḥammad b. Aḥmad Ibn Juzayy al-Gharnāṭī (d. 741/1340),[17] he says that the verse means that "one who believes their beliefs is one of them in all respects; [however] one who is opposed to their beliefs but is friendly with them is [only] one of them in his odiousness before God and is deserving of punishment."[18] The import of this interpretation is that a person who is friendly with unbelievers is a sinner, but not an unbeliever. In support of this contention, he relates the case, as reported by Aḥmad b. Muḥammad al-Burzulī (d. 841/1438),[19] of al-Muʿtamid Ibn ʿAbbād (d. 488/1095),[20] the well-known ruler of the taifa of Seville. Ibn ʿAbbād allied himself with a Christian kingdom in a battle against the Almoravids, but was eventually captured by Almoravids leader, Yūsuf Ibn Tashfīn (d. 500/1106).[21] The latter asked the jurists whether Ibn ʿAbbād should be killed as an apostate for fighting on the same side as the Christians. According to al-Burzulī, the majority of the jurists were of the opinion that Ibn ʿAbbād should not be considered an apostate and should not be killed. Ibn Tashfīn therefore did not execute him but instead exiled him to Aghmat where he remained impris-

16 Qur'ān 5: 51.

17 Brockelmann, *Geschichte der arabischen Litteratur*, 2: 264.

18 Muḥammad b. Aḥmad Ibn Juzayy, *Tafsīr Ibn Juzayy* (Beirut: Dār al-Kitāb al-ʿArabī, 1983), 102.

19 Brockelmann, *Geschichte der arabischen Litteratur*, 2: 247 and Supplement 2: 347–48.

20 *EI*^{2}, 7: 766.

21 Ibid., 11: 355.

oned until his death.[22] From this al-ʿAlawī draws the conclusion that even if a Muslim commits the reprehensible act of fighting on the side of the Christians, he is not to be considered an apostate, a category of person which is subject to the death penalty. He is, however, a rebel and, as such, although his weapons may be confiscated from him, he is not to be killed and retains possession of his family and property.[23]

Muḥammad b. Aḥmad ʿIllaysh (d. 1299/1882), who became the chief Mālikī *muftī* of Egypt,[24] replied to two separate petitions for *fatwās* regarding the French in Algeria. In contrast to al-Tasūlī and al-ʿAlawī who, when dealing with the issue of living under Christian rule, concentrated their attention on Europe as a military threat and gave little thought to it as a cultural threat, ʿIllaysh was greatly concerned with what he saw as the deleterious effects of European culture upon Muslims. The difference between their views was no doubt a product of the Egyptian intellectual environment of which ʿIllaysh was a part. Although originally from Tripolitania, ʿIllaysh had spent most of his adult life in Egypt, a society which had dealt with non-Muslim rule and influence for over thirty years before the French conquered Algeria. Egyptian intellectual elites had therefore spent longer than their Maghribī contemporaries in considering its legal and religious implications and ʿIllaysh was very much a part of this milieu.

The traditional nature of ʿIllaysh's position on living under Christian rule is made clear in his response to the following question which was put to him:

> What is your opinion regarding a Muslim region that, having been attacked and conquered, is ruled by the unbelieving enemy? Some of the mountains on the border of the aforementioned area have not been reached and controlled [by the enemy] and they are still protected by its peoples. Some of the residents of this area have migrated (*hājara*) to it with their families, property and progeny while others have remained under the rule of the unbelievers as their subjects. The unbelievers have imposed a tax (*kharāj*) upon them which resembles the well-known *jizya*. Among both those who migrated and those who remained are jurists. There is a dispute between these two groups of jurists. Those

22 al-Wazzānī, *al-Miʿyār al-jadīd*, 10: 293. On the conditions of his imprisonment, see Ronald Messier, *The Almoravids and the Meanings of Jihad* (Santa Barbara: Praeger, 2010), 106–107.

23 Ibid., 10: 294.

24 Brockelmann, *Geschichte der arabischen Litteratur*, 2: 738–739; Makhlūf, *Shajarat al-nūr*, 385 and Gilbert Delanoue, *Moralistes et politiques musulmans dans l'Égypte de XIXème siècle* (Cairo: Institut Français d'Archéologie Orientale, 1982), 127–40.

> who migrated with the Muslims to the aforementioned mountains say that *hijra* is obligatory. They rule that it is permissible to shed the blood, expropriate the property and take captive the families of those Muslims who remain under the [rule] of the unbelievers while having the ability to migrate. They base themselves on the fact that one who remains becomes someone who helps [the unbelievers] in fighting against the Muslims, plundering their property and striving for the victory of the unbelievers over them ... Those jurists who remain under [the rule of] the unbelievers and do not migrate say that *hijra* is not obligatory ... basing themselves upon the tradition, ... "There is no *hijra* after the conquest [of Mecca]," and other such traditions.[25]

The text neither mentions the name of the location to which the questioner refers nor the questioner's identity. From context, however, one can surmise that it concerns the situation of ʿAbd al-Qādir and his followers.[26] ʿIllaysh's response to the question is striking. He does not attempt to formulate his own opinion on the matter but simply quotes al-Wansharīsī's two *fatwā*s on the Mudéjars of Iberia. Thus it seems that, for ʿIllaysh, the situation of French rule in the 19th-century Maghrib was no different from that of Christian rule over Muslims living in Reconquista-era Iberia. Neither situation allowed for any dispensation to be given which would permit Muslims to remain in Christian territory.[27]

In other writings, ʿIllaysh gives greater insight into the factors which he feels make the rule of Europeans so corrupting of Islamic life. In a *fatwā* entitled, *Refutation of the Epistle 'Answers to the Perplexed Concerning the Status of the Hat of the Christians'*, which deals with the issue of Muslim students, studying in France, who wish to wear French hats, he discusses the cultural threat that Christian Europe poses to Muslims.[28] For ʿIllaysh, the desire to wear the hat is

---

25 Muḥammad ʿIllaysh, *Fatḥ al-ʿalī al-mālik fī al-fatāwā ʿalā madhhab al-Imām Mālik*, 375 ff.

26 On ʿAbd al-Qādir's possible authorship of this question, see Rudolph Peters, *Islam and Colonialism: The Doctrine of Jihad in Modern History* (The Hague: Mouton Publishers, 1979), 58 and 182 n. 58.

27 Interestingly, in a work of commentary, ʿIllaysh says that someone who converts to Islam in the abode of war but does not migrate is an unbeliever because migration is an indicator of the validity (*ṣiḥḥa*) of his Islam. Muḥammad ʿIllaysh, *Sharḥ manḥ al-Jalīl ʿalā mukhtaṣar al-ʿallāma Khalīl* (Beirut: Dār al-Fikr, 1989), 3: 318.

28 On this theme in ʿIllaysh's writings, see M. Hatina, "Fatwas as a Prism of Social History in the Middle East: The Status of Non-Muslims in the Nineteenth Century," in *Koexistenz und Konfrontation: Beiträge zur jüngeren Geschichte und Gegenwartslage der orientalischen Christen*, ed. M. Tamcke (Münster: Lit, 2003), 56–57 and W. Shadid and S. van Koningsveld,

a symbol of a much larger problem of Muslims seeking European wisdom and adopting European values. He criticizes European learning thus:

> Islamic law decrees that the branches of knowledge which are to be sought after are the theological sciences and their tools, i.e. the sciences of the Arabic language. Other knowledge is not to be sought after and, indeed, is to be proscribed. It is well-known that Christians know nothing at all of the theological sciences or of their tools, and that most of their sciences derive from weaving, weighing and cupping, which to the Muslims are among the meanest of occupations.[29]

Christians may have some preeminence in technology, says ʿIllaysh, but they entirely lack knowledge of the only science which is of any value, namely, theology. Although ʿIllaysh's critique of European culture is not particularly detailed, it was one of the first to be circulated in the Maghrib where previous authors had concentrated on the European military threat to the exclusion of the cultural threat. It is perhaps relevant to note that, later in life, ʿIllaysh's hostility to European influence led him to participate in the ʿUrābī revolt of 1881–82. He was, however, soon apprehended by the authorities and died in prison.

In his *al-Nawāzil al-ṣughrā*, al-Wazzānī includes an abbreviated *fatwā*[30] by Muḥammad b. Saʿd al-Tilimsānī (d. 1264/1848)[31] about the status of some tribes who defected to the French and lived under their protection. His *fatwā*, written in 1256/1841, is addressed to the *amīr al-muʾminīn*, which could either refer to the Moroccan Sultan or to ʿAbd al-Qādir, but almost certainly refers to the latter because of the incident that is described. The questioner asks what the legal status is of a tribe of the Banū ʿĀmir who defected to the French and lived under their protection. The Banū ʾĀmir were among ʿAbd al-Qādir's earliest supporters, but one of their tribes is indeed known to have defected

"Loyalty to a Non-Muslim Government: An Analysis of Islamic Normative Discussions and of the Views of Some Contemporary Islamicists," in *Political Participation and Identities of Muslims in Non-Muslim States*, ed. W.A.R. Shadid and P.S. van Koningsveld (Kampen: Kok Pharos, 1996), 91–92.

29 This treatise, which is not included in the printed version of ʿIllaysh's collected *fatwās*, is entitled *al-Radd ʿalā Risālat ajwibat al-hayārā ʿan ḥukm qalansuwwat al-naṣārā* (Cairo: al-Azhar Manuscript, *fiqh ʿām*, 305297), 5a-b, quoted in Pierre Cachia, *Ṭāhā Ḥusayn: His Place in the Egyptian Literary Renaissance* (London: Luzac, 1956), 86. Cf. W. Shadid and S. van Koningsveld, "Loyalty to a Non-Muslim Government," 92–93.

30 al-Wazzānī, *al-Nawāzil al-ṣughrā*, 1: 417–20.

31 Muḥammad Ḥajjī, *Mawsūʿat aʿlām al-Maghrib* (Beirut: Dār al-Gharb al-Islāmī, 1996), 7: 2581.

to the French shortly after ʿAbd al-Qādir's signing of the Desmichels Treaty (1834).[32] The abbreviated version of the *fatwā*, reproduced by al-Wazzānī, contains little more than quotations of previous *fatwās*. Most importantly, it contains quotations from the *fatwās* of Ibn Barṭāl (circa 8th/14th century),[33] ʿIsā b. Aḥmad b. Mahdī al-Māwāsī (d. 896/1491) and Aḥmad b. Muḥammad Ibn Zakrī (d. 900/1494) which allow for harsh measures to be taken against Muslims who cooperate militarily with the French. No information is provided, however, regarding what is to be done about Muslims who do not cooperate militarily with the French but who still live under French rule. There is no way of discovering al-Tilimsānī's opinion on this matter although it is perhaps telling that al-Tilimsānī himself had emigrated from his native Tlemcen after the French invasion.

ʿAbd al-Qādir on *Hijra* and Living under Christian Rule

In 1258/1843, ʿAbd al-Qādir wrote his own treatise on the obligation of *hijra* from lands controlled by the French. The doctrine of *hijra* was vital to the success of his operations. In addition to the fact that immigrants formed an important part of his armies, the complacency of Muslims with living under French rule nullified his dream of an independent Maghrib. Indeed, like ʿAbd al-Qādir, some French officials were well aware of the power of *hijra* to harm their interests. The French governor general of Algeria wrote: "We have everything to lose from the ruin of the Algerian people; the damage will be even greater if the Algerians begin to emigrate. This is quite easy for the population of the Ziban so close to Tunisia."[34] The French had therefore adopted an active policy of preventing migration to ʿAbd al-Qādir's territories.[35] ʿAbd al-Qādir also indicates, with some bitterness, that there were even jurists who had spoken against both his conception of *hijra* and against his demands for resistance against the French. One such jurist was his childhood teacher, Aḥmad Ibn Ṭahir, the *qāḍī* of Arzew, who was tortured to death and then executed by

---

32 Danziger, *Abd al-Qadir and the Algerians*, 94 ff. and al-Jazāʾirī, *Tuḥfat al-zāʾir*, 187–88.

33 On this jurists identity, see above, 22 n. 83.

34 Quoted in Julia Clancy-Smith, *Rebel and Saint: Muslim Notables, Populist Protest, Colonial Encounters (Algeria and Tunisia, 1800–1904)* (Berkeley: University of California Press, 1994), 125. On the extent of such migration, see Charles-Robert Ageron, "L'émigration des Musulmans algériens et l'exode de Tlemcen (1830–1911)," *Annales: economies, sociétiés, civilisations* 5 (1967), 1047–66.

35 al-Jazāʾirī, *Tuḥfat al-zāʾir*, 332.

ʿAbd al-Qādir's men.[36] ʿAbd al-Qādir's treatise is a response to the opposition of such jurists who, he says, fulfill the prediction of a tradition that states that "a time will come for the people when their scholars will reek more than the carcass of a donkey."[37]

In his treatise, ʿAbd al-Qādir cites the Islamic arguments directed against *hijra* by his opponents and systematically refutes them. I will give a sample of some of these arguments since they provide an interesting picture of the Islamic solutions that Muslims found to justify remaining in French-controlled territory. The argument that is most frequently raised is that *hijra* is an obligation which has been abrogated as indicated by the *ḥadīth* which declares that "there is no *hijra* after the conquest." ʿAbd al-Qādir agrees that this *ḥadīth* is of sound transmission. He says, however, that it refers only to a specific case, that of a person who, after the conquest of Mecca, wanted nonetheless to perform *hijra* from Mecca to Medina. In this *ḥadīth*, Muḥammad says that this particular *hijra* is no longer applicable in the same way that the ban on a migrant (*muhājir*) returning to his homeland (*waṭan*) is also no longer necessary if his homeland has become a part of the abode of Islam.[38]

Another argument against *hijra* which ʿAbd al-Qādir mentions is that *taqiyya* (religiously-sanctioned dissimulation) can replace the obligation of *hijra* and render it unnecessary. According to this view, living in a country in which the outward observances of Islam are banned is permissible so long as one can practice Islam inwardly. ʿAbd al-Qādir says that *taqiyya* was only permissible when the abode of Islam was so small that living under non-Muslim rule was unavoidable. When the abode of Islam became expansive, the concept of *taqiyya* was abrogated.[39] A further argument, he says, which people raise against *hijra* is based on a reading of the Qur'ānic story of Yūsuf. The argument uses the Qur'ānic verse, "He [Yūsuf] replied [to pharaoh]: 'Set me over the storehouses of the land. I am a knowing guardian,' "[40] as a precedent for accepting political appointments made by unbelievers. ʿAbd al-Qādir gives two different refutations of this view. He says that some claim that the pharaoh,

---

36 Danziger, *Abd al-Qadir and the Algerians*, 54–5, 75 and 80.

37 al-Jazāʾirī, *Tuḥfat al-zāʾir*, 416. I have been unable to locate the source of this tradition. ʿAbd al-Qādir's deputy, Qaddūr b. Muḥammad al-Ruwayla, speaks about many such jurists with similar distaste. His treatise on *hijra*, which consists almost entirely of quotations from al-Wansharīsī's *fatwās*, is unflatteringly addressed to the "*fuqahāʾ al-muslimīn al-dhimmiyyin*." See ʿAbd al-Karīm, *Ḥukm al-hijra min khilāl thalāth rasāʾil jazāʾiriyya*, 12.

38 al-Jazāʾirī, *Tuḥfat al-zāʾir*, 416.

39 Ibid., 416–17.

40 Qur'ān, 12: 55.

under Yūsuf's influence, had already converted to Islam and it was therefore legitimate for Yūsuf to accept an appointment from him. However, even if he had not converted, ʿAbd al-Qādir argues, permission to work for unbelievers only applies to captives, like Yūsuf, who have no other options.[41] It does not apply to Algerian Muslims who have the option of migrating to Muslim territory and who therefore never have the right to accept appointments offered by unbelievers.

ʿAbd al-Qādir then deals with the claim of those who believe that as long as a person has the protection of his clan (*ʿashīra*) he is able to remain among unbelievers. He says that this situation is not applicable in Algeria and asks:

> Is there a single individual among those people and tribes who have come under the protection (*dhimma*) of the unbelievers, who has a clan to protect him from the unbelievers when they seek to impose one of their laws upon him?... Only someone foolish and weak in both mind and faith could believe and trust in their pacts and covenants. Truly, the Wise Lawgiver does not accept their words and testimony and neither should we.[42]

He adds that it was this same mistaken belief that a Muslim can put his trust in unbelievers that led to the destruction of the Muslims of Cordoba. The Cordoban Muslims, he says, established a treaty with the unbelievers consisting of over sixty clauses, thinking that it would save them. Within a year, however, all of these clauses had been dishonored. A Muslim is therefore forbidden to remain in non-Muslim territory on the basis that non-Muslims have promised him the right to practice his religion because the promise of non-Muslims is not to be trusted.

Finally, ʿAbd al-Qādir deals with the claim of those who say that their loyalty to the unbelievers represents no more than a truce (*muhādana*) and is therefore sanctioned by Islamic law. ʿAbd al-Qādir responds that the concluding of a truce is the exclusive prerogative of the ruler or his deputy and cannot be assumed by anyone else. It is therefore not up to each and every Muslim to conclude his own truce with the enemy. Further, he says, the legitimacy of a truce is dependent upon the existence of a Muslim polity in which believers are free from the imposition of non-Islamic law. A truce is invalid if it simply means the incorporation of the Muslims into a non-Muslim polity. According to him, this is precisely what happened in Algeria where "the laws, legislation and

41 al-Jazāʾirī, *Tuḥfat al-zāʾir*, 417.

42 Ibid., 417–18.

regulations of the unbelievers are imposed upon elites and commoners alike." The result of this, he says, has been that Muslims living in these areas have completely allied themselves with their non-Muslim rulers. This has reached the point where, even if the non-Muslim ruler "wishes to raid the Muslims," his Muslim subjects pay his expenses, "bear his burdens," and fight against the Muslims as soldiers in his army.[43] Such a situation is not a truce, he says, but a complete annexation. It is therefore not legitimate to justify giving loyalty to the French on the basis that this is the same as concluding a truce with them.

I now discuss ʿAbd al-Qādir's own understanding of *hijra*. ʿAbd al-Qādir was probably the first in the nineteenth-century Maghrib to revive the concept of *hijra* by using it as a central part of his military strategy. Reference to the importance of migration from non-Muslim territory is attested in his thought as early as his secret treaty with the French of 1834, which contained a provision allowing for Muslims to leave lands controlled by the French.[44] For ʿAbd al-Qādir, the duty of *hijra* is enjoined by the Prophet Muḥammad's own actions and is confirmed by the consensus (*ijmāʿ*) of the Muslim jurists.[45] He justifies the wisdom of *hijra* by pointing to what he regards as complementary traditions, such as those which prohibit Muslims from forging ties with unbelievers.[46] *Hijra* is thus an obligation which is entirely in accordance with Islamic tradition. As such, it cannot have been abrogated and continues to be valid. According to ʿAbd al-Qādir, who seems to be using al-Wansharīsī's *fatwās* as his source, when a Muslim violates the obligation of *hijra*, he violates almost all the precepts of Islamic law. This is because Islamic observances, among which he mentions prayer, fasting, and charity, become devoid of value when practiced in the abode of war. It is therefore irrelevant whether a Muslim claims that he is able to observe Islamic regulations in the abode of war. He may think that he is practicing his religion but his actions are null and void.[47] Given the seriousness of the consequences of not performing *hijra*, ʿAbd al-Qādir indicates that few circumstances, other than extreme ill health, can excuse a person from this obligation. The fear of poverty cannot constitute an excuse, he says, because it

---

43 Ibid., 418.

44 For a reproduction of the treaty, see Danziger, *Abd al-Qadir and the Algerians*, 246–47. This principle is repeated in the famous Treaty of Tafna of May 30, 1837, see ibid., 253. This clause is inaccurately reproduced in al-Jazāʾirī, *Tuḥfat al-zāʾir*, 277.

45 al-Jazāʾirī, *Tuḥfat al-zāʾir*, 413. He supports his claim that there is a consensus mostly on the basis of quotations from al-Wansharīsī's *Asnā al-matājir*.

46 Ibid., 411–15.

47 Ibid., 415.

is God and not the land which provides. Similarly, the fact that a person's family is not able to migrate with him does not nullify his obligation.

ʿAbd al-Qādir is not, however, entirely consistent in his view on the status of Muslims who do not perform *hijra*. At the beginning of his treatise, he says that *hijra* is obligatory according to the consensus of the Muslims, and that someone who violates such consensus becomes an unbeliever (*kāfir*) and apostate whose life, according to Islamic law, is forfeit.[48] ʿAbd al-Qādir, however, seems to retreat from this position later in the same treatise. Perhaps he felt that such an uncompromising attitude would alienate many of his readers, especially those living under French rule, and prevent him from attaining the broad-based political and military support from Muslims which he needed. Instead, he introduces a different set of criteria according to which whether such Muslims are apostates depends not merely on their presence in the abode of war but also on their actions there. Thus Muslims living in Christian territory who give neither military nor financial assistance to Christians are still considered to be Muslims. He writes:

> Know that it is not permissible to kill one who enters their territory and receives their protection (*amān*) so long as he does not help them either with his person or his wealth… Although he is sinful (*ʿāṣī*), it is not permissible to take that which has been rendered inviolable by Islam, whether this is his life or property.[49]

Muslims who live in non-Muslim territory are therefore not apostates who must be punished by death. They are, however, sinful and this means that neither their testimony nor their judges can be accepted by Muslims.[50] In a similar category are those Muslims who help the enemy by supporting him with their property but do not themselves fight against the Muslims. These individuals are also not to be categorized as apostates, but they are nevertheless to be treated in the same way as those who help bandits.[51] Further, in view of their potential to cause harm with their property, it is important that it be expropriated. He adds that, according to the jurists, even the expropriation of the property of an entire tribe (*qawm*) is legitimate provided that they are found to be making sales to the enemy which weaken the Muslims.

---

48 al-Jazāʾirī, *Tuḥfat al-zāʾir*, 413.

49 Ibid., 420.

50 Ibid., 415.

51 Ibid., 419–20.

According to ʿAbd al-Qādir, Muslim residents of the abode of war who are considered apostates fall into two categories. First, there are those who take pleasure in living there because they appreciate non-Islamic culture. Among these, he says, are those Muslims who have assimilated into European culture to such an extent that they wear the European hat (*burnayṭah*).[52] Second, there are those who fight alongside non-Muslims against Muslims. Muslims belonging to either of these categories must be killed. He notes that although there is some debate among the jurists regarding whether their women and children can also be killed and enslaved, he thinks that there is no sin (*ithm*) in doing either.[53]

It is clear that ʿAbd al-Qādir did not implement all of the intricate distinctions that he makes in his treatise in his battles against Muslims who opposed his political program. It is noteworthy, however, that he chose to present his position in this way. It is also a considerably more nuanced position than was implied in some of his earlier petitions for *fatwās*. Not all Muslims living in the abode of war are to be considered apostates, but measures are nonetheless put in place which would allow him to combat them successfully in battle.

Fatwās which Limit *Hijra* and Give Support to Muslims Who Live under Christian Rule

The juristic opinions discussed above are in basic agreement that Muslims should perform *hijra* from Christian territory and only differ in the ways in which this project should be pursued. Political factors, however, caused a shift away from these views. This shift is most significantly seen in the thought of a single individual, the Moroccan Sultan, who had at first supported *hijra* but was forced to recant. Sultan ʿAbd al-Raḥmān had initially given financial grants to Algerian refugees whom he had praised for performing a religiously obligatory *hijra* from the abode of war at great personal cost.[54] He had seen the concept of *hijra* as a tool of low-key resistance against the French which involved

52 Ibid., 421.

53 Ibid., 421–22. Interestingly, as support for his position, he refers to the case, already cited by al-ʿAlawī, of al-Muʿtamid Ibn ʿAbbād who allied himself with the Christians in battle against Muslims. However, whereas al-ʿAlawī claimed that the majority of the jurists agreed that this did not make him an apostate, ʿAbd al-Qādir makes the opposite claim. He thus concludes that, according to the consensus of the jurists, participating in battle on the side of non-Muslims is apostasy and is punishable by death.

54 Bennison, *Jihad and Its Interpretations in Pre-Colonial Morocco*, 47–48.

neither significant military involvement nor great financial cost. Soon, however, both Sultan ʿAbd al-Raḥmān, and also some of the jurists, were forced to reevaluate their position. While it was true that *hijra* had the potential to disrupt the activities of the French, it had equal potential to destabilize the Moroccan regime. There was a limit to the number of migrants that the sultan's territories could absorb and migration to ʿAbd al-Qādir's camps strengthened a non-state actor who the sultan already had difficulty controlling. Once the French placed pressure on the sultan to rein in ʿAbd al-Qādir, the sultan realized that his rhetoric of support for *hijra* and resistance against the French needed to be curtailed. What was now required was a new Islamic discourse which minimized the importance of *hijra* and argued for the permissibility of coexistence with the European colonizers. Although arguments of this kind were not to be fully developed until the twentieth century, some attempts were made even as early as the 1830s.

One of the first jurists to provide a legal justification for living under French rule was Muḥammad Ibn al-Shāhid (d. 1253/1837 or 1255/1839), the *muftī* of Algiers.[55] His reasons for arguing this position were quite different from those of the Moroccan Sultan. Ibn al-Shāhid was concerned that the rhetoric of *hijra* and *jihād* of ʿAbd al-Qādir and others would undermine the authority of the jurists and bring chaos to all Algerian Muslims. His treatise is a response to some unnamed opponents who had sent a letter denouncing Algerian Muslims as unbelievers on account of their living under French rule.[56] In his treatise, Ibn al-Shāhid accepts that *hijra* is still a valid obligation that has not been abrogated. His argument, however, is that this obligation is only applicable under a certain set of circumstances which do not apply to Muslims in French-occupied Algeria. He analyses the classic Qurʾānic locus of the obligation of *hijra*, Qurʾān 4: 97–99, to determine under what circumstances *hijra* is obligatory. The passage reads:

> Those who wrong themselves and are taken by the angels will be asked, "In what circumstances were you?" They will say, "We were oppressed in the land." They will say, "Was not God's land spacious enough for you to

55 ʿAbd al-Karīm, *Ḥukm al-hijra min khilāl thalāth rasāʾil Jazāʾiriyya*, 7 and Abū al-Qāsim Saʿd Allāh, *Tārīkh al-Jazāʾir al-thaqāfī: Min al-qarn al-ʿāshir ilā al-rābiʿ ʿashar al-Hijrī (16–20 m.)* (Algiers: al-Sharika al-Waṭaniyya, 1981), 2: 284–85.

56 Abū ʿAbdallāh Muḥammad Ibn al-Shāhid, "Risālat Ibn al-Shāhid," in *Ḥukm al-hijra min khilāl thalāth rasāʾil Jazāʾiriyya*, 105–24. There is evidence that at least one of Ibn al-Shāhid's students, ʿAlī b. al-Ḥaffāf (d. 1307/1890), held views similar to those of the letter writers. See Jacques Berque, *L'Intérieur du Maghreb* (Paris: Gallimard, 1978), 416–18.

> migrate in it?" As for these [individuals], their abode is in hell, an evil journey's end, except in the case of the oppressed, be they men, women or children, who cannot devise something and are not guided to a way: [Regarding] these, it may be that God will pardon them. God is Pardoning and Forgiving.

According to this passage, Ibn al-Shāhid says, two conditions have to be in place in order for *hijra* to become obligatory. First, a Muslim has to be unable to perform that which is demanded by his religion. Second, this Muslim has to be able to leave for another land in which he will be able to practice his religion. If either of these conditions is not satisfied, he says, *hijra* ceases to be obligatory.[57] He then gives a number of arguments to show that neither of these conditions is fully in place for Algerian Muslims. Since tradition, he says, only censures those who, when living in non-Muslim territory, are unable to maintain their religion,[58] those who are able to maintain their religion there are permitted to remain. He argues that Algerian Muslims are indeed able to practice their religion and answers several objections to this contention. His opponents say that it is impossible to practice Islam in a place in which mosques and cemeteries are destroyed.[59] Ibn al-Shāhid responds that, even under such circumstances, Islam can be practiced because mosques are not essential to its observance. Prayer and other rituals are indeed obligatory, but they are not dependent upon the presence of a physical building and can be practiced in its absence. Moreover, he adds that the situation is not as dire as his opponents claim. Religion has not been corrupted in Algiers as a result of the presence of unbelievers. People continue to pray, young people learn the Qurʾān in schools, religious slaughter of meat continues and matters of marriage and inheritance remain in the hands of the jurists, as "the accursed unbeliever" does not rule over such matters.[60] When Ibn al-Shāhid's opponents claim that the rule of the unbelievers has had the effect of increasing "fornication" among women, he answers their charge thus:

---

57 Ibn al-Shāhid, "Risālat Ibn al-Shāhid," 108.

58 Ibid., 109–110.

59 Ibid., 114. The opponent is no doubt referring to the case of a military highway which was built through two Muslim cemeteries and to the conversion of a number of mosques into churches. On these events, see Martin, *Muslim Brotherhoods in Nineteenth-Century Africa*, 50.

60 Ibn al-Shāhid, "Risālat Ibn al-Shāhid," 114–15.

> If by "fornication" you mean the fornication of the prostitutes ... we say that fornication was already widespread both among us and among other [Muslim societies] before this at a time when Islam[ic government] was present ... We did not have control over it then ... we do not have the power to change it now.[61]

Thus, according to Ibn al-Shāhid, the presence of unbelievers has not disrupted the practice of Islam among Muslims in his land. Despite non-Muslim rule, Islamic norms and practices remain unaffected.

Ibn al-Shāhid then argues that even if it really was impossible for Algerian Muslims to practice Islam, it would still be impossible for them to emigrate. He argues that the Algerians are so destitute that they cannot afford the cost of travel. In view of their poverty, if they attempted to emigrate, they would probably die in transit. In the event that they actually managed to reach their final destination, they would either be beggars in their new country or would starve in the mountains.[62] Thus, even if the Algerians were unable to practice Islam in their homeland, they would not be blamed for neglecting *hijra* since they are unable to successfully make the journey to another land.

Having established that Algerian Muslims have no obligation to make *hijra*, Ibn al-Shāhid then argues that even if they did have such an obligation, they would not become unbelievers by abandoning it. People who abandon an obligation commit a sin, but committing a sin is not tantamount to unbelief. He reminds his readers of the seriousness of the charge of unbelief (*kufr*) and adds that, according to Islamic law, those who wrongly accuse someone of unbelief are guilty of unbelief themselves. A person, he says, can only be considered an unbeliever when he explicitly says something which indicates his unbelief.[63] Unbelief cannot be speculatively deduced from the observation of his actions. The speculative logic employed by his opponent, he says, is very dangerous because of what it implies. According to such reasoning, one might think that the venerable Shaykhs of the great seminary of al-Azhar should be regarded as unbelievers because they did not perform *hijra* after the European invasion—a prospect which Ibn al-Shāhid thinks should not even be contemplated. Before advocating that the *ʿulamāʾ* should migrate, Ibn al-Shāhid urges his opponent to think of the disastrous consequences of such an event. Without the *ʿulamāʾ*, he says, the Muslim masses would have no religious leaders to guide them

61 Ibid., 118–19.

62 Ibid., 116–18.

63 Ibid., 110–11.

and would immediately lapse into unbelief.[64] The injury to religion incurred by their remaining in non-Muslim territory is thus substantially less than the injury incurred by their leaving. In view of such circumstances, living under non-Muslim rule can occasionally be seen as necessary. As an example, he mentions the early *hijra* of the companions of Muḥammad to Abyssinia which was, he emphasizes, a part of the abode of unbelief.

Ibn al-Shāhid concludes by indicating that the motives of the Algerian Muslims are good and that the accusation that they enjoy living under Christian rule is false:

> Is it out of approval of unbelief and love of social relations with its people [that we live under Christian rule], or is it for another reason? How can you imagine that we approve of unbelief and love social relations with its people when prices have risen, our industries have been disrupted, our shops have been destroyed, making a profit has become difficult, our graves have been dug up and the tombs of our saints have been desecrated? These things came to pass only because of their [the European] invasion. So what glory is there in this such that we should approve of it?[65]

Finally, Ibn al-Shāhid does acknowledge that there is a minority of individuals who, for worldly reasons, cooperate with the French, and he agrees that they should be punished.[66] However, he says, the majority of Algerian Muslims are genuinely awaiting an opportunity to perform *hijra* and have to postpone doing so only because they are impoverished and unable to travel. They should under no circumstances be blamed for neglecting *hijra* on this account. Ibn al-Shāhid's treatise is thus not a rejection of *hijra*, but one which attempts to vastly limit its applicability to the situation of the Algerian Muslims.

The French diplomat Léon Roches claimed that he managed to secure a *fatwā* against *hijra* which was then widely circulated among Muslims in Algeria. He alleged that the *fatwā* itself was written by jurists belonging to the Tijāniyya *ṣūfī* order, but that it was later ratified by jurists from both al-Azhar and Mecca. The *fatwā*, he said, affirmed that since everything possible had already been done by the Algerian Muslims to oppose the French, it was now permissible to temporarily allow them to rule and wrong to revolt against them. His quotation of the *fatwā* reads:

---

64 Ibid., 112–13.

65 Ibid., 115.

66 Ibid., 116–18.

> Quand un peuple musulman, dont le territoire a été envahi par les infidèles, les a combattus aussi longtemps qu'il a conservé l'espoir de les en chasser, et, quand il est certain que la continuation de la guerre ne peut amener que misère ruine et mort pour les musulmans, sans aucune chance de vaincre les infidèles, ce people, tout en conservant l'espoir de secouer leur joug avec l'aide de Dieu, peut accepter de vivre sous leur domination à la condition expresse qu'ils conserveront le libre exercice de leur religion et que leurs femmes et leurs filles seront respectés.[67]

Thus, according to the *fatwā*, non-Muslim rule was to be tolerated providing that it allowed Islam to be freely observed and saw to it that the honor of Muslim women was respected. The authenticity of this *fatwā* has been called into question by a number of authors who claim that its existence was invented by Roches himself. They point to the fact that, other than the reference to the document in Roches' travelogue, there are no known copies of this *fatwā* and the French themselves never seem to have made any use of it.[68] In addition to this, there are grounds for believing that Roches never managed to travel to Mecca where he alleges that he had the *fatwā* approved by some Meccan jurists. However, although one should be wary of regarding this *fatwā* as genuine, other Maghribī jurists writing in the later nineteenth century expressed similar sentiments.[69] The content of the *fatwā* should therefore not be regarded as a reason for determining it to be a forgery.

Al-Wazzānī on Living under Christian Rule

Muḥammad al-Mahdī b. Muḥammad al-ʿImrānī, usually referred to as al-Mahdī al-Wazzānī (d. 1342/1923), was the *muftī* of Fez and one of the most prominent jurists of the region.[70] His *magnum opus* was entitled, *al-Nawāzil al-jadīda al-kubrā fī mā li-ahl Fās wa-ghayrihim min al-badw wa'l-qurā al-musammā bi'l-*

67 Léon Roches, *Dix ans a travers l'Islam: 1834–1844* (Paris: Perrin et cie, 1904), 241.

68 Marcel Émerit, "La Légende de Léon Roches," *Revue Africaine* 91 (1947), 81 ff. and Jean-Pierre Lehmann, "Léon Roches—Diplomat Extraordinary in the Bakumatsu Era: An Assessment of his Personality and Policy," *Modern Asian Studies* 14 (1980), 279 n. 18.

69 See, for example, Octave Depont and Xavier Coppolani, *Les Confréries religieuses musulmanes* (Algiers: Jourdan, 1897), 34 ff.

70 On his biography, see Muḥammad Ḥajjī, *Mawsūʿat aʿlām al-Maghrib* (Beirut: Dār al-Gharb al-Islāmī, 1996), 8: 2935–36; Muḥammad b. Muḥammad Makhlūf, *Shajarat al-nūr al-zakiyya fī ṭabaqāt al-Mālikiyya* (Beirut: Dār al-Kitāb al-ʿArabī, 197?), 1: 435–6; J. Berque, *Les Nawāzil el muzāraʿa du Miʿyār al Wazzānī* (Rabat: Editions Felix Moncho, 1940), 11 ff.;

Miʿyār al-jadīd al-jāmiʿ al-muʿrib ʿan fatāwā al-mutaʾakhkhirīn min ʿulamāʾ al-Maghrib.[71] It is generally referred to as *al-Miʿyār al-jadīd*, or "*The New Miʿyār*," and, as this title suggests, it was intended to update al-Wansharīsī's collection of *fatwā*s, *al-Miʿyār al-muʿrib*.

Al-Wazzānī's anthology provides some important examples of how the legal legacy of the jurists of the Reconquista period was reappropriated by later jurists. Although al-Wazzānī does not include any of his own *fatwā*s on the specific issue of living under Christian rule in his anthology, he does include some about a related problem: the immunity from Moroccan law sometimes granted by European consuls and merchants to Moroccan subjects who served as their aids in the pre-Protectorate period.[72] Many jurists regarded this problem as being equivalent to that of living under non-Muslim rule since, although the individuals receiving protection (protégées) lived in Muslim lands, they placed themselves under the protection and laws of Europeans, sometimes even holding European passports. The phenomenon of protégées seems to date to the reign of the Moroccan Sultan Muḥammad (r. 1171–1204/1757–1790). This sultan concluded treaties which granted some foreign consuls and merchants the privilege of extending their own rights and exemptions from local jurisdiction, taxes and conscription, to the Moroccans who served as their aids and representatives. By the late nineteenth century, many Moroccans held such protection and these individuals became the object of widespread resentment by Muslim political authorities, jurists, and the general public.[73]

Although most protégées in Morocco were non-Muslims, the protégées whom al-Wazzānī discusses are all Muslims. Al-Wazzānī seems to see most of

---

and Etty Terem, "The New *Miʿyar* of al-Mahdi al-Wazzani: Local Interpretation of Family Life in Late Nineteenth-Century Fez" (Ph.D. dissertation: Harvard University, 2007), 1–46.

71 The work was first printed in 1328/1910. On its composition, see Muḥammad Ḥajjī, *Naẓarāt fī al-nawāzil al-fiqhiyya* (Rabat: al-Jamʿiyya al-Maghribiyya li'l-Ta'līf wa'l-Tarjama wa'l-Nashr, 1999), 53–54.

72 On this issue, see ʿAbd al-Wahhāb Ibn Manṣūr, *Mushkilat al-ḥimāya al-qunṣuliyya bi'l-Maghrib min nash'atihā ilā mu'tamar Madrīd, sanat 1880* (Rabat: al-Maṭbaʿa al-Malakiyya, 1977) and Mohammed Kenbib, *Les Protégés: contribution à l'histoire contemporaine du Maroc* (Casablanca: Faculté des Lettres et des Sciences Humaines, 1996).

73 On this, see Muḥammad al-Manūnī, *Maẓāhir yaqẓat al-Maghrib al-ḥadīth*, 327 and 332–33; Ibn Manṣūr, *Mushkilat al-ḥimāya al-qunṣuliyya*, 49–51; Laroui, *Les Origines sociales et culturelles du nationalisme marocain*, 317–18; ʿAbd al-Raḥmān Ibn al-Zaydān, *al-ʿIzz wa'l-ṣawla fī maʿālim naẓm al-dawla* (Rabat: al-Maṭbaʿa al-Malakiyya, 1961), 1: 69 and Susan Miller and Amal Rassam, "The View from the Court: Moroccan Reactions to European Penetration during the Late Nineteenth Century," *International Journal of African Historical Studies* 16 (1983), 30 ff.

these protégées as seeking protection from non-Muslims for economic reasons or because of a desire for security for themselves and their families. He thinks that this is blameworthy, but he does not regard these actions as tantamount to an abandonment of Islam. He does, however, indicate that there are also protégées who seek out non-Muslim protectors because they prefer non-Muslim laws (*qānūn*) and government to those of the Muslims and therefore desire the victory of the unbelievers over the believers. These individuals, he says, are indeed to be considered unbelievers.[74] He bitterly describes the sentiment of such protégées: "They laugh at and scorn them [the believers], doing repugnant things to them to make them like themselves, [as it is said], 'they long for you to disbelieve as they disbelieve so that you will be equal to them' (Qur'ān 4: 89)."[75] Since these kinds of protégées are apostates, their testimony cannot be accepted, they cannot lead prayer, and their wealth is to be expropriated.[76] However, the protégées who belong to this category are not a group to whom al-Wazzānī devotes much attention, perhaps because he believes that they are a minority among the protégées. Instead, his *fatwā*s, as well as those of other jurists that he includes in his anthology, are directed at protégées who ally themselves with non-Muslims out of convenience rather than out of solidarity with their world view.

Most of al-Wazzānī's opinions on protégées are expressed in the context of a refutation of a *fatwā* which gives them considerable support. This *fatwā* is by Ibrāhīm al-Riyāḥī (d. 1266/1850), a well-known and accomplished reformist, whose distinctions included the founding of the Tījāniyya order in Tunisia, being appointed chief *muftī* of Tunisia, and later, rector of the Zaytūna Mosque.[77] Al-Riyāḥī's discussion of protégées comes in the context of a *fatwā* regarding the case of a judge (*qāḍī*) whose sons are kidnapped by a hostile tribe. Although the *qāḍī* pays the ransom that is demanded, the tribe still refuses to release his sons. In desperation, he asks the British consul to intervene and the latter secures their release. The petitioner asks al-Riyāḥī whether this act is blameworthy and, if so, whether the *qāḍī* should be stripped of his office. Al-Riyāḥī begins his *fatwā* by stating that he believes that the *Sharīʿa* permits a believer to seek protection (*iḥtimāʾ*) from an unbeliever, and that there is therefore no reason to blame the *qāḍī*. He argues that seeking protection is to be accepted because it was sanctioned by the companions of the

74 al-Wazzānī, *al-Miʿyār al-jadīd*, 3: 92–94.

75 Ibid., 3: 73.

76 Ibid., 3: 93–94.

77 Ibid., 3: 71. On his biography, see Makhlūf, *Shajarat al-nūr*, 386–89 and Aḥmad al-Ḥamrūnī, *ʿAlam al-Zaytūna al-Shaykh Ibrāhīm al-Riyāḥī* (Tunis: Mīdiyā Kum, 1996), 11 ff.

Prophet Muḥammad. As an example, he says that when Abū Bakr performed the *hijra* to Medina, he left his family and property in the care (*ḥimāya*) of a polytheist (*mushrik*). This precedent, he says, permits all Muslims to do the same under similar circumstances. The matter, he says, is rooted in the principle that when the safety of a Muslim's life or family is at stake, almost all actions become permitted including seeking the assistance of an unbeliever. He says that the matter is analogous to the case of the person who enters a wine-seller's establishment to avoid a vicious dog and is therefore not regarded as having committed a sin.[78] Al-Riyāḥī's message is that necessity requires a certain level of cooperation with non-Muslims who occupy positions of power in Muslim countries and that Islamic law sanctions this.

Al-Wazzānī refutes al-Riyāḥī's position, arguing that the situation of Abū Bakr is not analogous to that of the *qāḍī* described by the petitioner. The two situations are dissimilar because, whereas the protection that Abū Bakr sought was from the polytheists, the *qāḍī* sought protection from his fellow Muslims. One cannot therefore infer that it is permissible to seek aid from non-Muslims against Muslims on the grounds that Abū Bakr sought aid from non-Muslims against other non-Muslims. In fact, he says, the *Sharīʿa* demands the very contrary of al-Riyāḥī's opinion as it urges Muslims to exert forbearance when dealing with the harm caused by iniquitous Muslim rulers. This is enjoined, he says, because it is forbidden to owe obedience to an unbeliever.[79] Those who do so and die without a Muslim ruler over them die the death of the pagans (*al-jāhiliyya*).[80] He therefore believes that it is irrelevant whether or not the involvement of a Christian power can yield a more just outcome than relying on a Muslim one. Religion simply forbids leaving the protection of Muslims for that of non-Muslims. Thus al-Wazzānī entirely rejects al-Riyāḥī's leniency in this case of seeking the protection of Christians.

Al-Wazzānī does, however, approvingly cite the opinion of ʿAlī al-Mīlī al-Tūnisī (d. 1248/1832),[81] who argues that, under a certain set of rare circumstances, living under the protection of unbelievers or among them is permissible. Such a case does not include the situation in which a person fears for the safety of his own life or property, because religion takes precedence over such matters. However, if a person fears for his religion, he is permitted to seek the protection of an unbeliever if he thinks that this will be efficacious.

---

78 al-Wazzānī, *al-Miʿyār al-jadīd*, 3: 71–72.

79 Ibid., 3: 72–73.

80 Ibid., 3: 74, quoting *Ṣaḥīḥ al-Bukhārī*, no. 6531. Cf. Ibid., 3: 76.

81 Ismāʿīl Bāshā al-Baghdādī, *Hadiyyat al-ʿārifīn: Asmāʾ al-muʾallifīn wa-āthār al-muṣannifīn* (Beirut: Dār Iḥyāʾ al-Turāth al-ʿArabī, 1990), 1: 411.

This is because the legal principle of choosing the lesser harm applies in this situation.[82]

Al-Wazzānī's views on living under Christian rule can be deduced from his writings on the protégées. Since he does not think that it is permissible for Muslims to place themselves under non-Islamic law while living in their own lands, one can be certain that, *a fortiori*, he would not consider it permissible for them to do so while living in non-Muslim lands. Al-Wazzānī's views on the subject differ from al-Wansharīsī only in that his anthology preserves a much broader range of opinion on the issue. He includes, for example, some views which are more permissive than those of al-Wansharīsī regarding Muslims living under non-Muslim rule. For example, he includes a *fatwā* by al-ʿAbdūsī (d. 847/1442 or 849/1445) which grants considerable legitimacy to judges living in non-Muslim territory. Al-Wazzānī, however, also includes views which are less permissive of living under non-Muslim rule than al-Wansharīsī. For example, he notes that the student of al-Wansharīsī, Abū al-Ḥasan ʿAlī b. Hārūn al-Maṭaghrī (d. 951/1544),[83] viewed the abandonment of *hijra* as equivalent to apostasy.[84] The inclusion of a wide range of views is perhaps suggestive that al-Wazzānī recognized the inevitability of compromise on these issues given the possibility of further colonial encroachment on Muslim lands. Thus, while he clearly endorses a view similar to that of al-Wansharīsī, he ensures that his anthology contains a broad enough range of opinions to allow later jurists some flexibility in dealing with unknown future eventualities.

82 al-Wazzānī, *al-Miʿyār al-jadīd*, 3: 78.

83 Makhlūf, *Shajarat al-nūr*, 1: 278 and Ḥajjī, *Mawsūʿat aʿlām al-Maghrib*, 2: 874.

84 al-Wazzānī, *al-Miʿyār al-jadīd*, 3: 50. Al-Wazzānī includes al-Maṭaghrī's *fatwā* to indicate that some regard the abandonment of *hijra* as equivalent to apostasy and contrasts it with the opposing opinion of Abū ʿAbdallāh Muḥammad b. Aḥmad al-Nālī (d. 928/1522), see ibid., 3: 49–50 and Ḥajjī, *Mawsūʿat aʿlām al-Maghrib*, 2: 844. The actual details of the *fatwā* appear to be more complicated. Al-Maṭaghrī was asked about the case of a convert to Islam who was originally from the abode of war and who had made a few trips to his ancestral home after his conversion. While he was away on one of these trips, his wife, expecting that he would not return, married someone else. When he returned, she applied for an annulment of her marriage with him. In response, al-Maṭaghrī granted her the annulment on the ground that the convert, by returning to the abode of war, was guilty of apostasy (*ridda*). It does not seem likely that al-Maṭaghrī supported the view that any Muslim who travels to the abode of war is guilty of apostasy. It is more likely that he put forward this view as a legal loophole in order to excuse the convert's wife from the very serious consequences of a conviction for adultery.

Non-Juristic Approaches to the Issue of Non-Muslim Rule

This chapter has focused on the works of jurists who use traditional legal methodology, that is, jurists who attempt to situate their writings within the framework provided by their legal school. Although I have stressed that Islamic law was able to change in order to deal with new social realities, it is also important to emphasize that, by the end of the nineteenth century, some jurists began to feel that the legal tradition was insufficient for encapsulating their views on life under French rule. Influenced by currents in Salafī thought, they sought instead to express their views using the Qur'ān and *ḥadīth*, unmediated by the works of the jurists, as their sources for religious authority.[85] I will briefly consider two examples of such individuals. In the late nineteenth century, the jurist Muḥammad b. Jaʿfar al-Kattānī (d. 1345/1927)[86] wrote *Nasīḥat ahl al-Islām*, a work which was intended to provide advice to the Moroccan ruler on how to both organize a just polity and to prevent European military and cultural encroachments.[87] This Salafī-influenced work draws extensively on passages from the Qur'ān and the *ḥadīth* and almost entirely neglects the works of the jurists. Consequently, it has a much more radical tone than the works of the jurists that I have discussed. Al-Kattānī feels that the solution to the woes of Morocco is a radical reorganization of the state. He decries the corruption of those who hold power in Morocco who, he says, threaten to throw the entire area into turmoil (*fitna*).[88] Al-Kattānī's treatise is informed by an attitude of great pessimism. He believes that the entire Islamic world has been in decline for centuries. The successful early conquests of Islam, which he regards as signs of its former vibrancy, had come to an end and had been replaced by Christian

---

85 On the influence of Salafism in the Maghrib, see Abdallah Laroui, *Les Origines sociales et culturelles du nationalisme marocain (1830–1912)* (Paris: François Maspero, 1977), 305 ff.

86 Bettina Dennerlein, "Asserting Religious Authority in Late 19th Century/Early 20th Century Morocco: Muḥammad b. Jaʿfar al-Kattānī (d. 1927) and his *Kitāb salwat al-anfās*," in *Speaking for Islam: Religious Authorities in Muslim Societies*, ed. Gudrun Krämer and Sabine Schmidtke (Leiden: Brill, 2006), 136 ff.; ʿAbdallāh al-Fāsī, "al-ʿĀlim Muḥammad b. Jaʿfar al-Kattānī wa-kitābuhu *Salwat al-anfās* wa-muḥādathāt al-akyās mi-man uqbira min al-ʿulamāʾ wa'l-ṣulaḥāʾ bi-madīnat Fās," *al-Manāhil* 54 (1997), 116–62 and Evariste Lévi-Provençal, *Les Historiens du Chorfa* (Paris: Larose, 1920), 377 ff.

87 For an analysis of this work, see Henry Munson, Jr., *Religion and Power in Morocco* (New Haven: Yale University Press, 1993), 87–96. Another example of a similar work is Jaʿfar b. Idrīs al-Kattānī al-Ḥasanī, *al-Dawāhī al-madhiyya li'l-firaq al-maḥmiyya: Fī al-walāʾ wa'l-barāʾ*, ed. Abī Muḥammad al-Ḥasan b. ʿAlī al-Kattānī (Amman: Dār al-Bayāriq, 1999).

88 Abū ʿAbdallāh Muḥammad b. Abī al-Fayḍ Jaʿfar al-Kattānī, *Naṣīḥat ahl al-Islām*, ed. Idrīs al-Kattānī (Rabat: Maktabat Badr, 1989), 205.

rule over Muslim lands. This situation is, he says, the result of the neglect of the commandment of *jihād*. He writes:

> For this reason you see that the Muslims have become humiliated after having been powerful, poor after having been rich, fighting among themselves after having battled the unbelievers together, fragmented after having been united. The blessings have dwindled and the good things of the earth have disappeared. Shame has vanished and hypocrisy is everywhere. The rulers oppress and the wicked prevail. Affliction has descended upon us. Disasters, calamities, and suffering are great. The enemies have become insolent and many are the Muslims who have become their captives.[89]

A responsible ruler, al-Kattānī says, is one who leads the people in *jihād*. Neither the ruler nor the people are permitted to conclude a truce except under circumstances of absolute necessity because this amounts to an abandonment of the Qurʾānic injunction to wage *jihād*. If they do so, it must only be for a very short duration for the purpose of preparing and gathering an army, or for the purpose of a ruse (*ḥīla*) to trick the enemy. In the event that a truce is made, he says, it should not last beyond four months.[90] For al-Kattānī, one of the reasons that a truce must be of limited duration is that, without the activity of preparing for battle, Muslims settle down into business and agriculture and, once they are in this frame of mind, the enemy is in a good position to attack them.[91] The people are not to be excused from the precept of *jihād*, al-Kattānī says, on the ground that there is no ruler to lead them. In an offensive war, *jihād* is indeed a communal obligation which must be led by the ruler. Today, however, *jihād* is a defensive war and it has therefore become an individual obligation.[92] As a result of his views on the necessity of *jihād*, al-Kattānī does not permit Muslims to live under non-Muslim rule except in extreme circumstances of dire necessity.[93]

89 al-Kattānī, *Naṣīḥat ahl al-Islām*, 129, quoted in Henry Munson, Jr., *Religion and Power in Morocco*, 89.

90 al-Kattānī, *Naṣīḥat ahl al-Islām*, 148.

91 Ibid.

92 Ibid., 149.

93 Ibid., 167.

Another thinker who was influenced by such Salafī ideas[94] was Aḥmad b. Khālid al-Nāṣirī (d. 1315/1897).[95] Al-Nāṣirī comes to a conclusion opposite to that of al-Kattānī but, like al-Kattānī, he does not attempt to justify his position using Mālikī legal sources.[96] Al-Nāṣirī is clearly horrified by the encroachment of Christian cultural values on the Maghrib,[97] but this does not lead him to endorse either *hijra* or *jihād* due to the futility which he sees in both of these actions. He writes:

> It is clear that the Christians today are extremely strong and well prepared, while the Muslims ... are extremely weak and disorganized. This being the case, how can it be permissible from the point of view of an individual legal opinion and of state policy—not to speak of Islamic law—that the weak resist the strong and ... make war against those armed to the teeth?[98]

Even the cultural dangers to Islam must be stoically born. He writes: "I swear that in mixing and coming together with them, great harm is done to us. However, it is still less in comparison with the harm of war ... every man knows that peace is preferable to war."[99] He therefore regards the close contact with Christians forced upon the Maghrib by the French conquests as a tragic but entirely unavoidable fact of life to which Muslims must reconcile themselves. He does not attempt to formulate a legal justification for his views, they are simply put forward as a pragmatic solution to an otherwise insoluable problem. Al-Nāṣirī's most famous work was a monumental history of the Maghrib.

94 Kenneth Brown, *People of Salé: Tradition and Change in a Moroccan City, 1830–1930* (Cambridge: Harvard University Press, 1976), 79.

95 For his biography, see Kenneth Brown, "Profile of a Nineteenth-Century Moroccan Scholar," in *Scholars, Saints and Sufis: Muslim Religious Institutions in the Middle East since 1500* (Berkeley: University of California Press, 1972), 127–148 and Evariste Lévi-Provençal, *Les Historiens du Chorfa* (Paris: Larose, 1920), 10 ff.

96 On this, see Abdallah Laroui, *Les Origines sociales et culturelles du nationalisme marocain*, 324–26.

97 See also al-Nāṣirī's discussion on the Muslim observance of Christian festivals in his "Taʿẓīm al-minna bi-nuṣrat al-sunna," in Ismāʿīl Khaṭīb, *al-Mukhtār min Taʿẓīm al-minna wa'l-Miʿyār fī badʿ al-ʿibādāt wa'l-ʿādāt wa'l-ṭuruqiyya* (Tetouan: Jāmiʿat al-Baʿth al-Islāmī, 1996), 121–24.

98 Aḥmad b. Khālid al-Nāṣirī, *Kitāb al-istiqṣā li-akhbār duwal al-Maghrib al-Aqṣā* (Casablanca: Dār al-Kitāb, 1954), 4: 268, quoted in Brown, *People of Salé*, 183.

99 Ibid.

He ends this work by pondering the uncertainties of how Islam is to proceed in the face of such overwhelming European power:

> Know too that during these years the power of the Europeans has advanced to such a shocking degree that their triumph is without parallel. Their progress and advancement have grown steadily faster—like the [proverbial] doubling of the grains of wheat in the squares of the chessboard. Indeed, we are on the brink of a time of [total] corruption. Knowledge of the consequences of these things and their design belongs to God, may He be exalted, unique in [knowing] the divine secret. I know well today and the yesterday before it, but as for knowing what tomorrow holds, I am blind.[100]

For al-Nāṣirī, the only option available to Muslims is patience and trust in God. The solutions of *hijra* and *jihād* of the earlier part of the nineteenth century can only end in futile destruction. It is noteworthy that, despite their lack of use of Mālikī legal sources, the views of al-Kattānī and al-Nāṣirī are not greatly different in their practical effect from those which al-Wazzānī includes in his anthology. Their style, however, is more strident and could no doubt be counted on to appeal to a much broader audience than the more stylistically restrained works of the jurists.

100 al-Nāṣirī, *Kitāb al-istiqṣā*, 4: 279, quoted in Brown, *People of Salé*, 180.

Conclusion

For over a century, both Muslim and non-Muslim scholars have debated whether Islamic law can change and develop or whether its divine nature precludes this. The debate touches on an issue which is very central to Islamic thought: the reverence for tradition and the corresponding abhorrence of innovation (*bidʿa*). Jonathan Berkey emphasizes the centrality of this issue:

> The distinction between *sunna* [tradition] and *bidʿa* [innovation] is central to the normative framework of Islam. Innovations are inherently suspect because they represent a departure from the practice of the prophet Muhammad and his Companions … a principled aversion to any innovation remained an important, if not universal, element in the medieval Islamic discourse.[1]

The question which arises is what impact this dislike of innovation has had on the Islamic legal system. In this book I have discussed how one group of Islamic jurists negotiated the line between fealty to tradition and societal need for change. I have shown how Mālikī law did indeed change in order to address the new political and social circumstances wrought by the Reconquista, but did so while remaining firmly within the confines of the legal tradition. It is my hope that my observations on the processes of change that I have documented will be applied to studies of other legal issues or to patterns of development in other Islamic legal schools.

Perspectives on whether Islamic law changes can vary greatly depending on what legal genres one looks at. Scholarship on Islamic law has often suffered from the flaw that it draws conclusions on the general state of Islamic law from the study of only a single legal genre. For example, if one were to limit one's study of the jurists' views on the Reconquista to Mālikī legal manuals, one would have to conclude that the Mālikīs made no attempt to address the events of the Reconquista. One would have to further conclude that while change occurred in the formative period of the school, change almost entirely ceased to occur soon thereafter. Thus, for example, Saḥnūn (d. 240/854) provided for greater protection of Muslim property in the abode of war than his predecessor Mālik (d. 179/795), but further changes to these positions did not occur in manuals after Saḥnūn's time. One might therefore conclude from analyzing

1 Jonathan Berkey, "Tradition, Innovation and the Social Construction of Knowledge in the Medieval Islamic Near East," *Past & Present* 146 (1995), 41.

© KONINKLIJKE BRILL NV, LEIDEN, 2015 | DOI 10.1163/9789004284531_007

this genre of law that Islamic law is an idealistic law, a faithful interpretation of the divine word largely unsullied by the burden of having to conform to the needs of an imperfect world. If, however, one's research were to extend beyond the genre of legal manuals to the commentaries on these manuals, one would find more examples of legal change and increased sensitivity to contemporary events. Thus, for example, I showed that Ibn Nājī's commentary on a legal manual reflected his own experiences as a judge dealing with the Muslims of Christian Pantelleria. Ibn Nājī, and other jurists like him, felt that their personal experiences were relevant to the genre of commentary as it was deemed appropriate in this genre to explore and discuss the relevance of divine texts to human affairs. It is, however, in the *fatwā* genre that the jurists were most at liberty to relate the law to their own social circumstances. Compelled by the needs of the individuals who sought their help, the jurists transformed the law to make it a relevant source of guidance for their communities. On the basis of the study of *fatwā*s alone, one might answer the question, "does Islamic law develop?" by concluding that Islamic law is a plastic law almost endlessly changeable to fit societal needs. It is only by looking at a variety of legal genres that one can get an accurate picture of the jurists' attitudes to legal change. The Mālikī jurists appreciated the need for the divine law to remain unsullied by worldly circumstances in order to bear witness to God's will, but they also appreciated that the law sometimes needed to change in order to be pertinent to the life of the Muslim community. They resolved this tension by reserving their theological explorations of the law for legal manuals, but reserved other genres, particularly that of the *fatwā*, for its practical application. By taking into account a variety of legal genres, I have thus avoided the binary approach to legal change into which much contemporary scholarship on Islamic law has fallen.

I have further shown that the jurists' works on the Mudéjars are not simply a dialogue located within a closed set of legal texts. The term *hijra*, for example, was deliberately excluded from the legal tradition but could still re-enter that tradition via non-legal sources. I suggested that the use of the term in the Maghrib, in particular by the Almohads, gave it wide currency and that this had an impact on the jurists, some of whom then adopted the term in their legal works. Previous attempts to understand the jurists' use of *hijra* saw it as a *sui generis* juristic attempt to reintroduce a concept which appeared in the *Qurʾān* and *ḥadīth* in order to respond to the exigencies of frontier life. By looking outside of legal sources, I was able to show that the jurists' use of the term can be seen as evidence of their participation in a broader Maghribī cultural milieu.

The Reconquista-era jurists who required Muslims to leave Christian Iberia have not been favorably received by many contemporary scholars who tend to view their position as unproductive and irrational. Such scholars equate anti-coexistence or anti-accomodationist policies as stemming either from a psychosis brought about by the trauma of war and defeat, or from a religious "fundamentalism" that was unwilling to engage with the messiness of reality. However, it seems that the messy reality, as understood by both the Muslim jurists and the Christian rulers, was that Muslim populations in Iberia were of practical advantage to the Christians, and that Muslim abandonment of Iberia was of practical advantage to Muslim lands as a whole. Whether as soldiers, bureaucrats or tax payers, the Mudéjars gave considerable support to their Christian rulers. This was the case to such an extent that Christian rulers usually discouraged, or even banned, their migration to Islamic territory. The jurists' encouragement of migration can therefore be seen as a corresponding and politically necessary countermeasure. The jurists' response to Christian rule was therefore not a fundamentalist retreat to the world of Islamic texts, but a pragmatic one. The Islamic legal tradition did not compel jurists to prohibit or permit Muslims from living under Christian rule. There was enough variety in the tradition to accommodate either approach. What was fundamental for the jurists was developing a position which would be appropriate for their social and political circumstances. Their responses to the Reconquista are the result of a careful balancing of the needs of the Mudéjars with the needs of Muslims living in Islamic lands.

By the end of the Reconquista, the jurists had formulated a new body of law to deal with the crisis. This included a revivification of the concept of *hijra*, a hardening of the legal boundaries separating Muslims from Christians, and the introduction of laws designed to weaken the rights of Muslims who continued to live in Christian territory. Once the Mudéjar period was over and the Morisco period began, these new laws ceased to be of great importance due to the small size and isolated nature of Morisco communities. The corpus of law dealing with the Mudéjars was therefore largely neglected until the nineteenth century when jurists again faced a similar crisis of Christian rule and were forced to revisit it.

With the 1830 surrender of the Ottoman Dey of Algiers to the French, the jurists were again confronted with the question of the permissibility of life under Christian rule. Initially, many jurists evinced considerable sympathy for migration from French-controlled territory and armed resistance. They cited the legal sources developed during the Reconquista, especially the writings of al-Wansharīsī, as their authority for this position. This position, however, was short-lived. The sheer size of the Muslim population under French control was so great that it precluded the possibility of large-scale migration. Most jurists therefore soon acknowledged the futility of such calls for *hijra* in view of the overwhelming power which Muslims faced. They ceased the call for migration and began to shape Islamic law to deal with the difficulties of living under these new circumstances.

The issue of whether and how Muslims should live under non-Muslim rule continues to be of importance in the contemporary period and touches upon many of the central issues pertaining to what it means to be a Muslim and to the nature of Islam. Today, *fiqh al-aqalliyyāt* (the law governing Muslim minorities in non-Muslim countries) is a large and fast growing area of Islamic law which is characterized by considerable legal creativity and diversity of opinion. It is hoped that this study of the early history of the jurists' considerations of these issues will help to enliven scholarship in this area.

Appendix A

Al-Wansharīsī: On the Leader of the Muslims of Christian Marbella[1]

[Question]

Praise God, and blessings and peace on the Messenger of God. My master, please give your response to a case, may God be pleased with you and may He, through your life, bring joy to the Muslims.

The case concerns a Marbellan man, well-known for his virtue and piety, who rather than migrating together with his fellow townspeople, stayed behind in order to search for his brother who went missing while fighting the enemy in the land of war. He had until now searched for news of him but, not discovering any and despairing of him, was on the point of migrating when another obstacle arose. This [obstacle] was that he had become a spokesman and helper for the Muslim subject peoples (*dhimmiyyūn*) amongst whom he lived and also for their neighbors who lived in similar circumstances in Western al-Andalus. He represented them before the Christian rulers regarding whatever hardships fate dealt them, argued on their behalf, and frequently rescued them from great difficulties. Most of them are unable to perform these [services] themselves. If he were to migrate, few would be found to match him in this art. On account of his loss [of a brother], he had joined them, but the loss of him [the man himself] would cause them great harm. On the grounds that his residing there is of social benefit (*maslaḥa*) to those poor subject peoples, is it possible to grant him a dispensation to live under the rule of the unbelievers, even though he has the ability to migrate whenever he wills it? Or can one give no dispensation to him since [these subject peoples] also have no dispensation for residing there while subject to the laws of unbelief? This is especially the case given that they have been given permission [by the Christians] to migrate, and most of them have the ability to do so when they wish. [Further], if he were to be given a dispensation [to live there], would he also be given a dispensation to pray in his garments [in whatever degree of purity] he is able [to keep them]? This [would be required] because his clothing

---

1 al-Wansharīsī, *al-Miʿyār al-muʿrib*, 2:137–41. The translation of this *fatwā* was previously published in Alan Verskin, *Oppressed in the Land: Fatwās on Muslims Living under Non-Muslim Rule from the Middle Ages to the Present* (Princeton: Markus Wiener Publishers, 2012) and has been reproduced with permission. For earlier attempts to translate both this and the next fatwā by al-Wansharīsī into English, see Aboobaker Asmal, "Muslims under non-Muslim Rule: the Fiqhi (Legal) Views of Ibn Nujaym and al-Wansharisi" (Ph.D. dissertation: University of Manchester, 1998) and Jocelyn Hendrickson, "The Islamic Obligation to Emigrate: Al-Wansharīsī's Asnā al-Matājir Reconsidered" (Ph.D. Dissertation: Emory University, 2009).

© KONINKLIJKE BRILL NV, LEIDEN, 2015 | DOI 10.1163/9789004284531_008

would mostly not be free of impurities on account of his aforementioned frequent mixing with Christians, moving about among them, and sleeping and residing in their homes while in the service of the Muslim subject peoples.[2]

Explain for us God's ruling regarding this. If God wills it, may you be praised and rewarded and may abundant peace and the mercy and blessings of God, may He be exalted, support your exalted station.

[Answer]

He [al-Wansharīsī] answered him thus:

Praise is to God alone. Here is the answer [to your question], and it is God who bestows success through His grace. It is our one and victorious God who has set the poll-tax (*jizya*)[3] and abasement upon the necks of the accursed unbelievers as chains and fetters with which to roam about the land, cities, and towns, displaying the might of Islam and the nobility of the chosen prophet. Therefore, if one of the Muslims [138], may God guard and protect them, tries to invert these chains and fetters [by setting them] upon his own neck, he has acted against God and His messenger and has exposed himself to the anger of the Almighty and the Omnipotent. Indeed, it would be fitting for God to hurl him together with them into Hellfire: "God has decreed: I shall conquer, I and My messengers. God is Strong and Almighty" (Qur'ān 58: 21). It is obligatory for every believer with faith in God and the Last Day to endeavor to preserve this basic principle of faith by distancing himself and fleeing from the dwellings of the enemies of the Merciful One's ally [i.e., the Prophet].

To make excuses for the aforementioned virtuous man because of his intention of acting as an interpreter between the tyrant and his sinful Mudéjar[4] subjects does not free him from the obligation of migration. No one should be under the delusion that there is [any genuine] opposition to the obligation [of migration] in the prescriptions for evading it noted in the question—except someone who displays feigned or genuine ignorance of this inversion of Islam (*fiṭra*), or who has no knowledge of the sources from which the law is derived. Dwelling among the unbelievers, other than those who are protected

2 For views on how ritual impurity was transmitted from non-Muslims to Muslims, see below, page 9 n. 33.

3 The *jizya* or poll-tax is the tax levied upon "people of the book." On its origin and function, see Claude Cahen, "Djizya," in *The Encyclopedia of Islam, 2nd ed.*, 2: 559–62.

4 Arabic: *Ahl al-dajn*. A Mudéjar is defined as "a Muslim who, after the surrender of a territory to a Christian ruler, remained there without changing religion, and entered into a relationship of vassalage under a Christian king." L.P. Harvey, *Islamic Spain, 1250 to 1500*, 3.

and humbled peoples (*ahl al-dhimma wa'l-ṣaghār*), is not permitted and is not allowed for so much as an hour of a day. This is because of the filth, dirt, and religious and worldly corruption which is ever-present [among them].

[A List of Factors Precluding Muslims from Living in the Abode of Unbelief]

[1] Among these is that the purpose of Divine Law is for the word of Islam and witness to the truth to be raised high above all others, free from scorn and from the banners of unbelief triumphing over it. Their dwelling in humiliation and abasement necessitates that this noble, exalted and sublime word be abased rather than sublime, and be disdained rather than holy. [Knowing about] this violation of the Law's principles and foundations and about the one who, without necessity or compulsion, spends his life patiently enduring it, should be sufficient for you [to understand the position of the Law].

[2] Among these is the [issue of the] fulfillment of prayer, the fulfillment of which is second in virtue [only] to the two Declarations of Faith. Glorifying [God] and conducting prayer publicly cannot occur, or [even] be imagined to occur, except in an environment in which [Islam] is entirely out in the open, exalted, and free from scorn and contempt. However, dwelling among the unbelievers and intimately associating with the iniquitous exposes [Islam] to humiliation, disdain, derision and jest. God, may He be exalted, said: "When you make the call to prayer, they take it for a jest and sport. That is because they are a people who do not understand" (Qur'ān 5: 58).

[3] Among these is almsgiving (*zakāt*). It is clear to one who possesses understanding and an enlightened mind that, according to the basic tenets of Islam and the ordinances of all humankind, the collection of alms is the responsibility of the ruler. Where there is no ruler, because of the absence of this necessary condition, there is no collection of alms. There can be no alms because of the absence of the person who is entitled to collect it. This basic tenet of Islam is demolished by accepting the rule of unbelievers. As for [alms] being collected by someone who will use them against the Muslims, it is clear that this also involves opposing all the acts of worship mandated by the Law. [139]

[4] Among these is the fast of the month of Ramaḍān—which is clearly a duty incumbent upon every Muslim—as well as the alms given at the end of that month. The beginning and end [of the fast of Ramaḍān] are conditional on the sighting of the new moon. Under most circumstances this sighting can only

be established by a witness's testimony, and this testimony cannot be given except before Muslim rulers or their deputies. Where there is no Muslim ruler or deputy, there can be no testimony by witnesses. Therefore, with respect to legal practice, the [precise] beginning and end of the month is uncertain.

[5] Among these is pilgrimage to the House [the *ḥajj* pilgrimage to Mecca]. [Muslims] are still charged with performing the *ḥajj* pilgrimage even if this obligation is suspended because of their lack of ability to do so.

[6] The jihād for elevating the word of truth and annihilating unbelief is one of the basic tenets of Islamic practice. It is an obligation on the Muslim community as a whole (*farḍ ʿalā al-kifāya*), should the necessity arise, especially in the place of residence and vicinity in question. If their abandonment of jihād is not out of absolute necessity, then they are like someone who, out of no necessity, resolves to abandon [the obligation of] migration; and someone who determines to do so without necessity is like someone who freely and intentionally abandons it. As for those who defiantly pursue the opposite [of jihād] by aiding their [Christian] allies against the Muslims, either with their lives or their property, they, together with the polytheists, have the status of enemy combatants. This opposition and error should be sufficient for you [to understand the position of the Law].

This account has made it clear that the prayers, fasts, alms, and jihād [of Muslim residents of the abode of unbelief] are deficient. It indicates that they transgress by not exalting the word of God and witness to the truth and, [on the contrary], neglect to bring it to light, glorify it and elevate it above the scorn of the unbelievers and the derision of the iniquitous. How could a jurist or pious person hesitate to forbid residence [in the abode of unbelief] which involves opposition to all of these noble and sublime Islamic principles, together with the worldly degradation, abasement and humiliation that living in subjection generally involves. It moreover offends against the well-known glory of the Muslims and against their exalted rank by inciting people to despise and oppress the religion (*dīn*) [of Islam]. These are indeed matters which make one's ears ring.

[7] Among these is the humiliation, scorn and belittlement regarding which the Prophet, peace be upon him, has said: "It is incumbent on a Muslim not to abase himself,"[5] and he [also] said: "The upper hand is better than the lower hand."[6]

5 See, for example, *Jāmiʿ al-Tirmidhī* (Cairo: Dār al-Ḥadīth, 2001), n. 2204.

6 *Ṣaḥīḥ al-Bukhārī*, no. 1427.

[8] Among these is the scorn and mockery [of the unbelievers] which no one possessed of virtuous manliness (*murūwa*) would endure unless compelled by necessity. [140]

[9] Among these is the belittlement and harm to his honor, and perhaps also to his person and property. It is clear what this involves from the perspective of the Sunna and manliness.

[10] Among these is becoming engrossed in viewing objectionable things, being subjected to contact with ritual pollutants, eating forbidden things, and the like.

[11] Among these are the treaty violations by the [Christian] king and [his] control over life, wife, children and property, which are to be anticipated with dread.

It is reported that ʿUmar b. ʿAbd al-ʿAzīz[7] prohibited residing in the Andalusī peninsula. He did this despite it being, at that time, a frontier fortress, the virtue of which no one can be ignorant,[8] and despite the fact that the Muslims there had power, ascendancy, plentiful numbers and provisions. Despite all of this, the caliph of the time, whose virtue, piety, righteousness and good counsel of his subjects is agreed upon, prohibited [residence in al-Andalus] out of fear of corruption. How much more so would this be the case for someone who throws himself, his wife, and his children into their hands when they are powerful and ascendant and supported with great numbers and plentiful provisions, and then depends on them to fulfill their pacts in [accordance with] their law. [In contrast], we do not [even] accept their testimony as valid when it is given about themselves, let alone when it is given about us.[9] How can we rely on their claim to fulfill [their pact], given what has already happened and given the events to which anyone who investigates and examines reports of the region can attest?

---

7 This is the Umayyad caliph (r. 99/717 to 101/720) who, according to tradition, is renowned for his piety, see *Encyclopedia of Islam*, 2nd ed., s.v., "ʿUmar (II) b. ʿAbd al-ʿAzīz."

8 On the frontier fortress (*ribāṭ*) and its virtue, see Majid Khadduri, *War and Peace in the Law of Islam* (Baltimore: Johns Hopkins University Press, 1955), 81–82.

9 On the law regarding the acceptance or non-acceptance of the testimony of non-Muslims, see Antoine Fattal, *Le statut légal des non-Musulmans en pays d'Islam* (Beirut: Imprimerie Catholique, 1958), 361 ff.

[12] Among these, even if one assumes that their kings and notables will fulfill [their treaties], are fears for life, wife, children and also property, on account of their wicked people, fools and murderers. Their customs also bear witness to this and events confirm it.

[13] Among these is fear of religious corruption. Even if one concedes that those distinguished in wisdom might be secure [in their faith], who would there be to safeguard the young, the fools, the weak and the women when the notables and devils of the enemy call upon them?

[14] Among these is corruption through sexual relations. How will anyone who has a wife, daughter or pretty female relative safeguard her from a vulgar person from among the enemy's dogs or faithless pigs chancing upon her, and then beguiling and deceiving her respecting her religion? He would overpower her and she would be obedient to him, making apostasy and religious corruption separate her from her guardian. This resembles what happened to al-Muʿtamid Ibn ʿAbbād's [141] daughter-in-law and her children,[10] may God guard us against affliction and the enemies' malicious gloating.

[15] Among these is the spread of their reprehensible way of life, language, dress and customs to those who have lived among them for years. This is what happened to the people of Ávila[11] and of other such places who have lost knowledge of the Arabic language entirely. When knowledge of the Arabic language is entirely lost,[12] acts of worship are also lost. How can one even consider

10 The daughter-in-law of al-Muʿtamid Ibn ʿAbbād (r. 462–84/1069–1091), the last ruler of the ʿAbbādid dynasty, is reported to have become the mistress of King Alphonso VI of Castille and to have converted to Christianity. On this event, see E. Lévi-Provençal, "La 'mora Zaida', femme d'Alphonse VI de Castille et leur fils l'infant D. Sancho," *Hesperis* 18 (1934), 1–8.

11 It has been suggested that the text refers not to Ávila but to Ayelo in Valencia, see P.S. van Koningsveld and G.A. Wiegers, "The Islamic Statute of the Mudéjars in the Light of a New Source," *al-Qanṭara* 17 (1996), 28. Scholarship on the Muslims in Valencia, however, has shown that they continued to extensively use Arabic in documents into the 15th and 16th centuries. See María del Carmen Barceló Torres, "Las cartas árabes de Vila-Real. (Revisión del panorama mudéjar valenciano)," *Estudios Castellonenses* 1 (1982), 367.

12 On the issue of the loss of the Arabic language, see Gerard Wiegers, "Language and Identity: Pluralism and the Use of Non-Arabic Languages in the Muslim West," in *Pluralism and Identity: Studies in Ritual Behaviour*, ed. Jan Platvoet et al. (Leiden: Brill, 1995), 303 ff. and John Boswell, *The Royal Treasure* (New Haven: Yale University Press, 1977), 303 ff.

the abandonment of the verbal acts of worship which are so abundant in number and virtue?

[16] Among these is fear of [the unbelievers'] taking control over property by instituting heavy levies and unjust taxes. This leads to them expropriating property completely by encompassing it in the taxes of unbelief, whether all at once, on the pretext of some passing necessity, or through many payments. Or it might be that [their expropriations] rely upon some invented excuse or interpretation which it is impossible to make them reconsider or debate—even if these excuses are supremely weak, clearly feeble, and corrupt. They [the Mudéjars] do not have the audacity to do anything about this lest their actions cause the kindling of hatred and lead to the abrogation of the treaty [with the consequence that the Christians] will take control of their lives, wives and children. Events bear witness to this for one who has examined them. This has even occurred many times in the place in question as well as in other places. These present and anticipated corruptions firmly support the prohibition of residence [in the abode of unbelief] and the ban of this perversion of what is right. The different factors involved lead to a single conclusion. The leading jurists have already expanded this basic rule to other situations because of its strength and the clarity of its prohibition. The imām of Medina (*dār al-hijra*), Abū ʿAbdallāh Mālik b. Anas (d. 179/795), may God be pleased with him, said: "The Qurʾānic verses on migration teach that every Muslim must leave lands in which normative practices (*sunan*) are altered and in which other than what is right is in force," not to speak of leaving and fleeing from the lands of unbelief and the places of the iniquitous. God forbid that a virtuous and monotheistic community, while glorifying and praising God, be dependent on trinitarians and be content to dwell amongst impurity and filth. There is no scope for the aforementioned, virtuous [Marbellan] man to remain in the aforementioned place for [his] aforementioned objective. No dispensation can be given to him or to his companions regarding whatever impurities and pollutants attach themselves to their clothing and bodies. This is because pardon for these [impurities] is conditional upon the difficulty of guarding and protecting against these things and no such difficulty can attach to their choice of residing [in the abode of unbelief] and acting against what is right. God, may He be exalted, knows best and it is He who gives success.

This was written, with greetings to those for whom there is no God but God, by the poor and wretched slave who seeks God's forgiveness and desires blessings for one who applies himself to this [*fatwā*] and carries it out.

ʿUbaydallāh Aḥmad b. Yaḥyā b. Muḥammad b. ʿAlī al-Wansharīsī

Appendix B

Al-Wansharīsī's *"Asnā al-matājir,"* in *al-Miʿyār al-muʿrib*. Rabat: Wizārat al-Awqāf, 1981: 119–136.

The Most Exalted of all Transactions: A Clarification of the Laws Pertaining to One Whose Land has been Conquered by the Christians and has not Migrated and what Punishments and Restrictions Apply to Him

The shaykh, the great jurist, the excellent preacher, the enduring righteous model, the immaculate, excellent, just and pleasing totality, Abū ʿAbdallāh Ibn Quṭiyya, may God preserve his exaltedness and ascendancy, wrote this to me:

Praise is to God alone. Your answer regarding a case, please, my master, may God be pleased with you and bring joy to the Muslims through your life. The case concerns some Andalusīs who migrated from al-Andalus, leaving their houses, lands, gardens, vineyards and other types of real estate, and profusely spending their money [in order to do so]. They left the rule of the unbelieving community and claimed that they had fled to God, may He be exalted, with their religion, their lives, their families and their children, and that none of their [former] wealth remained with them. They settled, praise God the Exalted, in the abode of Islam in obedience to God and His Prophet and the Law of the Muslim covenant. [However,] after having reached the abode of Islam, they regretted their migration and grew angry, claiming that their present condition was one of hardship. They claimed that they could not find any means at all of sustaining a livelihood, nor any courteousness, ease, support or means of traveling safely and properly in the abode of Islam, [by which they meant] the Maghrib, may God safeguard and watch over her lands and give victory to her ruler. They clearly conveyed this sentiment with an assortment of repugnant words which indicated the weakness of their religion and their lack of certainty in their belief. They [people who knew the migrants] said that their migration had not been to God and His messenger, as they had claimed, but that it had been made for worldly aims which they expected to immediately attain upon their arrival in accordance with their desires. [120] When they did not realize these goals, they openly disparaged the abode of

© KONINKLIJKE BRILL NV, LEIDEN, 2015 | DOI 10.1163/9789004284531_009

Islam and its affairs. They abused and reviled that which had been the cause of their migration, and praised the abode of unbelief and its people, regretting having abandoned it. Someone even recalls that one of them had said, in denying [the obligation of] migration to the abode of Islam, which is this very land, may God safeguard it: "Is it [really] to here that one migrates from there? Nay, it is from here to there that one is obligated to migrate!" Another said, "If the ruler of Castille were to come to these parts, we would go to him and ask him to return us there," that is, to the abode of unbelief. Some also say that they search for whatever ruse they can find by which they can go back to the abode of unbelief and return to living under the unbelievers' pact of protection.

What is their status with respect to sin, neglect of religion and legal credibility? If they incline towards this and do not repent and return to God the Exalted, are they perpetrating the very disobedience [to Islam] from which they were fleeing? What about someone who, God forbid, returns to the abode of unbelief after having come to the abode of Islam? Is someone who hears them speaking openly about these matters or the like obliged to punish them or is he not obliged until they are warned and admonished? Is one who repents to God the Exalted to be left in peace with the hope that his repentance will be accepted and [only] the one who persists to be punished, or are they all to be avoided and each left to what he has chosen? Is it the case that God deems the intention valid and rewards anyone who is properly established in the abode of Islam, and God is angry [only] with someone who opts to return to the abode of unbelief and live under the pact of protection of the unbelievers? [If this is the case], is someone who openly disparages the abode of Islam to be left alone with nothing imposed on him?

Explain to us the law of God, may He be Exalted, regarding this. Is it a condition of [the obligation of] migration that no one migrate except to a place, in whatever region of the abode of Islam, which meets his desires and with guaranteed worldly goods which are acquired immediately upon his arrival? Or is this not a condition? Is migration obligatory from the abode of unbelief to the abode of Islam, whether to sweetness or bitterness, plenty or scarcity, hardship or ease, in accordance with the circumstances of the world? Surely its aim is the security of religion, family, children and the like, and to leave the rule of the unbelieving religious community for the rule of the Muslim community and whatsoever worldly circumstances God has willed, whether sweet or bitter, meager or plentiful living, and such like.

May God the Exalted reward you for your clear, succinct, lucid, healing and complete explanation. May a noble peace support your exalted station with the mercy and blessings of God, may He be exalted.

He [al-Wansharīsī] answered him thus: [121]

> Praise is to God alone and then blessings and peace on our master and Lord, Muḥammad.

Introduction

The answer to what you have asked, and it is God the Exalted who beneficently grants success, is that migration from the land of unbelief to the land of Islam is an obligation until the Day of Resurrection. This is also the case for migration from a land of sin and falsehood, whether on account of tyranny or corruption (*fitna*).[13] The Messenger of God, may God bless him and grant him peace, said: "The time is nigh when a Muslim's best property will be the sheep that he takes to the mountaintops and places of rainfall in order to flee with his religion from corruption." This tradition is included in the collections of al-Bukhārī, Abū Dāwūd, al-Nasāʾī and in the *Muwaṭṭaʾ*.[14] Ashhab[15] narrated a tradition on the authority of Mālik:[16] "No one should remain in a place in which anything other than truth is in force." [Ibn al-ʿArabī (d. 543/1148)] said in the *ʿĀrida*:[17]

> What if someone disputes this and says that there is no [place in existence] except [one in which "other than the truth is in force"]. We would

13 *Fitna* is a difficult word to render into English. It can be variously translated, depending on context, as temptation, trial, disorder, and sedition. I have preferred "corruption" as it seems to fit best in this context.

14 *Ṣaḥīḥ al-Bukhārī*, ed. Muḥammad Fuʾād ʿAbd al-Bāqī et al. (Dār al-Maʿrifa, 1959), no. 19. *Sunan Abī Dāwūd*, ed. Muḥammad Muḥyī al-Dīn ʿAbd al-Ḥamīd (Beirut: Dār al-Kutub al-ʿIlmiyya, 1985), no. 4267. *Sunan al-Nasāʾī*, ed. ʿAbd al-Fattāh Abū Ghudda (Beirut: Dār al-Bashāʾir al-Islāmiyya, 1988), no. 5036, Mālik, *al-Muwaṭṭāʾ*, ed. Muḥammad Fuʾād ʿAbd al-Bāqī (Cairo: Dār Iḥyāʾ al-Kutub al-ʿArabiyya, 1951), no. 16.

15 I.e., Abū ʿAmr Ashhab b. ʿAbd al-ʿAzīz b. Dāwūd al-Qaysī al-ʿĀmirī al-Jaʿdī (d. 204/819).

16 I.e., Mālik b. Anas (d. 179/795), the jurist for whom the Mālikī legal school is named, see *E.I.*^{2}, 6: 262.

17 Al-Wansharīsī's quotations from the *ʿĀriḍa* are not identical to those in the printed edition, see Ibn al-ʿArabī, *ʿĀriḍat al-aḥwadhī bi-sharḥ ṣaḥīḥ al-Tirmidhī*, ed. Jamal Marʿashlī (Dār al-Kutub al-ʿIlmiyya, 1997), 7: 88.

> answer that the place which is least sinful should be chosen. For example,[18] if there is a land in which there is unbelief, then a land in which there is injustice is better; or, if there is a land in which there is justice and prohibited things (*ḥarām*), then a land in which there is injustice and permitted things (*ḥalāl*) is better for residence; or a land in which there is disobedience under the jurisdiction of God is preferable to a land in which there is disobedience under the usurpations of man. This paradigm demonstrates what he [Ashhab] related. [Confirming this] ʿUmar Ibn ʿAbd al-ʿAzīz, may God be pleased with him, has said: "So-and-so is in Medina, so-and-so in Mecca, so-and-so in Yemen, so-and-so in Iraq and so-and-so in Syria—by God, the land is filled with injustice and wrongdoing."[19]

Evidence from the Qurʾān

This obligation of migration does not expire for those whose fortresses and lands the tyrant, may God curse him, occupies. It ceases only for those who are entirely unable by any means to migrate, not for those who do not migrate out of concern for their homeland or wealth—for that is invalid from the perspective of the Law. God, may He be exalted, said: "Except for the oppressed among the men, women, and children, who are unable to devise a plan and are not shown a way. As for these, it may be that God will pardon them. God is pardoning and forgiving" (Qurʾān 4: 98–99).[20] This condition of being oppressed, which excuses one who is afflicted by it, is not the same condition of being oppressed as is used as an excuse at the beginning and middle of the verse. For the [latter excuse] is made by those who wrong themselves [by falsely claiming]: "We were oppressed in the land." Indeed, God did not accept their words of excuse, and He indicated that they were able to migrate by some means. Through His words, "As for these, it may be

18 The text which follows is corrupt in Rabat text on which this translation is based. The text has been reconstructed on the basis of the above edition of *ʿĀriḍat al-aḥwadhī*, 7: 88–89.

19 Ibn al-ʿArabī, *ʿĀriḍat al-aḥwadhī*, 7: 88–89.

20 In this passage, al-Wansharīsī is commenting upon some verses that he does not quote in full. This is the complete passage: "As for those whom the angels take in death while they wrong themselves, [the angels] will ask: 'In what circumstances were you?' They will say: 'We were oppressed in the land.' [The angels] will say: 'Was not God's earth spacious that you could have migrated therein?' As for these, their abode will be hell, an evil journey's end. Except for the oppressed among the men, women, and children who are unable to devise a plan and are not guided to a way. As for these, it may be that God will pardon them. God is pardoning and forgiving (Qurʾān 4: 97–99).

that God will pardon them," He excused [only] those oppressed who were not able to devise a means and who could not discover a way [to migrate]. And a "perhaps" which emanates from God [will occur] of necessity. As for the one in the middle of the verse who [claims to be] oppressed and is punished, he is someone who is able by some means [to migrate]. The one who is [truly] oppressed is forgiven on account of his being entirely unable by any means [to migrate]. He is someone who is afflicted with residence [in the abode of unbelief] because of his inability to flee with his religion, being unable to find a path open to him and having no means [to migrate] revealed to him. He is not able [to migrate] by any means whatsoever and is thus equivalent to the cripple or the prisoner, or the very sick or very weak. One thus hopes that he will receive pardon for he becomes like someone who is coerced into [122] pronouncing words of unbelief. Nevertheless, he must still have the constant intention that, were he to have the ability or possibility of migrating, he would do so, and the accompanying resolution that if, one day, the possibility were to appear, he would migrate. As for someone who is able to make [migration] possible by some means or device, he is not to be excused [from the obligation] and he wrongs himself if he remains, as is implied by the [following] Qur'ānic verses and *ḥadīth*s:

[a] God, may He be Exalted, said:

> O you who believe! Do not take My enemy and your enemy as allies. Do you show them affection when they disbelieve in that truth which has come to you,... [driving out the messenger and you because you believe in God, your Lord? If you have come forth to strive in My way and seek My good pleasure, (do not show them affection). Do you show affection to them in secret, when I am well aware of what you hide and what you proclaim?] Whosoever of you does this has truly strayed from the right way (Qur'ān 60: 1).

[b] God, may He be Exalted, said:

> O you who believe! Do not take for your intimates other than yourselves, such people would spare no pains to ruin you; they yearn for you to suffer. Hatred is revealed by their mouths, but that which their breasts hide is greater. We have made plain for you the revelations if you will understand (Qur'ān 3: 118).

[c] And He, may He be exalted, said:

> Let not the believers take unbelievers as allies to the exclusion of believers. Whoever does so has no connection with God. However, this is not

the case if you do this to protect yourselves against them. God warns you to beware of Him. To God is the journeying (Qur'ān 3: 28).

[d] He, may He be exalted, said:

Do not acquiesce to those who do wrong so that the Fire touches you—you have no allies apart from God—and then you will not be helped (Qur'ān 11: 113).

[e] He, may He be exalted, said:

Give the hypocrites the tidings that there is a painful doom for them; those who take unbelievers as their allies instead of believers! Do they look for power at their hands? All power belongs to God... [He has already revealed to you in the Scripture that, when you hear God's revelations rejected and derided, you should not sit with them until they engage in some other conversation. If you did that, you are like them. God will gather hypocrites and unbelievers, all together, into hell. Those who wait about you and then,] if God gives you a victory, say: "Are we not with you?" and, if the unbelievers meet with a success, say: "Had we not mastery over you, and did we not protect you from the believers? God will judge between you on the Day of Resurrection, and God will not give the unbelievers a way over the believers (Qur'ān 4: 138–41).

[f] He, may He be exalted, said:

O you who believe! Do not choose unbelievers as allies to the exclusion of believers. Would you give God a clear warrant against you? (Qur'ān 4: 144).

[g] He, may He be exalted, said:

O you who believe! Do not take the Jews and Christians as allies. They are allies of one another. Whoever among you who takes them as allies is one of them. God does not guide people who do wrong (Qur'ān 5: 51).

[h] He, may He be exalted, said:

O you who believe, do not take those who make jest and sport of your religion as allies, whether they are from those who received the Scripture before you or from the unbelievers. Fear God if you are believers (Qur'ān 5: 57–58).

[i] He, may He be exalted, said:

Your ally can only be God, His messenger and those who believe, who establish worship, pay alms, and bow down. Whosoever takes God, His

> messenger and those who believe for allies—the party of God, they are the victorious (Qur'ān 5: 55–56).

[j] He, may He be exalted, said:

> As for those whom the angels take in death while they wrong themselves, [the angels] will ask: 'In what circumstances were you?' They will say: [123] 'We were oppressed in the land.' [The angels] will say: 'Was not God's earth spacious that you could have migrated therein?' As for these, their abode will be hell, an evil journey's end. Except for the oppressed among the men, women, and children who are unable to devise a plan and are not guided to a way. As for these, it may be that God will pardon them. God is pardoning and forgiving (Qur'ān 4: 97–99).

[k] He, may He be exalted, said:

> You see many of them becoming allies of those who disbelieve. Surely evil is that which they send on before them, for that God is angry with them and in the doom they will abide. If they believed in God and the Prophet and in that which is revealed to him, they would not take them as allies. But many of them are wrongdoers (Qur'ān 5: 80–81).

Those who "wrong themselves" in the earlier verse are none other than those who abandon migration while having the ability [to migrate] in accordance with God's words, "Was not God's earth spacious that you could have migrated therein?" They wrong themselves by abandoning it, that is, by residing among the unbelievers and increasing their multitude. There is an admonition in His words, "those whom the angels take," regarding the censuring and punishment of someone who dies still persevering in his residence [in the abode of unbelief]. But as for someone who repents of this and migrates, but whom death overtakes on the way, the King has taken him unto Him outside of them [the unbelievers], and it is hoped that his repentance will be accepted and that he will not die in a condition of wronging himself. This is also illustrated in the words of God, may He be exalted: "and whosoever forsakes his home, migrating to God and His messenger… [and death overtakes him, his reward is then incumbent on God]. God is ever forgiving and merciful" (Qur'ān 4: 100).

All of these Qur'ānic verses, or at least most of them, are texts prohibiting alliances with unbelievers—except His words, "You see many of them [becoming allies of those who disbelieve. Surely evil is that which they send on before them, for that God is angry with them and in the doom they will abide. If they believed in God and the Prophet and in that which is revealed to him, they would not take them as allies. But many of them are wrongdoers]" (Qur'ān 5: 80–81).

The [following] words of God, may He be exalted, indicate that there is no qualification of this prohibition: "O you who believe! Do not take the Jews and Christians as allies. They are allies of one another. Whoever among you who takes them as allies is one of them. God does not guide people who do wrong" (Qur'ān 5: 51). Similarly His words, may He be exalted, "O you who believe, do not take as allies those who make jest and sport of your religion, whether they are from those who received the Scripture before you or from the unbelievers. Fear God if you are believers" (Qur'ān 5: 57).

The repetition of verses with this meaning and their conforming to a single trend confirms this prohibition and removes any ambiguity that might attach to it. This is because ambiguity and doubt are removed if there is a meaning which is enshrined in a text and enforced through repetition. Regarding this matter, Qur'ānic texts, prophetic *ḥadīth*s, and the definitive consensus of scholars together give their support. You will not find disagreement among the people who pray towards Mecca and hold fast to the Precious Book, for "falsehood cannot come at it from in front or from behind it. It is a revelation from the Wise One and the Owner of Praise" (Qur'ān 41: 42). It is [124] a decisive religious prohibition like the prohibition against [eating] "carrion, blood and swine flesh,"[21] killing without justification, and similar cases among the five cardinal principles [religion (*dīn*), life, reason, property, lineage][22] which the leaders of [all] sects (*milal*) and religions (*adyān*) agree are sacrosanct. One who differs regarding this or who wants [to find] disagreement about residing with them and supports them by permitting this residence, making light of the matter and deeming the law trivial, has strayed from the religion and has quit the Muslim community. He is confuted [by arguments] from which no Muslim can defend himself, he is overcome by a scholarly consensus against which he has no way of disagreeing, and his argument is torn asunder.

---

21 Qur'ān, 16: 115.

22 For a general outline of these principles, see Bernard Weiss, *The Spirit of Islamic Law* (Athens: University of Georgia Press, 1998), 170.

Ibn Rushd (d. 520/1126) Prohibits Residence in the Abode of War

The leader of the jurists, the judge Abū al-Walīd Ibn Rushd (d. 520/1126),[23] may God have mercy on him, said in his *Muqaddimāt* in the section on trade in the abode of war:

> Migration (*hijra*) remains imperative until the Day of Resurrection. It is rendered obligatory by the consensus of the Muslims that someone who converts to Islam in the abode of war must not remain there where the laws of the polytheists are in force over him. Rather, he is to migrate and join the abode of the Muslims where their laws are in force over him.[24]

The messenger of God, may God bless him and grant him peace, said: "I am not responsible for any Muslim who resides among the polytheists."[25] However, this [obligation of] migration does not prohibit a migrant from returning to his homeland if it becomes an abode of faith and peace—whereas a return to Mecca had been forbidden for the migrants (*muhājirūn*) among the companions of the Prophet, may God bless him and grant him peace. God reserved this [law] for them on account of its merit. He [Ibn Rushd] said:

> Since the Book, the tradition and community consensus oblige someone who converts in the abode of war to migrate, join the abode of the Muslims, and not to reside with the polytheists or stay among them for [even] a night where their laws are in force over him, how can it be permitted for anyone to enter their lands where their laws are in force over him whether in trade or in other matters? Mālik, may God have mercy on him, already considered it reprehensible for anyone to dwell in a land in which the forbears are disrespected.[26] How then in a land in which the Merciful One is denied and in which idols are worshipped instead? No soul can be at peace with this except that of a Muslim of diseased faith.

---

23 This jurist was the grandfather of the philosopher known in the West as Averroes.

24 Muḥammad b. Aḥmad Ibn Rushd, *Kitāb al-muqaddimāt al-mumahhidāt*, ed. Muḥammad Ḥajjī (Beirut: Dār al-Gharb al-Islāmī, 1988), 4: 285.

25 *Sunan al-Tirmidhī*, no. 1604; *Sunan Abū Dāwūd*, no. 2645; and *Sunan al-Nasā'ī*, no. 4780.

26 I have been unable to find the source of this exact statement, but for a similar statement, see Ibn Abī Zayd al-Qayrawānī, *Kitāb al-Jāmiʿ fī al-sunan wa'l-ādāb wa'l-māghāzī wa'l-tārīkh*, ed. Muḥammad Abū al-Ajfān and ʿUthmān al-Baṭṭīkh (Beirut: Mu'assasat al-Risāla, 1985), 156, referred to in Michael Cook, *Commanding Right and Forbidding Wrong* (Cambridge: Cambridge University Press, 2001), 362.

A Discussion of the Views of Ibn Rushd

If you were to say: The statements of the *Muqaddimāt*'s author [Ibn Rushd] and the ancient jurists concern a case in which [a person's embrace of] Islam is a new development which occurs for [a person] residing among the polytheists. In contrast, the case in question is one in which residence [among the polytheists] is a new development while the original [state was the person's] Islam. There is a vast difference between these two cases and it is not appropriate to infer the law for the present case from [the first case].

I [al-Wansharīsī] say: The deliberations of the early jurists concerned the neglect of [the obligation of] migration in general, and they chose one such case as an example: the case in which a person converts to Islam while in the abode of war and remains there. The case [now] in question [125] is a second example of this. It is no different from the first example except for the detail about residence [in the abode of unbelief] being a new development. Thus, whereas in the first example, a [person's conversion to] Islam is a new development on [an original state] of residence [in the abode of unbelief], in the second case, residence [in the abode of unbelief] is a new development on an [original state of] Islam. The difference between them regarding which developed most recently is insignificant and does not warrant deeming the rule to be entirely restricted [to the first example]. Rather, the rightly guided imāms who preceded us focused their discussion on the case of someone who converted to Islam and did not migrate [only] because polytheistic rule [over Muslims] was absent in the early Islamic period. The events mentioned [by the questioner] only happened hundreds of years after the master-jurists (*mujtahid*) of the garrison towns had perished and there is no doubt that it was for this reason that none of them turned their attention to the legal rules [of this case]. Then when Christian rule [over Muslims] arose beginning in the fifth century after the [Prophet's] migration,[27] when the accursed Christians, may God destroy them, annexed the island of Sicily[28] and some parts of al-Andalus, some jurists were asked about it and about the legal rules which applied to someone who perpetrates [the act of remaining under Christian rule]. They answered: The rules are in accordance with the rules of someone who converts to Islam but does not migrate. They assimilated the latter [case] to the case in question on which the law was unestablished. They rendered the two groups equal with respect to the legal rules pertaining to their property and children and saw no difference between them. This is because both of them are under the rule of the

27 That is, the 11th century A.D.

28 The Norman offensive in Sicily began in 1068.

enemy, dwelling among them, consorting with them, enmeshed with them, and undistinguished from them. The neglect of the obligatory migration and flight and the other matters which these laws entail—which are [as yet] unestablished in the case in question—are [in fact] one and the same [in both cases]. So [the jurists], may God be pleased with them, assimilated the rule of that case to the one in which the ruling was unestablished.[29] Thus the independent judicial reasoning (*ijtihād*) of the later jurists merely involved assimilating the case on which the law was unestablished with that [of the case] in which it had been articulated, equating them in their underlying principle in all respects. The rulings of the jurists, may God be pleased with them, were made with correct speculation and cautious use of *ijtihād* and are supported by the positions of the rightly guided imāms who preceded them. They are therefore of the utmost excellence and beauty.

Evidence from the *Ḥadīth*

As for evidence from the tradition (*sunna*) regarding the prohibition against residence [in the abode of unbelief], consider [the tradition] included by al-Tirmidhī:

> The Prophet, may God bless him and grant him peace, dispatched a raiding party to Khathʿam. Some people sought protection by performing prostration,[30] but they quickly killed them. This news reached the Prophet, may God bless him and grant him peace. He ordered payment of half the blood money, saying "I am not responsible for any Muslim who resides among the polytheists." They said, "For what reason, O Messenger of God?" He said, "Their fires should not be in sight of one another."[31]

---

29 There is a dittography of *maskūt* in this line.

30 There is a difference of opinion as to what this prostration signifies. For Ibn al-ʿArabī, their prostration was a spur of the moment, improvised, attempt to convert to Islam (see below). This reading of the *ḥadīth* is supported by G.H.A. Juynboll, *Encyclopedia of Canonical Ḥadīth* (Leiden: Brill, 2007), 245. According to another scholar, the Banū Khathʿam were a tribe which had already converted to Islam at the time of Muḥammad's raid but were nonetheless in conflict with the Muslim community. The Banū Khathʿam made prostrations not to convert, but to demonstrate to the Muslim raiders that they were Muslims. See R.B. Serjeant "The 'Sunnah Jāmiʿah' Pacts with the Yathrib Jews, and the 'Taḥrīm' of Yathrib," *BSOAS* 41 (1978), 20.

31 *Sunan al-Tirmidhī*, no. 1604. "Their fires should not be in sight of one another," i.e., Muslims should not live so close to polytheists that they are able to see the fires of their hearths.

Also in the same chapter: "The Prophet, may God bless him and grant him peace, [126] said 'Do not dwell among and associate with the polytheists for one who dwells among and associates with them is one of them.'"[32] The textual evidence provided by these two *ḥadīth*s of what is intended is such that it will be apparent to anyone who possesses good insight and who can properly weigh the evidence. These two *ḥadīth*s have been established as sound (*ḥasān*)[33] in the six compilations of tradition around which the mill of Islam revolves. They said that there is nothing which opposes [these traditions]—no abrogation, nothing which would limit them to a special set of circumstances, etc. No Muslim disagrees regarding what these two traditions require and this is sufficient support for them—this together with the corroborating evidence in the very words of the Book and in the principles of the Law. In Abū Dāwūd's *Traditions*, there is a *ḥadīth* on the authority of Muʿāwiya,[34] who said: "I heard the Messenger of God, may God bless him and grant him peace, say '[The obligation of] migration will not cease until repentance ceases; and repentance will not cease until the sun rises in the West.' "[35]

There is also a *ḥadīth* on the authority of Ibn ʿAbbās (d. 68/687) which says, "The Messenger of God, may God bless him and grant him peace, said on the day of the conquest of Mecca, 'There is no [obligation of] migration after the conquest [of Mecca], but only *jihād* and intention; so if you are called [for *jihād*], offer yourself up.' "[36]

Ways of Reconciling Contrary *Ḥadīth*s on Migration

Abū Sulaymān al-Khaṭṭābī (d. 386/996 or 388/998)[37] said:

> At the beginning of Islam, migration was recommended but not obligatory, in accordance with the words of the Sublime, may He be exalted, "One who migrates in the way of God will find much refuge and

32 Ibid., no. 1650.

33 I.e., it has been determined by experts on *ḥadīth* that they genuinely emanated from the Prophet Muḥammad.

34 I.e., Muʿāwiya Ibn Abī Sufyān (d. 60/680), the Umayyad caliph.

35 For example, *Sunan Abī Dāwūd*, no. 2479 and *Sunan al-Nasāʾī*, no. 6711.

36 *Ṣaḥīḥ al-Bukhārī*, no. 2783 and *Ṣaḥīḥ Muslim* (Beirut: Dār al-Kutub al-ʿIlmiyya, 2003), no. 1353.

37 A Shāfiʿī scholar born in Bust (Sijistān), see Brockelmann, *Geschichte der arabischen Litteratur* (Leiden: Brill, 1949), 1: 165 and *Supplement*, 1: 275.

abundance in the earth" (Qur'ān 4: 100). This verse was revealed when the harm caused to the Muslims in Mecca by the idolaters became severe. It was then, when the Prophet, may God bless him and grant him peace, left for Medina, that migration became obligatory for Muslims. They were ordered to migrate to where he was in order to be together with him, to help one another, to make common cause in times of difficulty, and to study and come to understand religious matters. The greatest fear in that time was caused by the Quraysh tribe, who were the people of Mecca. When they [the Muslims] conquered Mecca and subdued them [the Quraysh], [migration] retained its meaning, but its obligation was removed, although it still remained recommended and desirable. There are two kinds of migration: one which is obligatory but which has been discontinued and one which remains [in effect], but is [only] recommended. This is how the two *ḥadīth*s are to be reconciled—although there is still the matter [of comparing] their chains of authority. The chain of authority of Ibn ʿAbbās's *ḥadīth* is authentic and traces back to the Prophet, the chain of authority of Muʿāwiya is contested.[38]

I [al-Wansharīsī] say: The two migrations mentioned in the *ḥadīth*s of Muʿāwiya and Ibn ʿAbbās are two [kinds] of migration whose obligation ceased with the conquest of Mecca. The first migration was made on account of fear for religion and life, like the migration of the Prophet, may God bless him and grant him peace, and his Meccan companions. This migration was an obligation for them without which their faith would not have sufficed. The second kind of migration was towards the Prophet, may God bless him and grant him peace, and to the abode in which he resided. Some made their oath of allegiance [to the Prophet] on the basis of their migration while others did so on the basis of their [faith in] Islam. But as for migration from the land of unbelief, it is an obligation until the Day of Resurrection.

Excerpts from Ibn al-ʿArabī's Works on the Status of Muslims Who Fail to Migrate

[127] Ibn al-ʿArabī said in the *Aḥkām*:

38 Abū Sulaymān al-Khaṭṭābī, *Kitāb Maʿālim al-Sunan*, published in the margins of *Sunan Abī Dāwūd*, ed. ʿIzzat ʿUbayd al-Daʿās and ʿĀdil al-Sayyid (Homs: Muḥammad ʿAlī al-Sayyid, 1969), 3: 8.

> Travel is divided into six categories. The first is migration and it is defined as leaving the abode of war for the abode of Islam. It was an obligation at the time of the Prophet, peace be upon him. This migration remains obligatory until the Day of Resurrection. The migration which ceased with the conquest [of Mecca] was that of journeying to the Prophet, may God bless him and grant him peace, in whatever place he was. If [someone] remains in the abode of war, he commits a sin, although there is a difference of opinion regarding his status.

You should [also] examine the remaining categories of migration [in Ibn al-ʿArabī's *Aḥkām*].[39]

Ibn al-ʿArabī: Even Those Who Barely Qualify as Muslims Because They Had Improper Conversions Receive Protection for their Lives and Property

[Ibn al-ʿArabī] said in *al-ʿĀriḍa*:[40]

> At first, God forbade Muslims to remain among the polytheists in Mecca and obligated them to join the Prophet in Medina. When God conquered Mecca, the obligation of migration expired but the prohibition against residing among the polytheists remained. Those [people of Khathʿam] who sought protection by performing prostration had not converted to Islam and resided among the polytheists. Their supplication for protection [through prostration] was [contrived] at the spur of the moment. It is true that, according to the consensus of the imāms, it is not permissible to kill someone who suddenly converts to Islam when he sees the sword over his head. They were killed, however, for one of two reasons. Either it was because prostration [in and of itself] does not oblige protection, since it is faith attested to by two pronouncements of the Declaration of Belief [that obliges protection]; or it was because those who killed them did not know that [prostration] had protected them. [The latter] is the

39 Muḥammad b. ʿAbdallāh Ibn al-ʿArabī, *Aḥkām al-Qurʾān*, ed. ʿAlī Muḥammad al-Bajāwī (Cairo: ʿĪsā al-Bābī al-Ḥalabī, 1967), 1: 484.

40 Ibn al-ʿArabī, *ʿĀriḍat al-aḥwadhī bi-sharḥ ṣaḥīḥ al-Tirmidhī*, ed. Jamal Marʿashlī (Beirut: Dār al-Kutub al-ʿIlmiyya, 1997), 7: 105–106.

correct explanation. This is because, [in another case], when Khālid[41] hastened to kill the Banū Jadhīma, they said, "We have left one religion for another" and they did not say, more appropriately, "We have converted to Islam," and therefore Khālid killed them. The Prophet, may God bless him and grant him peace, paid blood money to them on account of the error of Khālid. The errors of the ruler and his agents are recompensed by the treasury.[42]

He [Ibn al-ʿArabī] said: "This indicates that the pronouncement of 'There is no God but God, Muḥammad is the messenger of God" is not in actual fact a condition of conversion to Islam. [Conversion occurs even if a person merely says that he is a Muslim.][43] Indeed, [the Prophet] paid half of the blood money to [the people of Khathʿam] only on account of the truce and social welfare (*maslaḥa*). In the case of the people of Jadhīma, he paid double that in accordance with what the circumstances of each individual necessitated, taking [their estimations of this] at their word."[44]

Disagreements Regarding the Kinds of Protection Afforded to Muslims Living in the Abode of War

[Ibn al-ʿArabī continued:] "There is disagreement regarding someone who converts to Islam, remains in the abode of war and is then killed or his family taken prisoner and his money confiscated. Mālik said: 'His blood is protected, but anyone may take his property until he [re]takes

---

41 I.e., Khālid b. al-Walīd (d. 21/642) who was an Arab commander during the early conquests. See P. Crone, "Khālid b. al-Walīd," in *Encyclopaedia of Islam*, 2nd edition, 4: 928–29.

42 That is, because the Banū Khathʿam were Muslims, they would have been entitled to full blood money, but this was reduced on account of the special circumtances of the case. Muḥammad had sent a raiding party against them and this raiding party had to overwhelm the Banū Khathʿam before they were willing to submit. Thus the amount to which they would have been entitled was reduced as if by way of penalty. See the beginning of the *ḥadīth* upon which Ibn al-ʿArabī is commenting, *ʿĀriḍat al-aḥwadhī*, 7: 104. Cf. *Muṣannaf Ibn Abī Shayba fī al-aḥādīth wa'l-āthār* (Beirut: Dār al-Fikr, 1994), 8: 462.

43 This text, missing in al-Wansharīsī, appears in Ibn al-ʿArabī, *ʿĀriḍat al-aḥwadhī*, 7: 105.

44 The Banū Jadhīma were treated better than the Banū Khathʿam because Khālid's war against the Banū Jadhīma was initiated against the wishes of the Prophet. According to the sources, the Prophet expressed his disapproval of Khālid, deeply regretted the event, and compensated the tribe in excess of their losses. See ʿAbd al-Malik Ibn Hishām, *The Life of Muḥammad*, tr. A. Guillaume (Oxford: Oxford University Press, 1982), 561–62.

> possession of it in the abode of Islam.' [However,] it is [also] said that [this convert] possesses ownership of his property and family, and this is supported by the opinion of al-Shāfiʿī."[45]

This matter is recognized as one of those on which there is disagreement, a disagreement based on the issues of whether the resident of the abode of war can lawfully own property, and of whether what provides inviolability is Islam [itself] or [residence in] the abode [of Islam].[46] One who is of the opinion that [the Muslim convert residing in the abode of war] lawfully owns property adheres to the words of the Prophet, peace be upon him, "Has ʿAqīl left us any home?"[47] and to the Prophet's words, may God bless him and grant him peace, "I ordered that the people be fought until they say, 'There is no God but God,' and when they say it, they receive protection from me for their lives and their property, except by legal right."[48] [The Prophet] treated blood and property equally and used a possessive grammatical construction to show the relationship between them, and the possessive construction necessarily signifies ownership. He [the Prophet] then relates that those of them who convert to Islam possess inviolability, which means that no one [128] may in any way [wrongfully take what is theirs]. One who holds that [the convert living in the abode of war can] own property is also supported by the words of the Prophet, may God bless him and grant him peace: "One who converts for the sake of [maintaining ownership] over property retains ownership of it." [And are also supported] by the words of the Prophet, may God bless him and grant him peace: "The property of a Muslim man is not licit except by his consent." [However,] according

---

45 Ibn al-ʿArabī, *ʿĀriḍat al-aḥwadhī*, 106. Al-Shāfiʿī (d. 204/ 820) is the jurist for whom the Shāfiʿī legal school is named.

46 On the concept of "inviolability" in Islamic law, see Baber Johansen, "Der *ʿIṣma*-Begriff im Ḥanafitischen Recht," in *Contingency in a Sacred Law* (Leiden: Brill, 1999), 238–62.

47 This terse passage is the response which Muḥammad gave when he was asked whether he would stay in the house of his uncle, Abū Ṭālib, in which he had spent much of his youth. Since his uncle Abū Ṭālib had not converted to Islam, and there is a principle that Muslims cannot inherit from non-Muslims, only those of Abū Ṭālib's children who were non-Muslim, among whom was his son ʿAqīl, inherited from him. His Muslim sons, Jaʿfar and ʿAlī inherited nothing. It was thus up to ʿAqīl to decide whether he would allow Muḥammad to use his property. Those who claim that residents of the abode of war have the right to own property rely on this passage because it indicates that Muḥammad believed that non-Muslims, like Abū Ṭālib and ʿAqīl, have ownership rights which must be respected. See *Ṣaḥīḥ al-Bukhārī*, no. 4282 and *Ṣaḥīḥ Muslim*, no. 1351.

48 *Ṣaḥīḥ al-Bukhārī*, no. 20 and 2946 and *Ṣaḥīḥ Muslim*, no. 20.

to Mālik, Abū Ḥanīfa,[49] and those who agree with them, it is the abode which provides inviolability. A Muslim's property and children, the ownership of which have not been established in the abode of Islam and which are taken in the abode of unbelief, have the status of booty for the Muslims. It is as if, according to [Mālik and Abū Ḥanīfa], the unbelievers cannot hold [valid] ownership, and their property and children, like their lives, are licit for anyone who is able [to take them]. It is as if, when an unbeliever converts to Islam and does not establish ownership of his property or children in the abode of Islam, he has no property or children. It is as if they belong to the unbelievers just as their abode belongs to them and no Muslim has ownership while he dwells among them.

Does Islam or the Abode of Islam Provide Protection?

Ibn al-ʿArabī also said:[50]

> It is Islam which provides inviolability for a Muslim's life, but the abode which provides inviolability for his property. Al-Shāfiʿī said: "Islam provides inviolability for both of them." Abū Ḥanīfa said: " 'Effective protection' is from the abode but 'moral protection' is from Islam."[51] This means that, in the case of someone who converts to Islam but does not migrate and is killed, an act of atonement to God is required, but not blood money or retaliation. [However,] if this person had migrated, both an act of atonement to God and the blood money would have been obligatory for the patron responsible for these payments. It is thus said that, according to Mālik and al-Shāfiʿī, this convert's blood is [entirely] protected, whereas for Abū Ḥanīfa, an act of atonement to God is made, but blood money is not paid for his accidental killing. They adduce as evidence what is clear from what the Qurʾānic commentators say regarding His words, may He be exalted: "Those who believed but did not migrate from their homes, you have no duty to protect them until they leave their homes" (Qurʾān 8: 72), and His words, may He be exalted: "If he [the vic-

49 This jurist, for whom the Ḥanafī legal school is named, died in 150/767.

50 It is not possible to identify the work from which this passage was taken. It is possible that it was taken from Ibn al-ʿArabī's lost work, *al-Inṣāf fī masāʾil al-khilāf*.

51 That is, while a person deserves to have both his life and property protected by virtue of being a Muslim, in actual practice such protection can only be guaranteed by living in the abode of Islam.

tim] is of a people who are hostile to you, and he is a believer, then [the act of penance is] to set free a believing slave" (Qur'ān 4: 92)[52]—and [note that] blood money is not mentioned [in these verses]. [The commentators] said that the believer to which [this latter verse] refers is the Muslim who has not migrated and therefore, because he lives among the enemy, is [considered to be] one of them, in accordance with His words, may He be exalted, "Whoever among you who takes them as allies is one of them" (Qur'ān 5: 51). [The person referred to] is therefore a believer who lives among the enemy. When the beginning of the verse [4: 92] mentions blood money, it refers [both] to that for a believer in general and, at the end of the verse, to a believer who lives under a people who are under our pact or covenant, that is, the *dhimmīs* (non-Muslim subjects). It is silent [about blood money] for the believer who lives among the enemy and this indicates that it is not paid and that only an act of atonement to God is obligatory. This is the law of the blood [of Muslims who live among the unbelievers].

Ibn al-ʿArabī said:

This was an issue of great significance in Khurāsān[53] which the Mālikīs did not face and which the Iraqis did not know about, and so how [much less so] the Maghribī jurists who were followers of legal precedent, [not innovators]. Abū Ḥanīfa's companions adduce evidence for the claim that it is the abode which provides inviolability from the fact that it is fortresses and strongholds which guard, protect, and fend off [dangers]. [Consequently], the life and property of an unbeliever who comes to our abode are protected. His situation is like that of property: If it is [129] abandoned on the road, the punishment of [hand] amputation is not obligatory [for someone who takes it]; if it is held in someone's possession, it is guaranteed by the punishment of amputation.[54] Al-Shāfiʿī

52 That is, this act of penance is due if a believer is accidentally killed.

53 Khurāsān is a region which comprises parts of present-day northeastern Iran, southern Turkmenistan and northern Afghanistan.

54 I.e., the theft of property can only be punished if it has an established owner. If property lies abandoned in the road, there is no crime in taking it. An unbeliever's life and property can be taken in the abode of war because the abode of war is regarded as a kind of "no man's land" in which no ownership or protection can be established. However, if an unbeliever enters the abode of Islam, no doubt with the appropriate permission, he receives protection for his life and property.

> adduces evidence for his claim from the words of the Prophet, may God bless him and grant him peace: "I ordered that the people be fought [until they say, 'There is no God but God,' and when they say it, they receive protection from me for their lives and property, except by legal right]." This text indicates that it is Islam which provides inviolability for life and property. Even if a Muslim were to enter the abode of war, his life and property would be inviolable and [his location in that] abode would be of no account. [Therefore] the view of our companions [the Mālikīs] that Islam gives inviolability to life but not to children or property, and the view of the Ḥanafīs that protection and inviolability can only be bestowed through fortresses is incorrect. This is because they are based on a concept of *de facto* immunity[55] which can be achieved [even] by the unbeliever and by the bandit (*muḥārib*), but which is not acknowledged by the Law [to have value]—but surely the discussion should proceed according to what the Law acknowledges?! Can you not see that Muslim bandits and unbelievers can secure themselves in fortress, but it is [still] permissible to take their lives and property—in the case of [an unbeliever] under all circumstances, and in the case of [a bandit] provided that he stubbornly perseveres [in his activities]. Property, however, is only protected by its owner's keeping it with him in safekeeping.[56]

I [al-Wansharīsī] say: The opinion of Ashhab and Saḥnūn[57] agrees with the opinion of al-Shāfiʿī, and this is the opinion chosen by Abū Bakr Ibn al-ʿArabī, according to his words included here. The opinion of Abū Ḥanīfa and Asbagh Ibn al-Faraj[58] agrees with that of Mālik. This is the opinion chosen by Ibn Rushd and it is [also] the generally accepted view on the authority of Mālik, may God have mercy on him. Their source of disagreement is in accordance with what has been determined.

The famous jurist and judge, Abū ʿAbdallāh Ibn al-Ḥājj (d. 529/1134), and other later jurists, [also] discussed the property of the Muslim in question, [that is], the one who resides in the abode of war and does not leave after the tyrant comes to govern it. They compared it to the earlier disagreement among the scholars of the garrison towns regarding the property of someone who converts to Islam and remains in the abode of war. Then, after connecting and equating these rules, Ibn al-Ḥājj draws a distinction which indicates that

55 Literally, tangible immunity (*al-ʿiṣma al-ḥissiyya*).

56 Ibn al-ʿArabī, *Aḥkām al-Qurʾān*, 1: 477.

57 I.e., Saḥnūn b. Saʿīd (d. 240/854), see *EI*², 8: 843–45.

58 An Egyptian Mālikī jurist who died in 225/839.

property owned prior to conversion to Islam, in contrast to the property of a Muslim, is licit [as booty]. This is because the Muslim's ownership was never interrupted. His ownership was never preceded by an unbelief which would have made his property and children licit for the Muslims and no one, therefore, can have a [legitimate] claim against him. This [according to Ibn al-Ḥājj] is the preponderant opinion and is evident from ratiocination and from inferential reasoning from texts. This is [all] patently clear from contemplating the previously explained source of disagreement. Ibn al-Ḥājj supports the distinction [he has drawn] with a case included in the book of *jihād* in the *Samāʿ Yaḥyā*, and here it is, verbatim:

> I asked him [Ibn Nāfiʿ(d. 186/802–3)] about a Muslim Barcelonan who failed to leave that town within the year appointed for this after its conquest and who made raids against the Muslims, fearing that they would kill him if they were victorious. [Ibn Nāfiʿ] said, "I view his status as being no different from that of a bandit who robs [130] Muslims in the abode of Islam. This is because he remains within the religion of Islam. If he is apprehended, his case is brought before the ruler who judges it as he would judge people of corruption and banditry. As for his property, I do not think that it is licit for anyone to take it.

The relevant part of the passage ends here. Ibn Rushd said:

> Ibn Nāfiʿ's statement that those [Muslim residents of the abode of war] who make raids against Muslims are equivalent to bandits is correct. There is no disagreement about it because if a Muslim engages in banditry, he receives the same judgment, whether he engages in it in the lands of Islam or in the lands of unbelief. As for Ibn Nāfiʿ's statement that it is not licit for anyone to take [such a Muslim's] property, this is in clear disagreement with Mālik's statement in the *Mudawwana* regarding someone who converts to Islam in the abode of war after which the Muslims raid that abode taking his family and property. These things are all [legitimate] booty and [Mālik] does not distinguish between whether the army gains his property and children as booty before he leaves the abode [of war] or after.

I [al-Wansharīsī] say: It is clear that Ibn Rushd's statement indicates a different determination of evidential preponderance regarding the property and children of those in question than that of his contemporary and fellow townsman, the judge Abū ʿAbdallāh Ibn al-Ḥājj. So consider this matter. Some of the best authorities show that the rules which apply to the lives, children and property [of those who convert to Islam in the abode of war also] apply to those [Muslims] who dwell among Christian residents of the abode of war, but still take into account the difference of opinion on this issue and its settlement by way of a determination of preponderance. [According to these authorities], if they fight us with their allies, the view permitting the taking of their lives gains preponderance; and if they help them with their property in fighting us, then the view permitting the taking of their property gains preponderance. Permission for capturing their children has already been determined to have preponderance in order to free the children from their control and raise them among Muslims, safe from religious corruption and protected from the sin entailed in abandoning migration.

The Law Regarding Those Who Defame the Abode of Islam

Regarding the claim mentioned in the question [which prompted this *fatwā*], made by those who had migrated from the abode of war to the abode of the Muslims and then had angrily regretted it: From the perspective of the magnanimous *Sharīʿa*, their claim regarding the difficulty of earning a livelihood and loss of subsistence is an invalid claim and a worthless imagining. Only someone of weak conviction, or rather someone deficient in intellect and religion, could imagine or consider this notion to have any worth. How could someone imagine that this notion presents proof of the expiration of the obligation migration from the abode of war, while in the lands of Islam, may the word of God be exalted, there is a wide expanse for the powerful and for the weak, for the heavy and for the light?[59] God has made these lands expansive so that those who have been hurt by the unbelievers' assault and the Christian strike against religion, wife and children may seek refuge in them. A large and noble group of the greatest companions [of the Prophet], may God be pleased with them, migrated to the land of Abyssinia, fleeing with their religion from the persecution of the Meccan polytheists. [131] Among them were Jaʿfar b. Abī Ṭālib, Abū Muslima b. ʿAbd al-ʾAsad, ʿUthmān b. ʿAffān, and Abū ʿUbayda b. Jarrāh.[60] The event of [the migration to] Abyssinia is well-known. Others migrated to other places, leaving behind their homelands, property, children,

59 This sentence is perhaps modeled on the wording of Qurʾān 9: 41.

60 For an outline of this event, see Montgomery Watt, *Muḥammad at Mecca* (Oxford: Oxford University Press, 1953), 115 ff.

and ancestors, and rejecting, fighting and making war against [the polytheists], cleaving to their religion and spurning worldly concerns.

How [can someone propose this] when it so happens that abandoning [the abode of unbelief] does not infringe upon his ability to earn a living among the Muslims, and his rejecting it does not impact upon the abundance [available] to those seeking to acquire a livelihood. This is especially the case in the pious Maghrib, may God preserve it, increase its glory and nobility, and guard it from the vicissitudes of fortune and distress, from its heartlands to its frontier. God has made this land fertile and has spread it far and wide, especially the city of Fez and its districts, its surrounding region and area. If someone were indeed to accept this vain imagining [that is, imagining the superiority of the abode of war], then he is, God save us, devoid of complete reason, fully-developed views and understanding, and he has established both a sign and a proof of his despicable and contemptible soul by demonstrating the preponderance of his vile, worldly aims over the pious labors relating to the Hereafter. Giving such preference is truly wretched and [this person] has become lost and has gone astray by pursuing it. The migrant who regrets his migration from an abode in which the trinity is invoked, church bells are struck and in which Satan is worshipped has truly committed an act of unbelief against the Merciful One. A human being truly has nothing except his religion, for in it is his eternal salvation and his happiness in the Hereafter. Regarding someone who forsakes his precious soul by preferring abundant wealth, God, may He be exalted, said: "O you who believe! Let neither your wealth nor your children distract you from remembrance of God. Those who do so, they are the losers" (Qur'ān 63: 9). And He, may He be exalted, said: "Your wealth and your children are only a temptation whereas, by God, with Him is an immense reward" (Qur'ān 64: 15). According to the wise, the greatest and most sublime benefit of property is spending it in the way of God for the sake of pleasing Him. How could someone obstinately and hurriedly hurl himself into submission to the rule of the enemy when He, may He be exalted, said: "You see those in whose heart is a disease race towards them, saying: 'We fear lest a misfortune befall us.' [And it may happen that God will secure a victory for you, or a commandment from His presence. Then they will repent for their secret thoughts" (Qur'ān 5: 52). The misfortune referred to in this case is the relinquishing of real estate. [The person who perceives this to be a misfortune] is described as possessing a sick mind or weak conviction because, if he were strong in religion, firm in conviction, placing his confidence in God, may He be exalted, and fully relying on Him, he would not have neglected the principle of trust in God which is of the utmost degree of importance and of great profit and is a witness to the truth of faith and the firmness of conviction. [132] This having been established, there can be no concession of any kind for any of those who have been mentioned which would allow for a return [to the abode of unbelief] or for the abandonment of migration. [A person] cannot in any way be excused from this whether by claiming the presence of an oppressive difficulty or by making use of a delicate ruse (*ḥīla*). Rather, he must discover any means he can to release himself from the unbeliever's noose. [Even] under circumstances in which he cannot find a tribe to defend him and patrons to shelter him, and is [therefore] content to reside in a place in which religion is harmed and in which the public affirmations of Islamic norms are prohibited (*iẓhār shaʿāʾir al-muslimīn*), he [is considered to have] abandoned the religion and set out upon the path of the apostates. Fleeing from a territory conquered by the depraved polytheists to a territory in which there is peace and faith is an obligation. For this reason, they were given His words in answer to their excuse [for not migrating]: 'Was not God's earth spacious [that you could have migrated therein?' As for these, their abode will be hell, an evil journey's end]" (Qurʾān 4: 97). That is, wherever the migrant turns, even if he is weak, he will find spacious and adjacent land. There is therefore no excuse for someone who is able to migrate even if there is hardship involved in devising a strategy, earning a livelihood and maintaining a subsistence. There is only an exception for the oppressed person (*mustaḍaʿf*) who is constitutionally incapable, that is, who is unable to devise a strategy and who is not guided to any way [of migrating]. He who hurries to flee or hastens to depart from the abode of perdition to the abode of the pious has a manifest sign in the present world for what will become of him in the Hereafter. This is because there is an expectation of triumph and success for someone for whom the performance of virtuous deeds is made easy, but there is an apprehension of perdition and degradation for someone for whom the performance of evil deeds is made easy. May God make you and us among those who for whom prosperity is made easy and who benefit from admonition.

As for what you have mentioned about these migrants' repugnant words, their disparagement of the abode of Islam, their wish to return to the abode of polytheism, idols and other detestable abominations—these could only emanate from wicked people. They deserve disgrace in this world and in the Hereafter and must be brought down to the worst of abodes. It is obligatory for someone to whom God has given power in the land and for whom he has made prosperity easy to seize these people and impose a severe punishment on them, making a severe example of them by beating and imprisoning them so that they do not transgress the divine ordinances. This is because the corruption of these people is a worse harm than corruption proceeding from hunger, fear, kidnapping, and stealing property. This is because someone who is destroyed by the latter is given the mercy of God, may He be exalted, and His most noble pardon, whereas someone whose religion is destroyed is given the curse of God and His greatest anger. Love of polytheistic governance, dwelling among Christians, determination to reject migration, trusting in unbelievers, and contentment with paying the poll tax (*jizya*), with the Christian ruler's victory and with humiliation, while rejecting Islamic glory and obedience and allegiance to the Islamic ruler—these are great abominations, mortal blows almost tantamount to unbelief, God save us!

The Legal Credibility of Muslims Who Reside in the Abode of Unbelief

As for the legal credibility of those who remain [in the abode of unbelief], return there after having migrated, or who hope to return, they fall short of the religious perfection required for judging, witnessing and leading prayer. [133] This is an obvious and unquestionable matter for someone with even the weakest grasp of [the science of] interpreting substantive law and legal matters. Similarly, neither their testimony nor the communications of their judges are to be accepted. Ibn ʿArafa (d. 803/1401), may God have mercy on him, said: "It is stipulated that the acceptance of a judge's communications is dependent upon his valid appointment by someone who is himself validly appointed. This was done as a precaution against the communications of the Mudéjar judges, like the judges of Valencia, Tortosa, Pantelleria, and others like that."

The Legitimacy of Judges and Professional Witnesses Who Reside in the Abode of Unbelief

Imām Abū ʿAbdallāh al-Māzarī (d. 536/1141), may God have mercy on him, was asked in his time about whether or not, given the necessity [of their offices], one can accept the rulings of the Sicilian judges and the testimony of their professional witnesses when it is not known whether their residence under the unbelievers is by compulsion or by choice. He answered:

> Their testimony might be impugned in two ways. The first pertains to the issue of the judge's probity (*ʿadāla*) and his testimonial evidence—for residing in the abode of war under the leadership of the unbelievers is not permitted. The second pertains to his appointment, [that is,] whether he has been appointed by the unbelievers. Regarding the first, the principle which should be relied upon in this matter, and those like

it, is that of thinking well of Muslims and of disassociating Muslims from sinful acts. One should not deviate from this principle by harboring false thoughts and unfounded suspicions. Thus one approves [the testimony] of someone who has the appearance of probity although it is possible that he may in reality have secretly committed a grave sin—not only of someone whose freedom from sin is established. The [latter] possibility is rejected and the ruling based upon appearance has preponderance. An exception to this occurs if indications arise which might require this [presumption of] probity to be abandoned. Under such circumstances, it is obligatory to suspend judgment until the matter is clarified and the ruling [on his probity] becomes dependent on whatever is most probable.[61] I have already written about this in *Sharḥ al-Burhān* where I discussed the approaches of Abū al-Maʿālī and myself regarding the disagreements and disputes among the companions, may God be pleased with them.

As for [the judge's] residence in the abode of war, if it is under compulsion, it is clear that his probity is not impugned. This is also the case if he has a sound explanation [for being there]. For example, if his residence among [134] the people of war is out of hope of giving them [religious] guidance or delivering them from some error. This is stated by al-Bāqillānī (d. 403/1013). Mālik's companions have similarly permitted entering [the abode of war] for the purpose of ransoming prisoners. Moreover, if [the judge] resides there by choice, in ignorance of the law and without an explanation, this does impugn his probity. There is disagreement in the [Mālikī] school regarding whether to reject the evidence of someone who enters [the abode of war] by choice for the purpose of trading—and the disagreement regarding the interpretation of the *Mudawwana* is even more intense. In principle, [a Muslim resident of the abode of war] who appears to have probity, but regarding whom there is some doubt as to [the status of] his residence, is to be excused. This is because most of the aforementioned probable [reasons for his residence] indicate that he is to be excused. One cannot reject [his testimony] on the grounds of a single possibility except if there is evidence testifying that his residence was by choice, not on account of a [legitimate]

61 The following line, which seems to be corrupt, appears here in al-Wansharīsī's quotation of the *fatwā*, but not in Turki's edition: "A ruling is based upon circumscribed evidence whereas probity is based upon unrestricted evidence and so it is discounted [under these circumstances]." See Abdel-Magid Turki, "Consultation juridique d'al-Imām al-Māzarī sur le cas des musulmans vivant en Sicile sous l'autorité des Normands," *Mélanges de l'Université Saint-Joseph* 50 (1984), 689–704.

> cause. As for the second [factor which may compromise his probity], it is the issue of the unbeliever's appointment of judges, officials and others. If it [the appointment of a judge by non-Muslims] is for the purpose of restraining people [from harming] one another, then it is obligatory. To such an extent is this the case that some of the Mālikīs have declared it to be a rational obligation despite the fact that the judge's appointment by an unbeliever is [usually considered to be] void. On account of the people's need for him and his residing there out of necessity on their account, his authority is not impugned and the implementation of his rulings is not impaired—it is as if a Muslim ruler appointed him.
>
> In the [*Mudawwana*'s] book of oaths, in the case of someone who swears to grant a claim within an allotted time, he [Saḥnūn] established that the shaykhs of a locale stand in place of the ruler when he is absent out of fear that [the locale] might lack the exercise of justice.[62]

According to Muṭarrif (d. 282/895) and ʿAbd al-ʿAzīz Ibn al-Mājishūn (d. 164/780), the rulings of a just judge appointed by someone who rebelled against the ruler and conquered a territory are legally valid.

I [al-Wansharīsī] say: The Andalusī shaykhs issued a *fatwā* concerning those living under the rule of the apostate, ʿUmar Ibn Ḥafṣūn (305/918).[63] It said that neither their testimony nor the communications of their judges can be accepted. There is disagreement regarding whether [the authority] of judges appointed by an unjust ruler are to be accepted. In the *Garden of the Souls on the Generations of the Scholars of Ifrīqiya*[64] by [Abū Bakr ʿAbdallāh Ibn Muḥammad] al-Mālikī (d. 453/1061), Saḥnūn said:

> There was a disagreement between Abū Muḥammad ʿAbdallāh Ibn Farrūkh (d. 175/791) and Ibn Ghānim (190/806), the judge of Ifrīqiya. Both are among those who narrated from Mālik,[65] may God be pleased with him. Ibn Farrūkh said, "A judge should not accept a judicial post if

62 On the basis of Turki's edition of this *fatwā*, one can deduce that it ends here.

63 Ibn Ḥafṣūn was the leader of a rebellion (267–305/880–918) against the Umayyads in the Andalusian province of Reiyo (Málaga). Many of the jurists accused Ibn Ḥafṣūn, rightly or wrongly, of renouncing Islam and converting to Christianity. See Maribel Fierro, "Four Questions in Connection with Ibn Ḥafṣūn," in *The Formation of al-Andalus, Part 1: History and Society* (Aldershot: Ashgate, 1998), 292–328.

64 In Arabic: *Riyāḍ al-nufūs fī ṭabaqāt ʿulamāʾ Ifrīqiya.*

65 That is, they were both students of Mālik.

he is appointed by an unjust ruler." Ibn Ghānim said: "He is permitted to assume authority, even if the ruler is unjust." They wrote about this to Mālik. Mālik said: "The Persian, that is Ibn Farrūkh, is correct, and the one who claims he is an Arab, that is Ibn Ghānim, errs." Ibn ʿArafa said: "They [the Mālikīs] did not invalidate accepting [the authority] of the ruler's usurper for fear of suspending justice."[66]

The Fate in the Hereafter of Muslims Who Live in the Abode of Unbelief

[The above] has pertained to the worldly rules concerning [Muslims living in the abode of unbelief. The following] concerns the otherworldly [fate] of someone who passes through life, ruining his youth and old age by dwelling under their governance, not migrating or migrating and then returning to the land of unbelief, and persisting until death in committing this major act of disobedience, [135] God save us. The tradition and the scholars say that [such people] are given a severe punishment—although not an eternal one. This is based on their belief that the punishment for perpetrators of major sins ceases when, according to what is mentioned in sound reports, they are released through the intercession of our lord, prophet and master, Muḥammad, the elected and chosen one, may God bless him and grant him peace. An indication of this is contained in the words of God, the mighty and exalted: "God does not forgive a partner being associated with Him. He forgives all except that to whom He wills" (Qur'ān 4: 48). And His words: "Say: 'My servants who have exceeded the bounds, despair not of God's mercy, Who forgives all sins. He is the Forgiving, the Merciful' " (Qur'ān 39: 53). And His words: "Your Lord is full of forgiveness for humankind despite their wrongdoing" (Qur'ān 13: 6). There is an exception to this in His words which are very severe regarding them: "Whoever among you who takes them as allies is one of them" (Qur'ān 5: 51) and in the words

66 This is in potential conflict with Ibn ʿArafa's above statement (*al-Miʿyār al-Muʿrib*, 2: 133): "It is stipulated that the acceptance of a judge's communications is dependent upon his valid appointment by someone who is himself validly appointed. This was done as a precaution against the communications of the Mudéjar judges, like the judges of Valencia, Tortosa, and Pantelleria, and others like that." One pre-modern jurist understands Ibn ʿArafa's statement that the Mālikīs accept the authority of the ruler's usurper as referring to a situation prior to the advent of Christian rule over Muslims. After this point, the law changed. See Muḥammad b. Yūsuf al-ʿAbdārī al-Mawwāq, *al-Tāj wa'l-iklīl li-Mukhtaṣar Khalīl* (Ṭarābulus: Maktabat al-Najāḥ, 1969), 6: 143. For different versions of Ibn ʿArafa's statement, see *Fatāwā al-Burzulī* (Beirut: Dār al-Gharb al-Islāmī, 2002), 4: 49 and *al-Miʿyār al-muʿrib*, 10: 66 and 109.

of [the Prophet], peace be upon him: "I am not responsible for any Muslim who resides among the polytheists,"[67] and in the words of [the Prophet], peace be upon him: "... for one who dwells among and associates with them is one of them."[68]

The statements that you mentioned by the fool who is ignorant of religion are the epitome of scorn and contempt, including his statement: "Is it [really] to here that one migrates [from there]?!" Regarding the fool's other statement, "If the ruler of Castille were to come to these parts, we would go to him [and ask him to return us there]," his words are repugnant and his tone is abominable.

The odiousness expressed in both of these statements is obvious to you, just as it is obvious that each deserves censure and severe reproach. Indeed, no one would utter such a thing or deem it permissible, save for one who would debase himself, who has lost—God save us—his senses, and who desires to overturn that which is authentic in both its chain of transmission and its content, and whose meaning no one in all the Islamic world, from east to west, disputes. He does this as a result of aims which are invalid in the eyes of the Law and which are nonsensical. These foolish aims could only issue from someone over whose heart Satan has gained mastery and who has made him forget the sweetness of faith and where faith is geographically located.

Whoever commits and is ensnared in this sin has hastened the punishment for which his vile and despicable soul is liable [both] in this world and in the Hereafter. He is not, however, equal in disobedience [to God], sin, animus, abhorrence, odiousness, remoteness from God, impairment, blameworthiness, and deservedness of censure as someone who completely abandons [the obligation of] migration by living under the governance of the enemy and dwelling among those who are remote from God. This is because the full extent of what has issued from these repugnant people is a resolution—that is, a determination and mental preparation for action—but they have not carried it out.

Is There Such a Thing as "Thought Crime" in Islamic Law or are Punishments Only for Evil Acts?

Our Ashʿārī[69] imāms have disagreed regarding the assignment of blame [for bad thoughts]. The imām, Abū ʿAbdallāh al-Māzarī, may God have mercy on him, transmitted on the authority of many [scholars] the tradition that, in principle,

67 *Sunan al-Tirmidhī*, no. 1604; *Sunan Abū Dāwūd*, no. 2645; and *Sunan al-Nasāʾī*, no. 4780.

68 *Sunan al-Tirmidhī*, no. 1650.

69 A theological school named for Abū al-Ḥasan al-Ashʿarī (d. 324/935–6). See *Encyclopedia of Islam*, 2nd ed., s.v., "Ash̲ʿariyya."

one does not assign blame for them, this being on account of the words of [the Prophet], [136] peace be upon him, "God disregards the [evil] inner thoughts of His community [so long as they do not voice and act upon them]."[70] The judge, Abū Bakr al-Bāqillānī, said: "He is assigned blame for them." He drew his proof from the *ḥadīth*: "If two Muslims cross swords, then both the killer and the killed go to hell. It was said, 'O Messenger of God, this for the murderer, but why for the murdered?' He said, 'Surely he [too] was desirous of killing his companion,'"[71] his sin was thus his desire. [Al-Bāqillānī] was answered: "The meeting and sword drawing was an action"—that was the "desire" that was intended. It is said in Qāḍī ['Iyāḍ]'s *Ikmāl*:[72]

> On account of the many *ḥadīth*s that indicate that blame is assigned for actions of the heart, most of the early jurists, the theologians and *ḥadīth* transmitters construed the *ḥadīth*s which did not assign blame to refer to having something in mind [*hamm*], [rather than having a firm resolution (*'azm*)]. [Sufyān] al-Thawrī (d. 161/ 778) was asked, "Can we be blamed for having something in mind?" He responded: "[Only] if it was a resolution (*'azm*)." But they [the jurists also] said: "One is blamed for the evil of a resolution because it is an act of disobedience to God, but not for the evil of what is intended, because that has not [yet] been accomplished. If he does it, he is inscribed for a second sin, but if he restrains himself from committing it, he is inscribed for a good deed according to the *ḥadīth*: "Indeed, he abandoned it for My sake."[73] Muḥyī al-Dīn al-Nawawī (d. 676/1277) said: "The texts have given clear evidence regarding blame on account of resolution. For example, His words, may He be exalted, 'Those who love slander to be spread about those who believe [will have a painful punishment in this world and the Hereafter]' (Qur'ān 24: 19). And His words, may He be exalted, 'Avoid much suspicion, for some suspicion is a sin' (Qur'ān 49: 12). The community thus came to a consensus on prohibiting the envying and scorning of people and the desiring of repugnant things."

The [above] argument could be objected to on the grounds that the "resolution" regarding which there is disagreement is one which has an external

70 *Ṣaḥīḥ al-Bukhārī*, no. 5269 and *Ṣaḥīḥ Muslim*, no. 127.

71 *Ṣaḥīḥ al-Bukhārī*, no. 31 and *Ṣaḥīḥ Muslim*, no. 2888.

72 I.e., 'Iyāḍ Ibn Mūsā (d. 544/1149), *Ikmāl al-Mu'lim bi-fawā'id Muslim*.

73 *Ṣaḥīḥ Muslim*, no. 205.

expression, for example, fornication and wine drinking. As for one which has no external expression, like beliefs and evil thoughts such as envy and the like, these are not subject to disagreement. This is because the prohibition against these is in itself. It is on account of the act itself [thinking these thoughts] that the commandment exists, [and the prohibition] is not justified on the basis of any consensus regarding it.

Conclusion

So let this be the end of the written answer to the instructive question by the great jurist, the excellent preacher, the enduring righteous model, the immaculate and excellent, just and pleasing totality, Abū ʿAbdallāh Ibn Quṭiyya, may God preserve his exaltedness and ascendancy. It is appropriate to give this *fatwā* a title: "The Most Exalted of All Transactions: A Clarification of the Laws Pertaining to One Whose Land Has Been Conquered by the Christians and Has Not Migrated and What Punishments and Restrictions Apply to Him." By God, I ask that this response be of benefit and that my reward be doubled on account of it. This was written by the poor slave who seeks God's forgiveness, ʿUbaydallāh Aḥmad b. Yaḥyā b. Muḥammad b. ʿAlī al-Wansharīsī, may God grant him success. It was completed on Sunday, the 19th of the holy month of Dhū al-Qaʿda in the year 896.[74] May God acquaint us with His good.

74 The Gregorian equivalent is (approximately) September 23, 1491. Van Koningsveld and Wiegers suggest that this date might be incorrect as the day of the week does not correctly correspond to the date—the 19th is a Friday, not a Sunday. This in itself would not be enough to reject the date recorded in the printed editions as such two-day discrepancies can occur in dating systems which depend on local sightings of the moon. Van Koningsveld and Wiegers do, however, cite the catalog of Michael Casiri which lists a version of this manuscript as having been composed in 898 (1493). This year has the advantage that 19 Dhū al-Qaʿda occurs on a Sunday. There is no satisfactory way of arbitrating between these two datings. See P.S. van Koningsveld and G.A. Wiegers, "The Islamic Statute of the Mudéjars," 53 and Michael Casiri, *Bibliotheca arabico-hispaña escurialensis* (Madrid: Antonius Perez de Soto, 1760–70), 2: 170, no. 1753. 2.

Bibliography

Sources in Arabic

ʿAbbās, Iḥsān. *al-ʿArab fī Ṣiqilliyya*. Beirut: Dār al-Thaqāfa, 1975.

ʿAbd al-Karīm, Muḥammad. *Ḥukm al-hijra min khilāl thalāth rasāʾil jazāʾiriyya*. Algiers: al-Sharika al-Waṭaniyya li'l-Nashr wa'l-Tawzīʿ, 1981.

ʿAbd al-Wahhāb al-Baghdādī. *al-Ishrāf ʿalā nukat masāʾil al-khilāf*, ed. Abū ʿUbayda Mashhūr b. Ḥasan Āl Salmān. 6 vols. Riyadh: Dār Ibn al-Qayyim, 2008.

———. *al-Maʿūna ʿalā madhhab ʿālim al-Madīna*, ed. Ḥasan Muḥammad Ḥasan Ismāʿīl al-Shāfiʿī. 2 vols. Beirut: Dār al-Kutub al-ʿIlmiyya, 1998.

———. *Kitāb al-talqīn fī al-fiqh al-Mālikī*. Rabat: al-Mamlaka al-Maghribiyya, Wizārat al-Awqāf wa'l-Shuʾūn al-Islāmiyya, 1993.

Abū Dāwūd. *Sunan*. Cairo: al-Maktaba al-Tijāriyya al-Kubrā, 1935.

Abū al-Fatḥ, Aḥmad. *Kitāb al-mukhtārāt al-fatḥiyya fī tārīkh al-tashrīʿ wa-uṣūl al-fiqh*. Cairo: Maṭbaʿat al-Nahḍa, 1924.

al-ʿAdawī, ʿAlī b. Aḥmad al-Ṣaʿīdī. *Ḥāshiya ʿalā kifāyat al-ṭālib al-rabbānī li-Risālat Ibn Abī Zayd al-Qayrawānī*. 2 vols. Cairo: Muṣṭafā al-Bābī al-ḥalabī, 1938.

Anon., *al-Ḥadīqa al-mustaqilla al-naḍira fī al-fatāwā al-ṣādira ʿan ʿulamāʾ al-ḥaḍra*, ed. Jalāl ʿAlī Juhānī. Beirut: Dār Ibn Ḥazm, 2003.

al-Anṣārī, Abū Yūsuf Yaʿqūb b. Ibrāhīm. *al-Radd ʿalā siyar al-Awzāʿī*. Cairo: Maktabat Dār al-Hidāya, n.d.

al-Baghdādī, Ismāʿīl Bāshā. *Hadiyat al-ʿārifīn: asmāʾ al-muʾallifīn wa-āthār al-muṣannifīn*. 2 vols. Beirut: Dār Iḥyāʾ al-Turāth al-ʿArabī, 1990.

al-Bājī, Abū al-Walīd Sulaymān b. Khalaf. *al-Muntaqā: Sharḥ Muwaṭṭaʾ Mālik*, ed. Muḥammad ʿAbd al-Qādir Aḥmad ʿAṭā. 9 vols. Beirut: Dār al-Kutub al-ʿIlmiyya 1999.

al-Balghaythī, Aḥmad b. al-Maʾmūn, *Kitāb ḥusn al-naẓra fī aḥkām al-hijra*. Cairo: Maṭbaʿat ʿAbd al-Raḥmān, 1970.

al-Barādhiʿī, Khalaf b. Abī al-Qāsim. *Tahdhīb masāʾil al-Mudawwana* (*al-Tahdhīb fī ikhtiṣār al-Mudawwana*), ed. Aḥmad Farīd al-Mazīdī. 2 vols. Beirut: Dār al-Kutub al-ʿIlmiyya, 2006.

al-Bayhaqī, Aḥmad b. al-Ḥusayn. *Sunan al-Kubrā*. 10 vols. Hyderabad: Maṭbaʿat Majlis Dāʾirat al-Maʿārif al-Niẓāmiyya, 1925.

Bello, Muhammad. *Infāq al-maysūr*. Legon: Institute of African Studies, University of Ghana, 1964.

al-Bukhārī, Muḥammad b. Ismāʿīl. *Ṣaḥīḥ al-Bukhārī*, ed. Muṣṭafā Baghā. 7 vols. Beirut: Dār Ibn Kathīr, 1993.

al-Burzulī, Abū al-Qāsim b. Aḥmad. *Fatāwā al-Burzulī: Jāmiʿ masāʾil al-aḥkām limā nazala min al-qaḍāyā biʾl-muftīn waʾl-ḥukkām*, ed. Muḥammad al-Ḥabīb al-Hayla. 7 vols. Beirut: Dār al-Gharb al-Islāmī, 2002.

al-Dabbāgh, ʿAbd al-Raḥmān b. Muḥammad. *Maʿālim al-īmān fī maʿrifat ahl al-Qayrawān*, ed. Ibrāhīm Shabbūḥ. Cairo: Maktabat al-Khānjī, 1968.

al-Fāsī, ʿAbdallāh. "al-ʿĀlim Muḥammad b. Jaʿfar al-Kattānī wa-kitābuhu Salwat al-anfās wa-muḥādathāt al-akyās mi-man uqbira min al-ʿulamāʾ waʾl-ṣulaḥāʾ bi-madīnat Fās." *al-Manāhil* 54 (1997): 116–162.

Faṭṭānī, Ismāʿīl Luṭfī. *Ikhtilāf al-dārayn wa-atharuhu fī aḥkām al-munākaḥāt waʾl-ʿāmalāt*. Cairo: Dār al-Salām liʾl-Ṭibāʿa waʾl-Nashr waʾl-Tawzīʿ waʾl-Tarjama, 1990.

Gannūn, Muḥammad b. al-Madanī. "Risāla fī al-hijra min arḍ al-ʿadūw." In *al-Tasliya waʾl-salwān li-man ibtilā biʾl-idhāya waʾl-buhtān*. Fez: lithograph, 1884.

al-Ghāmidī, ʿAlī b.ʿAbdallāh b. Musfir Āl Shuwayl. *al-Aḥkām al-fiqhiyya al-mutaʿalliqa biʾl-dākhil fī al-Islām*. Mecca: self-published, 2006.

al-Gharnāṭī, Abū Ḥayyān. *Al-Baḥr al-muḥīṭ*. 8 vols. Beirut: Dār Iḥyā al-Turāth al-ʿArabī, 1990.

Ḥajjī, Muḥammad. *al-Ḥarakah al-fikriyya biʾl-Maghrib fī ʿahd al-Saʿdīyīn*. 2 vols. Rabat: Dār al-Maghrib liʾl-Taʾlīf waʾl-Tarjama waʾl-Nashr, 1977.

———. *Mawsūʿat aʿlām al-Maghrib*. 10 vols. Beirut: Dār al-Gharb al-Islāmī, 1996.

———. *Naẓarāt fī al-nawāzil al-fiqhiyya*. Rabat: al-Jamʿiyya al-Maghribiyya liʾl-Taʾlīf waʾl-Tarjama waʾl-Nashr, 1999.

al-Ḥamrūnī, Aḥmad. *ʿAlam al-Zaytūna al-Shaykh Ibrāhīm al-Riyāḥī*. Tunis: Mīdiyā Kum, 1996.

al-Ḥaṭṭāb, Muḥammad b. Muḥammad. *Mawāhib al-jalīl li-sharḥ mukhtaṣar Khalīl*. 6 vols. Cairo: Maṭbaʿat al-Saʿāda, 1911.

Ibn ʿAbd al-Barr, Yūsuf b. ʿAbdallāh. *al-Kāfī fī fiqh ahl al-madīna al-Mālikī*. Beirut: Dār al-Kutub al-ʿIlmiyya, 2002.

Ibn Abdūn, Muḥammad b. Aḥmad. *Risāla fī al-qaḍāʾ waʾl-ḥisba*, ed. Fāṭimah al-Idrīsī. Beirut: Dār Ibn Ḥazm liʾl-Ṭibāʿa waʾl-Nashr waʾl-Tawzīʿ, 2009.

Ibn Abī Zayd al-Qayrawānī, Abū Muḥammad ʿAbdallāh. *Kitāb al-jāmiʿ fī al-sunan waʾl-ādāb waʾl-māghāzī waʾl-tārīkh*, ed. Muḥammad Abū al-Ajfān and ʿUthmān al-Baṭṭīkh. Beirut: Muʾassasat al-Risāla, 1985.

———. *Kitāb al-jihād min Kitāb al-nawādir waʾl-ziyādāt* (*Der heilige Krieg* (*ğihād*) *aus der Sicht der mālikitischen Rechtsschule*), ed. Mathias von Bredow. Beirut: Franz Steiner Verlag, 1994.

———. *al-Nawādir waʾl-ziyādāt ʿalā mā fī al-mudawwana min ghayrihā min al-ummahāt*, ed. ʿAbd al-Fattāḥ Muḥammad al-Ḥulw. 15 vols. Beirut: Dār al-Gharb al-Islāmī, 1999.

———. *Risāla*, ed. Léon Bercher. Algiers: Jules Carbonel, 1949.

Ibn al-ʿArabī, Muḥammad b. ʿAbdallāh. *Aḥkām al-Qurʾān*, ed. ʿAlī Muḥammad al-Bajāwī. 4 vols. Cairo: ʿĪsā al-Bābī al-Ḥalabī, 1967.

———. *ʿĀriḍat al-aḥwadhī li-sharḥ Ṣaḥīḥ al-Tirmidhī*. 7 vols. Beirut: Dār al-Kitāb al-ʿArabī, 1992.

———. *Kitāb al-qabas fī sharḥ Muwaṭṭaʾ Mālik ibn Anas*, ed. Muḥammad ʿAbdallāh Walad Karīm. 3 vols. Beirut: Dār al-Gharb al-Islāmī, 1992.

Ibn al-ʿArabī, Muḥyī al-Dīn. *al-Waṣāyā li-Ibn al-ʿArabī*. Cairo: Dār al-Ghad al-ʿArabī, 1988.

Ibn ʿArafa, Muḥammad b. Muḥammad. *Tafsīr Ibn ʿArafa*, ed. Jalāl al-Asyūṭī. 4 vols. Beirut: Dār al-Kutub al-ʿIlmiyya, 2008.

Ibn ʿĀṣim, al-Gharnāṭī, Abū Yaḥyā Muḥammad b. Muḥammad. *Jannat al-riḍā fī al-taslīm li-mā qaddara Allāhu wa-qaḍā*, ed. Ṣalāḥ Jarrār. 3 vols. Amman: Dār al-Bashīr, 1989.

Ibn ʿAskar, Muḥammad b. ʿAlī. *Dawḥat al-nāshir li-maḥāsin man kāna biʾl-Maghrib min mashāyikh al-qarn al-ʿāshir*, ed. Muḥammad Ḥajjī. Casablanca: Markaz al-Turāth al-Thaqāfī al-Maghribī, 2003.

Ibn ʿAṭīya, ʿAbd al-Ḥaqq b. Ghālib, *al-Muḥarrar al-wajīz fī tafsīr al-Kitāb al-ʿazīz*. Beirut: Dār al-Kutub al-ʿIlmiyya, 1993–95.

Ibn Baṭṭāl, ʿAlī b. Khalaf. *Sharḥ Ibn Baṭṭāl ʿalā Ṣaḥīḥ al-Bukhārī*, ed. Muṣṭafā ʿAbd al-Qādir ʿAṭā. 10 vols. Beirut: Manshūrāt Muḥammad ʿAlī Bayḍūn, Dār al-Kutub al-ʿIlmiyya, 2003.

Ibn Bassām al-Shantarīnī, Abū al-Ḥasan ʿAlī. *al-Dhakhīra fī maḥāsin ahl al-Jazīra*, ed. Iḥsān ʿAbbās. 8 vols. Beirut: Dār al-Thaqāfa, 1979.

Ibn Farḥūn, Ibrāhīm b. ʿAlī. *al-Dībāj al-mudhahhab fī maʿrifat aʿyān ʿulamāʾ al-madhhab*. Cairo, 1932.

Ibn Fūdī, ʿUthmān, *Bayān wujūb al-hijra ʿalā al-ʿibād*, ed. F.H. El Masri. Oxford: Oxford University Press, 1978.

Ibn Hajar al-ʿAsqalānī, Shihāb al-Dīn Aḥmad. *al-Durar al-kāmina fī aʿyān al-miʾah al-thāmina*, ed. Muḥammad Sayyid Jād al-Ḥaqq. 5 vols. Cairo: Dār al-Kutub al-Ḥadītha, 1967.

Ibn al-Hājib, ʿUthmān b. ʿUmar. *Jāmiʿ al-ummahāt*, ed. Abū ʿAbd al-Raḥmān al-Akhḍar al-Akhḍarī. Damascus: al-Yamāma, 1998.

Ibn al-Ḥājj al-ʿAbdarī al-Fāsī, Muḥammad b. Muḥammad. *al-Madkhal*. 4 vols. Beirut: Dār al-Kitāb al-ʿArabī, 1972.

Ibn Hanbal, Aḥmad b. Muḥammad. *Musnad al-Imām Aḥmad*. 8 vols. Beirut: Dār Iḥyā al-Turāth al-ʿArabī, 1993.

Ibn Ḥazm, Abū Muḥammad b. Aḥmad. *al-Muḥallā*, ed. Aḥmad Muḥammad Shākir. 11 vols. Cairo: Idārat al-Ṭibāʿa al-Munīriyya, 1934.

Ibn al-Jallāb, ʿUbaydallāh b. al-Ḥusayn. *al-Tafrīʿ*, ed. Ḥusayn b. Sālim al-Dahmānī. 2 vols. Beirut: Dār al-Gharb al-Islāmī, 1987.

Ibn Jubayr, Muḥammad b. Aḥmad. *Riḥla*, ed. W. Wright and M.J. de Goeje. Leiden: Brill, 1907.

Ibn Juzayy al-Gharnāṭī, Muḥammad b. Aḥmad. *Qawānīn al-aḥkām al-shar'iyya wa-masā'il al-furū' al-fiqhiyya*. Beirut: Dār al-'Ilm li'l-Malāyīn, 1968.

———. *Tafsīr Ibn Juzayy*. Beirut: Dār al-Kitāb al-'Arabī, 1983.

Ibn al-Khaṭīb, *al-Iḥāṭa fī akhbār Gharnāṭa*, ed. Muḥammad 'Abdallāh 'Inān. 4 vols. Cairo: Maktabat al-Khānjī, 1973.

Ibn Manṣūr, 'Abd al-Wahhāb. *Mushkilat al-ḥimāya al-qunṣuliyya bi'l-Maghrib min nash'atihā ilā mu'tamar Madrīd, sanat 1880*. Rabat: al-Maṭba'a al-Malakiyya, 1977.

Ibn Nājī, Qāsim b. 'Īsā. *Sharḥ Ibn Nājī al-Tanūkhī 'alā matn al-Risāla li'l-Imām Abī Muḥammad 'Abdallāh b. 'Abd al-Raḥmān Ibn Abī Zayd al-Qayrawānī*, ed. Aḥmad Farīd al-Mazīdī. 2 vols. Beirut: Dār al-Kutub al-'Ilmiyya, 2007.

Ibn Rushd, Muḥammad b. Aḥmad (*al-jadd*). *al-Bayān wa'l-taḥṣīl wa'l-sharḥ wa'l-tawjīh wa'l-ta'līl fī masā'il al-mustakhraja*, ed. Muḥammad Ḥajjī. 20 vols. Beirut: Dār al-Gharb al-Islamī, 1984.

———. *Fatāwā Ibn Rushd*, ed. al-Mukhtār b. al-Ṭāhir al-Talīlī. 3 vols. Beirut: Dār al-Gharb al-Islāmī, 1987.

———. *al-Muqaddimāt al-mumahhidāt*, ed. Muḥammad Ḥajjī. 3 vols. Beirut: Dār al-Gharb al-Islāmī, 1988.

Ibn al-Qaṭṭān al-Marrākushī, Ḥasan b. 'Alī. *Naẓm al-jumān li-tartīb mā salafa min akhbār al-zamān*, ed. Maḥmūd 'Alī Makkī. Beirut: Dār al-Gharb al-Islāmī, 1990.

Ibn al-Qūṭiyya, Muḥammad b. 'Umar. *Tārīkh iftitāḥ al-Andalus*, ed. P. de Gayangos, E. Saavedra and F. Codera. Madrid: Revista de Archivos, 1926.

Ibn Rushd, Muḥammad. b. Aḥmad (*al-ḥafīd*). *Bidāyat al-mujtahid*. 2 vols. Beirut: Dār al-Ma'rifa, 1982.

Ibn Sahl, Abū al-Aṣbagh 'Īsā. *Dīwān al-aḥkām al-kubrā: al-Nawāzil wa'l-a'lām li-Ibn Sahl*, ed. Rashīd al-Na'īmī. 2 vols. Riyadh: Rashīd al-Na'īmī, 1997.

Ibn Sallām al-'Ibāḍī, *Kitāb fīhi bad' al-Islām wa-sharā'i' al-dīn*, ed. Werner Schwartz. Wiesbaden: Franz Steiner, 1986.

Ibn Sarrāj al-Andalusī, Abū al-Qāsim. *Fatāwā Qāḍī al-Jamā'a Abī al-Qāsim Ibn Sarrāj al-Andalusī*, ed. Muḥammad Abū al-Ajfān. Abu Dhabi: al-Majma' al-Thaqāfī, 2000.

Ibn al-Shāhid, Abū 'Abdallāh Muḥammad. "Risālat Ibn al-Shāhid." In *Ḥukm al-hijra min khilāl thalāth rasā'il jazā'iriyya*, ed. Muḥammad 'Abd al-Karīm, 105–24. Algiers: al-Sharika al-Waṭaniyya li'l-Nashr wa'l-Tawzī', 1981.

Ibn Shās, Jalāl al-Dīn 'Abdallāh b. Najm. *'Iqd al-jawāhir al-thamīna fī madhhab 'ālim al-Madīna*, ed. Muḥammad Abū al-Ajfān and 'Abd al-Ḥafīẓ Manṣūr. 3 vols. Beirut: Dār al-Gharb al-Islāmī, 1995.

Ibn Tūmart, Muḥammad. *Kitāb Muḥammad Ibn Tūmart mahdī al-muwaḥḥidīn*, ed. I. Goldziher. Algiers: P. Fontana, 1903.

Ibn Ward, Aḥmad b. Muḥammad. *Ajwibat Ibn Ward al-Andalusī al-musammāh bi-"al-jawābāt al-ḥisān 'an al-su'ālāt dhawāt al-afnān li-Qāḍī al-Jamā'a Abī al-Qāsim Aḥmad Ibn Ward al-Tamīmī"*, ed. Muḥammad al-Sharīf. Rabat: Ṭūb Barīs, 2008.

Ibn Zarb, Muḥammad b. Yaḥyā. *Kitāb al-Khiṣāl*, ed. ʿAbd al-Ḥamīd al-ʿAlamī. Rabat: Wizārat al-Awqāf wa'l-Shu'ūn al-Islāmiyya, al-Mamlaka al-Maghribiyya, 2005.

Ibn al-Zaydān, ʿAbd al-Raḥmān. *al-ʿIzz wa'l-ṣawla fī maʿālim naẓm al-dawla*. 2 vols. Rabat: al-Maṭbaʿa al-Malakiyya, 1961.

al-Ifrānī, Muḥammad al-Ṣaghīr b. Muḥammad. *Nuzhat al-ḥādī bi-akhār mulūk al-qarn al-ḥādī*, ed. O. Houdas. Paris: Leroux, 1888.

ʿIllaysh, Muḥammad b. Aḥmad. *Fatḥ al-ʿalī al-mālik fī al-fatāwā ʿalā madhhab al-Imām Mālik*. 2 vols. Beirut: Dār al-Maʿrifa, n.d.

———. *al-Radd ʿalā Risālat ajwibat al-hayārā ʿan ḥukm qalansuwwat al-naṣārā*. Cairo: Al-Azhar Manuscript, *fiqh ʿām*, 305297.

———. *Sharḥ manḥ al-jalīl ʿalā mukhtaṣar al-ʿallāma Khalīl*. 4 vols. Beirut: Dār al-Fikr, 1989.

ʿIyāḍ b. Mūsā al-Yaḥsubī, known as Qāḍī ʿIyāḍ. *Kitāb al-shifā bi-taʿrīf ḥuqūq al-Muṣṭafā*, ed. ʿAlī Muḥammad al-Bajāwī. 2 vols. Cairo: Maṭbaʿat ʿĪsā al-Bābī al-Ḥalabī, 1977.

———. *Al-Tanbīhāt al-mustanbaṭa ʿalā al-kutub al-mudawwana wa'l-mukhtalaṭa*, ed. M. al-Wathīq. 4 vols. Beirut: Dār Ibn Ḥazm, 2011.

———. *Tarājim Aghlabiyya mustakhraja min madārik al-qāḍī ʿIyāḍ*, ed. Muḥammad al-Ṭālibī. Tunis: al-Jāmiʿa al-Tūnisiyya, 1968.

———. *Tartīb al-madārik wa-taqrīb al-masālik li-maʿrifat aʿlām madhhab Mālik*, ed. Aḥmad Bukayr Maḥmūd. 5 vols. Beirut: Maktabat al-Ḥayāh, 1967.

al-Jazā'irī, Muḥammad Bāshā. *Tuḥfat al-zā'ir fī tārīkh al-Jazā'ir wa'l-amīr ʿAbd al-Qādir*, 2nd edition, ed. Mamdūḥ Ḥaqqī. Beirut: Dār al-Yaqẓa al-ʿArabiyya li'l-Ta'līf wa'l-Tarjama wa'l-Nashr, 1964.

al-Jīdī, ʿUmar b. ʿAbd al-Karīm. *Mabāḥith fī al-madhhab al-Mālikī bi'l-Maghrib*. Rabat: al-Hilāl al-ʿArabiyya li'l-Ṭibāʿa wa'l-Nashr, 1993.

———. *al-ʿUrf wa'l-ʿamal fī al-madhhab al-Mālikī wa-mafhūmuhumā ladā ʿulamā' al-Maghrib*. n.l.: Ṣundūq Iḥyā' al-Turāth al-Islāmī, 1984.

al-Jisr, Ḥusayn. *Kitāb al-risāla al-ḥamīdiyya fī ḥaqīqat al-diyāna al-Islāmiyya wa-ḥaqīqat al-sharīʿa al-Muḥammadiyya*. Cairo: al-Maṭbaʿa al-Ḥamīdiyya al-Miṣriyya, 1905.

Kaḥḥalah, ʿUmar Riḍā. *Muʿjam al-mu'allifīn: Tarājim muṣannifī al-kutub al-ʿArabiyya*. 15 vols. Damascus: al-Maktaba al-ʿArabiyya, 1961.

Karam, Idrīs. *al-ʿAlāqāt al-ijtimāʿiyya min khilāl al-nawāzil al-fiqhiyya bi'l-Maghrib*. Rabat: Éditions IDGL, 2005.

al-Kattānī, ʿAbd al-Ḥayy b. ʿAbd al-Kabīr. *Fihris al-fahāris wa'l-ithbāt wa-muʿjam al-maʿājim wa'l-mashyakhāt wa'l-musalsalāt*, ed. Iḥsān ʿAbbās. 3 vols. Beirut: Dār al-Gharb al-Islāmī, 1982.

al-Kattānī, Muḥammad b. Jaʿfar. *Naṣīḥat ahl al-Islām*, ed. Idrīs al-Kattānī. Rabat: Maktabat Badr, 1989.

———. *Salwat al-anfās wa-muḥādathat al-akyās bi-man uqbira min al-ʿulamā' wa'l-ṣulaḥā' bi-Fās*, ed. ʿAbdallāh al-Kāmil al-Kattānī, et al. 4 vols. Rabat: Dār al-Thaqāfa, 2004.

al-Kattānī, Jaʿfar b. Idrīs. *al-Dawāhī al-madhiyya li'l-firaq al-maḥmiyya: fī al-walā' wa'l-barā'*, ed. Abī Muḥammad al-Ḥasan b. ʿAlī al-Kattānī. Amman: Dār al-Bayāriq, 1999.

Khalīl b. Isḥāq al-Jundī, *Mukhtaṣar Khalīl*, ed. Ṭāhir Aḥmad al-Zāwī. Cairo: Dār Iḥyā' al-Kutub al-ʿArabiyya, 1980.

Khallāf, Muḥammad ʿAbd al-Wahhāb. *Wathā'iq fī aḥkām qaḍā' ahl al-dhimma fī al-Andalus: Mustakhrajah min makhṭūṭ al-Aḥkām al-kubrā li'l-Qāḍī Abī al-Aṣbagh ʿĪsā Ibn Sahl.* Cairo: Markaz al-ʿArabī, 1980.

Khaṭīb, Ismāʿīl. *al-Mukhtār min Taʿẓīm al-minna wa'l-Miʿyār fī badʿ al-ʿibādāt wa'l-ʿādāt wa'l-ṭuruqiyya.* Tetouan: Jāmiʿat al-Baʿth al-Islāmī, 1996.

al-Khaṭṭābī, Abū Sulaymān. *Kitāb Maʿālim al-Sunan*, in *Sunan Abī Dāwūd*, ed. ʿIzzat ʿUbayd al-Daʿās and ʿĀdil al-Sayyid. 3 vols. Homs: Muḥammad ʿAlī al-Sayyid, 1969.

al-Khuḍarī, Muḥammad. *Tārīkh al-tashrīʿ al-Islāmī*, 3rd ed. Cairo: Maṭbaʿat Dār Iḥyā' al-Kutub al-ʿArabiyya, 1930.

al-Maghīlī, Muḥammad b. ʿAbd al-Karīm. *Ajwibat al-Maghīlī ʿan as'ilat al-Amīn al-Ḥājj Muḥammad Askiyā*, ed. and tr. John O. Hunwick. London: Oxford University Press, 1985.

Makhlūf, Muḥammad b. Muḥammad. *Shajarat al-nūr al-zakiyya fī ṭabaqāt al-Mālikiyya.* 2 vols. Beirut: Dār al-Kitāb al-ʿArabī, 197?.

Makkī, Maḥmūd ʿAlī. "Wathā'iq ta'rīkhiyya jadīda ʿan aṣr al-murābiṭīn." In *Revista del Instituto de Estudios Islámicos en Madrid* 7–8 (1959–60): 109–98.

al-Mālikī, Abū Bakr ʿAbdallāh b. Muḥammad. *Kitāb riyāḍ al-nufūs fī ṭabaqāt ʿulamā' al-Qayrawān wa-Ifrīqiya*, ed. Bashīr al-Bakkūsh. 3 vols. Beirut: Dār al-Gharb al-Islāmī, 1983.

al-Manūfī al-Shādhilī, ʿAlī Abū al-Ḥasan. *Kifāyat al-ṭālib al-rabbānī li-Risālat Ibn Abī Zayd al-Qayrawānī*, in *Ḥāshiyah ʿalā Kifāyat al-ṭālib al-rabbānī*. 2 vols. Cairo: Muṣṭafā al-Bābī al-Ḥalabī, 1938.

al-Manūnī, Muḥammad. *al-Maṣādir al-ʿArabiyya li-tārīkh al-Maghrib.* 3 vols. Rabat: al-Mamlaka al-Maghribiyya, Jāmiʿat Muḥammad al-Khāmis, Kullīyat al-Ādāb wa'l-ʿUlūm al-Insāniyya, 1983.

———. *Maẓāhir yaqẓat al-Maghrib al-ḥadīth.* 2 vols. Beirut: Dār al-Gharb al-Islāmī, 1985.

al-Mawsūʿah al-fiqhiyya. 45 vols. Kuwait City: Dawlat al-Kuwayt, Wizārat al-Awqāf wa'l-Shu'ūn al-Islāmiyya, 1987-.

al-Mawwāq, Muḥammad b. Yūsuf al-ʿAbdārī. *al-Tāj wa'l-iklīl li-Mukhtaṣar Khalīl.* 6 vols. Tripoli: Maktabat al-Najāḥ, 1969.

al-Māzarī, Muḥammad b. ʿAlī. *Īḍāḥ al-maḥṣūl min Burhān al-uṣūl*, ed. ʿAmmār al-Ṭālibī. Beirut: Dār al-Gharb al-Islāmī, 2001.

Mazīn, Muḥammad. "Ḥaṣīlat isti'māl kutub al-nawāzil al-fiqhiyya fī al-kitāba al-tārīkhiyya al-Maghribiyya." In *al-Baḥth fī tārīkh al-Maghrib*, 73–93. Rabat: al-Mamlaka al-Maghribiyya, Jāmi'at Muḥammad al-Khāmis, Kullīyat al-Ādāb wa'l-'Ulūm al-Insāniyya bi'l-Ribāṭ, 1989.

Muslim Ibn al-Ḥajjāj. *Saḥīḥ Muslim*, ed. Muḥammad Fu'ād 'Abd al-Bāqī. 5 vols. Cairo: Dār Iḥyā' al-Kutub al-'Arabiyya, 1955.

al-Nafrāwī, Aḥmad b. Ghunaym. *Kitāb al-fawākih al-dawānī 'alā Risālat Ibn Abī Zayd al-Qayrawānī*. 2 vols. Cairo: Maṭba'at al-Sa'āda, 1913.

al-Nāṣirī, Aḥmad b. Khālid. *Kitāb al-istiqṣā li-akhbār duwal al-Maghrib al-aqṣā*, ed. Ja'far al-Nāṣirī and Muḥammad al-Nāṣirī. 9 vols. Casablanca: Dār al-Kitāb, 1954–1956.

Nu'mān b. Muḥammad, Abū Ḥanīfah, known as al-Qāḍī al-Nu'mān. *Risālat iftitāḥ al-da'wa*, ed. Wadād al-Qāḍī. Beirut: Dār al-Thaqāfa, 1970.

Nuwayhiḍ, 'Ādil. *Mu'jam a'lām al-Jazā'ir min ṣadr al-Islām ḥattā muntaṣaf al-qarn al-'ishrīn*. Beirut: al-Maktab al-Tijārī li'l-Ṭibā'a wa'l-Nashr wa'l-Tawzī', 1971.

al-Qādirī, Muḥammad b. al-Ṭayyib. *Nashr al-mathānī li-ahl al-qarn al-ḥādī 'ashar wa'l-thānī*, ed. Muḥammad Ḥajjī and Aḥmad al-Tawfīq. 4 vols. Rabat: Maktabat al-Ṭālib, 1982.

al-Qarāfī, Shihāb al-Dīn Aḥmad b. Idrīs, *al-Dhakhīra*, ed. Muḥammad Ḥajjī. 15 vols. Beirut: Dār al-Gharb al-Islāmī, 1994.

———. *Sharḥ tanqīḥ al-fuṣūl fī ikhtiṣār al-maḥṣūl fī al-uṣūl*, ed. Ṭāhā 'Abd al-Ra'ūf Sa'd. Cairo: Maktabat al-Kulliyyāt al-Azhariyya, 1973.

al-Qurṭubī, Muḥammad b. Aḥmad al-Anṣārī. *al-Jāmi' li-aḥkām al-Qur'ān*. 20 vols. Cairo: Dār al-Kātib al-'Arabī, 1967.

Razzūq, Muḥammad. *al-Andalusiyyūn wa-hijrātuhum ilā al-Maghrib*. Casablanca: Ifrīqiya al-Sharq, 1989.

Sa'd Allāh, Abū al-Qāsim. *Tārīkh al-Jazā'ir al-thaqāfī: Min al-qarn al-'āshir ilā al-rābi' 'ashar al-Hijrī (16–20 m.)*. 2 vols. Algiers: al-Sharika al-Waṭaniyya, 1981.

Saḥnūn b. Sa'īd al-Tanūkhī. *al-Mudawwana al-kubrā*. 4 vols. Beirut: Dār al-Kutub al-'Ilmiyya, 1994.

al-Ṣamadī, Muṣṭafā. *Fiqh al-nawāzil 'inda al-Mālikiyya: Tārīkh*^{an} *wa-manhaj*^{an}. Riyadh: Maktabat al-Rushd Nāshirūn, 2007.

Ṣaqr, Nādiya Ḥusnī. *Dawr 'Abd al-Raḥmān al-Nāṣir fī irjā' ḥarakat al-istirdād*. Mecca: al-Maktaba al-Fayṣaliyya, 1985.

al-Ṣāwī, Aḥmad b. Muḥammad. *Bulghat al-sālik li-aqrab al-masālik ilā madhhab al-Imām Mālik 'alā al-Sharḥ al-ṣaghīr li'l-quṭb al-shahīr Aḥmad b. Muḥammad b. Aḥmad al-Dardīr*. 2 vols. Cairo: Muṣṭafā al-Bābī al-Ḥalabī, 1952.

al-Sayyid, Riḍwān. "al-Dār wa'l-hijra wa-aḥkāmuhumā 'inda Ibn al-Murtaḍā." *al-Ijtihād* 12 (1991): 213–40.

Sharḥabīlī, Muḥammad b. Ḥasan. *Taṭawwur al-madhhab al-Mālikī fī al-gharb al-Islāmī ḥattā nihāyat al-'aṣr al-Murābiṭī.* Rabat: al-Mamlaka al-Maghribiyya, Wizārat al-Awqāf wa'l-Shu'ūn al-Islāmiyya, 2000.

al-Sharīf, Muḥammad. *al-Maghrib wa-ḥurūb al-istirdād.* Tetouan: Jāmi'at 'Abd al-Mālik al-Sa'dī, Kullīyat al-Ādāb wa'l-'Ulūm al-Insāniyya, 2005.

al-Shāṭibī, Ibrāhīm b. Mūsā. *Fatāwā al-Imām al-Shāṭibī*, ed. Muḥammad Abū al-Ajfān. Tunis: n.p., 1985.

Shaykha, Jum'a. "Ba'd al-Maẓāhir al-dīniyya fī riḥlat 'Abdallāh b. al-Ṣabāḥ al-Andalusī." *Dirāsāt Andalusiyya* 12 (1994): 38–45.

al-Subkī, Taqī al-Dīn 'Alī b. 'Abd al-Kāfī. *Fatāwā al-Subkī.* 2 vols. Cairo: Maktabat al-Qudsī, 1936.

al-Ṭabarī, Muḥammad b. Jarīr. *Kitāb ikhtilāf al-fuqahā*, ed. Joseph Schacht. Leiden: Brill, 1933.

Ṭāḥā, 'Abd al-Wāḥid Dhannūn. "Aḥmiyyat al-kutub al-fiqhiyya fī dirāsat tārīkh al-Andalus." In *al-Ḥaḍāra al-Andalusiyya fī al-zamān wa'l-makān*, 119–55. Mohammedia: Jāmi'at al-Ḥasan al-Thānī, Kullīyat al-Ādāb wa'l-'Ulūm al-Insāniyya III, 1993.

al-Tasūlī, 'Alī b. 'Abd al-Salām. *Ajwibat al-Tasūlī 'an masā'il al-Amīr 'Abd al-Qādir fī al-jihād*, ed. 'Abd al-Laṭīf Aḥmad al-Shaykh Muḥammad Ṣālih. Beirut: Dār al-Gharb al-Islāmī, 1996.

al-Tha'ālibī, 'Abd al-Raḥmān. *al-Jawāhir al-ḥisān fī tafsīr al-Qur'ān*, ed. 'Ammār al-Ṭālibī. 5 vols. Algiers: al-Mu'assasa al-Waṭaniyya li'l-Kitāb, 1985.

al-Tunbuktī, Aḥmad Bābā. *Kitāb nayl al-ibtihāj bi-taṭrīz al-Dībāj.* Cairo: 'Abbās b.'Abd al-Salām b. Shaqrūn, 1932.

al-Tunbuktī, Aḥmad b. al-Qāḍī. *Muṣliḥ Fūlānī fī bilād al-Maghrib: Naṣīḥat Aḥmad ibn al-Qāḍī al-Tunbuktī ilā awwalī al-amr bi-Tūnis wa'l-Maghrib*, ed. Muḥammad al-Manṣūr and Fāṭimah al-Ḥarrāq. Rabat: Ma'had al-Dirāsāt al-Ifrīqiya, 2000.

al-Turūdī, 'Abdallāh Ibn Muḥammad. *Tazyīn al-waraqāt*, ed. M. Hiskett. Ibadan: Ibadan University Press, 1963.

al-'Umrānī, 'Abd al-Ḥayy Ḥasan. *al-Madhhab al-Mālikī wa-madā akhdhihi bi'l-maṣālīḥ al-mursala.* Rabat: al-Mamlaka al-Maghribiyya, Wizārat al-Awqāf wa'l-Shu'ūn al-Islāmiyya, 2003.

al-'Utbī, Muḥammad b. Aḥmad. *al-Mustakhraja min al-asmi'a mimmā laysa fī al-Mudawwana* [*al-'Utbīyah*]. In Ibn Rushd, *al-Bayān wa'l-taḥṣīl*, ed. Muḥammad Ḥajjī. 20 vols. Beirut: Dār al-Gharb al-Islamī, 1984.

al-Wansharīsī, Aḥmad b. Yaḥyā. *al-Mi'yār al-mu'rib wa'l-jāmi' al-mughrib 'an fatāwā ahl Ifrīqiya wa'l-Andalus wa'l-Maghrib*, ed. Muḥammad Ḥajjī. 13 vols. Rabat: Wizārat al-Awqāf wa'l-Shu'ūn al-Islāmiyya li'l-Mamlaka al-Maghribiyya, 1981.

———. *'Uddat al-burūq fī jam' mā fī al-madhhab min al-jumū' wa'l-furūq*. Beirut: Dār al-Gharb al-Islāmī, 1990.

al-Wansharīsī, Aḥmad b. Yaḥyā and Husayn Mu'nis (ed.). "Asnā al-matājir fī bayān aḥkām man ghalaba 'alā waṭanihi al-Naṣārā wa-lam yuhājir wa-mā yatarattabu 'alayhi min al-'uqūbāt wa'l-zawājir." *Revista del Instituto de Estudios Islamicos en Madrid* 5 (1957): 129–91.

al-Wazzānī, al-Mahdī (Muḥammad al-Mahdī b. Muḥammad al-'Imrānī). *al-Mi'yār al-jadīd (al-Nawāzil al-jadīda al-kubrā fī mā li-ahl Fās wa-ghayrihim min al-badw wa'l-qurā al-musammāh bi'l-Mi'yār al-jadīd al-jāmi' al-mu'rib 'an fatāwā al-muta'akhkhirīn min 'ulamā' al-Maghrib)*. 12 vols. Rabat: Wizārat al-Awqāf wa'l-Shu'ūn al-Islāmiyya li'l-Mamlaka al-Maghribiyya, 1996.

———. *al-Nawāzil al-ṣughrā al-musammāh al-minaḥ al-sāmiyah fī al-nawāzil al-fiqhiyya*. 4 vols. Rabat: al-Mamlaka al-Maghribiyya, Wizārat al-Awqāf wa'l-Shu'ūn al-Islāmiyya, 1992.

al-Yūbī, Laḥsan. "al-faqīh 'Alī b. 'Abd al-Salām al-Tasūlī wa-nawāziluhu." In *al-Nawāzil al-fiqhiyya wa-atharuhā fī al-fatwā wa'l-ijtihād*, 227–44. Casablanca: Jāmi'at al-Ḥasan al-Thānī, Kullīyat al-Ādāb wa'l-'Ulūm al-Insāniyya, 2001.

———. *al-Fatāwā al-fiqhiyya fī ahamm al-qaḍāyā min 'ahd al-Sa'dīyīn ilā mā qabla al-ḥimāya: Dirāsa wa-taḥlīl*. Rabat: al-Mamlaka al-Maghribiyya, Wizārat al-Awqāf wa'l-Shu'ūn al-Islāmiyya, 1998.

al-Zarrūq, Aḥmad b. Aḥmad. *Sharḥ Risālat Ibn Abī Zayd al-Qayrawānī*, ed. Aḥmad Farīd al-Mazīdī. 2 vols. Beirut: Dār al-Kutub al-'Ilmiyya, 2006.

al-Zayyātī, 'Abd al-'Azīz b. al-Ḥasan. *al-Jawāhir al-mukhtāra fī mā waqaftu 'alayhi min al-nawāzil bi-jibāl ghumāra*. 2 vols. Bibliothèque Nationale du Royaume du Maroc, ms. 1698.

Non-Arabic Secondary Sources

Abou El Fadl, Khaled. "Islamic Law and Muslim Minorities: The Juristic Discourse on Muslim Minorities from the Second/Eighth to the Eleventh/Seventeenth Centuries." *Islamic Law and Society* 1 (1994): 141–187.

———. "Striking a Balance: Islamic Legal Discourses on Muslim Minorities." In *Muslims on the Americanization Path?*, ed. Yvonne Yazbeck Haddad and John L. Esposito, 47–64. Atlanta: Scholars Press, 1998.

———. *Rebellion and Violence in Islamic Law*. Cambridge: Cambridge University Press, 2001.

Abun-Nasr, Jamil M. *A History of the Maghrib in the Islamic Period*. Cambridge: Cambridge University Press, 1987.

———. *The Tijaniyya: A Sufi Order in the Modern World*. London: Oxford University Press, 1965.

Adeleye, R.A. "The Dilemma of the Wazir: The Place of the *Risālat al-wazīr ilā ahl al-ʿilm wa al-tadabbur* in the History of the Conquest of the Sokoto Caliphate." *Journal of the Historical Society of Nigeria* 4 (1968): 285–311.

Ageron, Charles-Robert. "L'émigration des Musulmans algériens et l'exode de Tlemcen (1830–1911)." *Annales: economies, sociétiés, civilisations* 5 (1967): 1047–66.

Ahmad, Muhammad Mushtaq. "The Notions of *Dār al-Ḥarb* and *Dār al-Islām* in Islamic Jurisprudence with Special Reference to the Ḥanafī School." *Islamic Studies* 47 (2008): 5–37.

Al-Hajj, Muhammad. "The Thirteenth-Century in Muslim Eschatology: Mahdist Expectation in the Sokoto Caliphate." *Research Bulletin: Centre of Arabic Documentation Research Bulletin, University of Ibadan* 3 (1967): 100–13.

Arcas Campoy, María. "Algunas consideraciones sobre los tratados de jurisprudencia malikí de al-Andalus." *Miscelánea de Estudios Árabes y Hebraicos* 37 (1988): 13–21.

———. "Valoración actual de la literatura jurídica de al-Andalus." In *Actas del II coloquio hispano-marroquí de ciencias históricas*, 31–49. Madrid: Agencia Española de Cooperación Internacional, 1992.

Arié, Rachel. *L'Espagne musulmane au temps des Nasrides (1232–1492)*. Paris: Éditions de Boccard, 1973.

Asmal, Aboobaker M. "Muslims under Non-Muslim Rule: The *Fiqhi* (Legal) Views of Ibn Nujaym and al-Wansharisi." Ph.D. dissertation, University of Manchester, 1998.

Athamina, Khalil. "*Aʿrāb* and *Muhājirūn* in the Environment of *Amṣār*." *Studia Islamica* 66 (1987): 5–25.

Bakker, Johan de. *The Jihad Waged by the First ʿAlawī Sultans of Morocco (1660–1727): A Major Contribution to their Legitimacy as Rulers*. Amsterdam: Middle East Research Associates, 1991.

Barceló Torres, María del Carmen. "Las cartas árabes de Vila-Real. (Revisión del panorama mudéjar valenciano)." *Estudios Castellonenses* 1 (1982): 365–397.

Bello, Omar. *ʿUlama and Colonialism in Nigeria: Risālah ilā al-muʿāṣirīn by al-Qāḍī ʿAbdallāh*. Sokoto: The Islamic Academy, n.d.

Bennison, Amira K. *Jihad and its Interpretations in Pre-Colonial Morocco: State-Society Relations during the French Conquest of Algeria*. London: RoutledgeCurzon, 2002.

Bennison, Amira and M.A. Gallego. "Religious Minorities under the Almohads: An Introduction." *Journal of Medieval Iberian Studies* 2 (2010): 143–54.

Berque, Jacques, *L'intérieur du Maghreb*. Paris: Gallimard, 1978.

———. *Les Nawāzil el muzāraʿa du Miʿyār al Wazzānī*. Rabat: Editions Felix Moncho, 1940.

———. *Opera Minora*. 3 vols. Saint-Denis: Bouchène, 2001.

———. "Ville et université, aperçu sur l'histoire de l'école de Fès." *Revue historique de droit française et étranger* 26 (1949): 64–117.

Biberstein Kazimirski, A. de. *Dictionnaire Arabe-Français*. 4 vols. Paris: Maisonneuve et cie, 1860.

Blasco Martínez, Asunción. "Notarios Mudéjares de Aragón (siglos xiv–xv)." In *Aragón en la Edad Media* 10–11 (1993): 109–34.

Boronat y Barrachina, Pascual. *Los moriscos españoles y su expulsión: Estudio histórico-crítico*. 2 vols. Valencia: Imprenta de Francisco Vives y Mora, 1901.

Boswell, John. *The Royal Treasure: Muslim Communities under the Crown of Aragon in the Fourteenth Century*. New Haven: Yale University Press, 1977.

Bosworth, C.E. "A Note on *Ta'arrub* in Early Islam." *Journal of Semitic Studies* 34 (1989): 355–63.

Bresc, Henri. "Pantelleria entre l'Islam et la Chrétienté." *Cahiers de Tunisie* 19 (1971): 105–27.

Brett, Michael. "The Lamp of the Almohads: Illumination as a Political Idea in Twelfth Century Morocco." In *Ibn Khaldun and the Medieval Maghrib*, 1–27. Aldershot: Ashgate, 1999.

———. "Le mahdi dans le Maghreb medieval." *Revue des Mondes Musulmans et de la Méditerranée* 91–4 (2000): 93–105.

———. "Muslim Justice under Infidel Rule: The Normans in Ifriqiya 517–555 H/1123–1160 AD." *Cahiers de Tunisie* 43 (1991): 325–68.

———. *The Rise of the Fāṭimids*. Leiden: Brill, 2001.

Brockelmann, Carl. *Geschichte der arabischen Litteratur* (GAL). 5 vols. Leiden: E.J. Brill, 1996.

Brown, Kenneth. *People of Salé: Tradition and Change in a Moroccan City, 1830–1930*. Cambridge: Harvard University Press, 1976.

———. "Profile of a Nineteenth-Century Moroccan Scholar." In *Scholars, Saints and Sufis: Muslim Religious Institutions in the Middle East since 1500*. Berkeley: University of California Press, 1972.

Brunschvig, Robert. *La Berbérie orientale sous les ḥafṣides des origines à la fin du XV siècle*. 2 vols. Paris, Librairie d'Amérique et d'orient, 1947.

Burns, Robert I. "Immigrants from Islam: The Crusaders' Use of Muslims as Settlers in Thirteenth-Century Spain." *The American Historical Review* 80 (1975): 21–42.

———. *Medieval Colonialism: Postcrusade Exploitation of Islamic Valencia*. Princeton: Princeton University Press, 1975.

Burns, Robert I. and Paul E. Chevedden. *Negotiating Cultures: Bilingual Surrender Treaties in Muslim-Crusader Spain under James the Conqueror*. Leiden: Brill, 1999.

Burton, John. *The Sources of Islamic Law: Islamic Theories of Abrogation*. Edinburgh: Edinburgh University Press, 1990.

Bustani, A. and C. Quirós. *Fragmentos de la época sobre noticias de los Reyes nazaritas o capitulaciones de Granada y emigración de los andaluces a Marruecos*. Larache: Artes gráficas Boscá, 1940.

Buzineb, H. "Respuestas de jurisconsultos maghrebíes en torno a la inmigración de los musulmanes hispánicos." *Hesperis-Tamuda* 26–27 (1988): 53–66.

Cachia, Pierre. *Ṭāhā Ḥusayn: His Place in the Egyptian Literary Renaissance*. London: Luzac, 1956.

Cagigas, Isidro de las. *Los Mudéjares*. 2 vols. Madrid: Consejo Superior de Investigaciones Científicas, Instituto de Estudios Africanos, 1948.

Carmona, Alfonso. "Le Malékisme et les conditions requises pour l'exercice de la judicature." *Islamic Law and Society* 7 (2000): 122–58.

———. "The Introduction of Mālik's Teachings in al-Andalus." In *The Islamic School of Law*, ed. P. Bearman et al., 41–56. Cambridge: Harvard University Press, 2005.

Casiri, Michael. *Bibliotheca arabico-hispaña escurialensis*. 2 vols. Madrid: Antonius Perez de Soto, 1760–70.

Catlos, Brian A. *The Victors and the Vanquished: Christians and Muslims of Catalonia and Aragon, 1050–1300*. Cambridge: Cambridge University Press, 2004.

Chalmeta, Pedro. "Precisiones acerca de Ibn Hafsun." In *Actas de las II Jornadas de Cultura Árabe e Islámica*. Madrid: Instituto Hispano-Arabe de Cultura, 1985: 163–75.

Cigar, Norman. *Muhammad al-Qadiri's Nashr al mathani: The Chronicles*. London: Oxford University Press, 1981.

Clancy-Smith, Julia A. *Rebel and Saint: Muslim Notables, Populist Protest, Colonial Encounters (Algeria and Tunisia, 1800–1904)*. Berkeley: University of California Press, 1994.

Coleman, David. *Creating Christian Granada: Society and Religious Culture in an Old-World Frontier City, 1492–1600*. Ithaca: Cornell University Press, 2003.

Cook, Michael. *Commanding Right and Forbidding Wrong*. Cambridge: Cambridge University Press, 2001.

———. *Early Muslim Dogma: A Source-Critical Study*. Cambridge: Cambridge University Press, 1981.

Cossé Brissac, Philippe de. *Les Rapports de la France et du Maroc pendant la conquête de l'Algérie (1830–1847)*. Paris: Larose, 1931.

Coulson, Noel James. "Doctrine and Practice in Islamic Law: One Aspect of the Problem." *Bulletin of the School of Oriental and African Studies* 18 (1956): 211–26.

Cressier, Patrice, Maribel Fierro, Luis Molina (eds.). *Los Almohades: problemas y perspectivas*. Madrid: Consejo Superior de Investigaciones Científicas, 2005.

Crone, Patricia. "The First-Century Concept of *Hiǧra*." *Arabica* 61 (1994): 352–87.

———. *God's Rule: Government and Islam*. New York: Columbia University Press, 2004.

Cuperly, Pierre. *Introduction à l'étude de l'ibāḍisme et de sa théologie*. Algiers: Office des Publications Universitaires, 1984.

Dachraoui, Farhat. "Intégration ou exclusion des minorités religieuses. La conception islamique traditionnelle." In *L'expulsió dels moriscos: conseqüències en el món islàmic i el món cristià*, 195–203. Barcelona: Generalitat de Catalunya, Departament de Cultura, 1994.

Daga Portillo, Rocío. "Los nawazil y géneros relacionados en la literatura juridica: fetuas y masa'il." *Miscelanea de Estudios Árabes y Hebraicos* 40–1 (1991–2): 79–85.

———. "Organización jurídica y social en la España musulmana." Ph.D. dissertation, Universidad de Granada, 1990.

Danziger, Raphael. *Abd al-Qadir and the Algerians: Resistance to the French and Internal Consolidation*. New York: Holmes & Meier Publishers, 1977.

Davis-Secord, Sarah. "Muslims in Norman Sicily: The Evidence of Imām al-Māzarī's Fatwās." *Mediterranean Studies* 16 (2007): 46–66.

Delanoue, Gilbert. *Moralistes et politiques musulmans dans l'Egypte du XIX*e *siècle (1798–1882)*. 2 vols. Cairo: Institut français d'archéologie orientale du Caire, 1982.

Dennerlein, Bettina. "Asserting Religious Authority in Late 19th Century/Early 20th Century Morocco: Muḥammad b. Ja'far al-Kattānī (d. 1927) and his *Kitāb salwat al-anfās*." In *Speaking for Islam: Religious Authorities in Muslim Societies*, ed. Gudrun Krämer and Sabine Schmidtke, 128–52. Leiden: Brill, 2006.

———. "Legitimate Bounds and Bound Legitimacy. The Act of Allegiance to the Ruler (*bai'a*) in 19th Century Morocco." *Die Welt des Islams*, New Series, 41 (2001): 287–310.

Depont, Octave and Xavier Coppolani, *Les Confréries religieuses musulmanes*. Algiers: Jourdan, 1897.

Drory, Joseph. *Ibn al-'Arabi mi-Sevilya*. Ramat-Gan: Bar-Ilan University, 1993.

Echevarría, Ana. "De cadí a alcalde mayor. La élite judicial mudéjar en el siglo XV." *Al-Qanṭara*, 24 (2003): 139–168 and 273–289.

———. *Knights on the Frontier: The Moorish Guard of the Kings of Castile (1410–1467)*, tr. M. Beagles. Leiden: Brill, 2009.

Émerit, Marcel. "La légende de Léon Roches." *Revue Africaine* 91 (1947): 81–105.

Emon, Anver. *Islamic Natural Law Theories*. Oxford: Oxford University Press, 2010.

Encyclopedia of Islam, 2nd ed. (EI^2), 13 vols. Leiden: Brill, 1960–2009.

Ennahid, Said. *Political Economy and Settlement Systems of Medieval Northern Morocco: An Archaeological-Historical Approach*. Oxford: Archaeopress, 2002.

Epalza, Míkel de. "Caracterización del exilio musulmán: La voz de Mudéjares y Moriscos." In *Destierros aragoneses*. 2 vols., 1: 217–28. Saragossa: Institución Fernando el Católico, 1988.

———. "La voz oficial de los musulmanes hispanos, mudéjares y moriscos, a sus autoridades cristianas: cuatro textos, en árabe, en castellano y en catalán—valenciano." *Sharq al-Andalus* 12 (1995): 279–97.

Epstein, Michael. "The Connection between *Hijra* and *Jihād* in Classical Islam." *Jamā'a* 15 (2005–6): 53–85.

Fadel, Mohammad. "Adjudication in the Mālikī Madhhab: A Study of Legal Process in Medieval Islamic Law." Ph.D. diss., University of Chicago, 1995.

———. "Rules, Judicial Discretion and the Rule of Law in Naṣrid Granada: An Analysis of *al-Ḥadīqa al-mustaqilla al-naḍra fī al-fatāwā al-ṣāḍira 'ulamā' al-ḥaḍra.*" In *Islamic Law: Theory and Practice*, ed. R. Gleave and E. Kermeli, 49–86. London: I.B. Tauris, 1997.

Fancy, Hussein. "Theologies of Violence: The Recruitment of Muslim Soldiers by The Crown of Aragon." *Past and Present* 221 (2013), 39–73.

Febrer Romaguera, Manuel Vicente. "Los Bellvís. Una dinastí Mudéjar de alcadíes generals de Valencia, Aragón y el principado de Cataluña." In *Actas del III Simposio Internacional de Mudéjarismo*, 277–90. Teruel: Instituto de Estudios Turolenses, 1986.

Fernández Félix, Ana. "Children on the Frontiers of Islam." In M. García Arenal (ed.), *Conversions islamiques. Identités religieuses en Islam méditerranéen.* Paris: Maisonneuve et Laros, 2002.

———. "Cristianos y conversos al Islam en al-Andalus bajo los Omeyas: Una aproximación al proceso de islamización a través de una fuente legal andalusí del s. III/I." In *Visigodos y omeyas*, 415–28. Madrid: Consejo Superior de Investigaciones Científicas, Instituto de Historia, Departamento de Historia Antigua y Arqueología, 2000.

———. *Cuestiones Legales del Islam Temprano: La Utbiyya y el proceso de formación de la sociedad Islámic Andalusí.* Madrid: Consejo Superior de Investigaciones Científicas, 2003.

Fernández y González, Francisco. *Estado social y político de los Mudéjares de Castilla.* Madrid: de J. Muñoz, 1866.

Fierro, Maribel. "Accusations of 'Zandaqa' in al-Andalus." *Quaderni di Studi Arabi* 5–6 (1987–8): 251–8.

———. "Christian Success and Muslim Fear in Andalusī Writings during the Almoravid and Almohad Periods." In *Dhimmis and others: Jews and Christians and the World of Classical Islam*, ed. U. Rubin and D. Wasserstein, 155–78. Winona Lake: Eisenbrauns, 1997.

———. "La emigración en el Islam: Conceptos antiguos, nuevas problemas." *Awrāq* 12 (1991): 11–41.

———. *La heterodoxia en al-Andalus durante el período Omeya.* Madrid: Instituto Hispano-Arabe de Cultura, 1987.

———. "The Legal Policies of the Almohad Caliphs and Ibn Rushd's *Bidāyat al-Mujtahid.*" *Journal of Islamic Studies* 10 (1999): 226–248.

———. "Le Mahdi Ibn Tūmart et al-Andalus: l'élaboration de la légitimité almohade." *Revue des Mondes Musulmans et de la Méditerranée* 91–4 (2000): 107–24.

———. "Mawālī and Muwalladūn in al-Andalus." In *Patronate and Patronage in Early and Classical Islam*, ed. M. Bernards and J. Nawas, 195–245. Leiden: Brill, 2005.

———. "A Muslim Land without Jews or Christians: Almohad Policies Regarding the 'Protected People.'" In *Christlicher Norden - Muslimischer Süden. Ansprüche und Wirklichkeiten von Christen, Juden und Muslimen auf der Iberischen Halbinsel im Hoch- und Spätmittelalter*, M. Tischler and A. Fidora, 231–47. Munich: Aschendorff Verlag, 2011.

———. "Proto-Malikis, Malikis, and Reformed Malikis in al-Andalus." In *The Islamic School of Law*, ed. P. Bearman et al., 57–76. Cambridge: Harvard University Press, 2005.

———. "The *Qāḍī* as Ruler." In *Saber religioso y poder político en el Islam: actas del Simposio Internacional, Granada, 15–18 octubre 1991*, 71–116. Madrid: Agencia Española de Cooperación Internacional, 1994.

Fierro, Maribel and Saadia Faghia, "Un nuevo texto de tradiciones escatológicas sobre al-Andalus," *Sharq al-Andalus* 7 (1990): 99–111.

Fisher, Humphrey J. "What's in a Name? The Almoravids of the Eleventh Century in the Western Sahara." *Journal of Religion in Africa* 22 (1992): 290–317.

Florencia Mendizábal, María. "La comunidad Mudéjar de Ávila. Notas para su estudio." *Fundación* 7 (2004–5): 77–88.

Friedmann, Yohanan. *Tolerance and Coercion in Islam: Interfaith Relations in the Muslim Tradition*. Cambridge: Cambridge University Press, 2003.

García Sanjuán, Alejandro. "Del Dar al-Islam al Dar al-Harb: la cuestion Mudéjar y la legalidad Islamica." In *Congreso conmemorativo del 750 aniversario de la Toma de Carmona*, 177–188. Carmona: Diputacion de Sevilla, 1998.

———. *Till God Inherits the Earth: Islamic Pious Endowments in al-Andalus (9–15th Centuries)*. Leiden: Brill, 2007.

García-Arenal, Mercedes. *Messianism and Puritanical Reform: Mahdīs of the Muslim West*, tr. Martin Beagles. Leiden: Brill, 2006.

Gay, Jules. *L'Italie méridionale et l'Empire byzantin depuis l'avènement de Basile Ier jusqu'a la prise de Bari par les Normands (867–1071)*. Paris: Albert Fontemoing, 1904.

Gil, Moshe. "Muslim Rule in Sicily." In *Jews in Islamic countries in the middle ages*. Brill: Leiden, 2004.

Goldziher, I. *Livre de Mohammed Ibn Toumert*. Algiers: P. Fontana, 1903.

———. "Muruwwa and Dīn." In *Muslim Studies*, ed. S.M. Stern, 1: 11–44. London: George Allen & Unwin Ltd, 1967.

Granja, Fernando de la. "Fiestas cristianas en al-Andalus." *al-Andalus* 35 (1970): 119–42.

Graulle, A. (tr.). "La '*Daouhat an-nâchir*' de Ibn Askar." *Archives Marocaines* 19 (1913): 1–341.

Guichard, Pierre. "Littérature jurisprudentielle et histoire de l'Espagne Musulmane: la lente integration des *fatwā*/s mālikites à l'historiographie d'al-Andalus." *Comptes-rendus des séances de l'Académie des Inscriptions et Belles-Lettres* 143 (1999): 757–779.

———. *Les Musulmans de Valence et la Reconquête (XIe–XIIIe siècles)*. 2 vols. Damascas: Institut français de Damas, 1990.

Hallaq, Wael B. "Murder in Cordoba: *Ijtihād, Iftā'* and the Evolution of Substantive Law in Medieval Islam," *Acta Orientalia* 55 (1994): 55–83.

Halm, Heinz. *The Empire of the Mahdi: The Rise of the Fatimids*, tr. Michael Bonner. Leiden: Brill, 1996.

Halperin-Donghi, Tulio. *Un conflict nacional: Moriscos y Cristianos viejos en Valencia.* Valencia: Institución Alfonso el Magnánimo, 1980.

Hamet, Ismaïl. *Le gouvernement marocain et la conquête d'Alger (documents chérifiens)*. Algiers: Chihab Editions, 1900.

Hammoudi, Abdellah. *Master and Disciple: The Cultural Foundations of Moroccan Authoritarianism*. Chicago: University of Chicago Press, 1997.

Harvey, L.P. "Crypto-Islam in Sixteenth-Century Spain." In *Actas del primer congreso de studios árabes e islámicos*, 163–78. Madrid: Comité Permanente del CEAI, 1964.

———. *Islamic Spain, 1250 to 1500*. Chicago: University of Chicago Press, 1990.

———. *Muslims in Spain, 1500 to 1614*. Chicago: University of Chicago Press, 2005.

Hatina, Meir. "Fatwas as a Prism of Social History in the Middle East: The Status of Non-Muslims in the Nineteenth Century." In *Koexistenz und Konfrontation: Beiträge zur jüngeren Geschichte und Gegenwartslage der orientalischen Christen*, ed. Martin Tamcke, 51–74. Münster: Lit, 2003.

Hendrickson, Jocelyn. "The Islamic Obligation to Emigrate: Al-Wansharīsī's *Asnā al-Matājir* Reconsidered." Ph.D. Dissertation: Emory University, 2009.

———. "Is al-Andalus Different? Continuity as Contested, Constructed, and Performed across Three Mālikī *Fatwās*," *Islamic Law and Society* 20 (2013): 371–424.

———. "Muslim Legal Responses to Portuguese Occupation in Late Fifteenth-Century North Africa," *Journal of Spanish Cultural Studies* 12 (2011): 309–325.

Hess, Andrew C. *The Forgotten Frontier: A History of the Sixteenth-Century Ibero-African Frontier*. Chicago: University of Chicago Press, 1978.

Hiskett, Mervyn. *The Sword of Truth: The Life and Times of the Shehu Usuman Dan Fodio*, 2nd ed. Evanston: Northwestern University Press, 1994

Hopkins, J.F.P. and Nehemia Levtzion. *Corpus of Early Arabic Sources for West African History*. Princeton: Markus Wiener Publishers, 2000.

Huici Miranda, Ambrosio. "Un fragmento inédito del Ibn 'Iḏārī sobre los Almorávides." *Hespéris Tamuda* 2 (1961): 43–111.

———. "El reinado del califa almohade al-Rašīd, hijo del al-Ma'mūn." *Hespéris* 41 (1954): 9–45.

Ibn Jubayr, Muḥammad b. Aḥmad. *The Travels of Ibn Jubayr*, tr. R.J.C. Broadhurst. London: Jonathan Cape, 1952.

Idris, Hady Roger. *La Berbérie orientale sous les Zīrīdes, xe–xiie siècles*. 2 vols. Paris: Librairie d'Amérique et d'Orient, Adrien-Maisonneuve, 1962.

———. "Commerce maritime et *ḳirāḍ* en Berbérie orientale: d'après un recueil inédit de *fatwās* médiévales." *Journal of the Economic and Social History of the Orient* 4 (1961): 225–39.

———. "Contribution à l'étude de la vie religieuse en Ifrīqiya Zīrīde (xème–xième siècles)." In *Mélanges Louis Massignon*, 2 vols., 2: 327–59. Damascus: Institut d'Études Islamiques de l'Université de Paris et de l'Institut Français de Damas, 1957.

———. "Réflexions sur le Mālikisme sous les Umayyades d'Espagne." In *Atti del terzo congresso di studi arabi e islamici. Ravello, 1–6 settembre* 1966, 397–414. Napoli: Istituto universitario orientale, 1967.

Jackson, Sherman A. *Islamic Law and the State: The Constitutional Jurisprudence of Shihāb al-Dīn al-Qarāfī*. New York: E.J. Brill, 1996.

James, David. *Early Islamic Spain: the History of Ibn al-Qūṭīya: A Study of the Unique Arabic Manuscript in the Bibliothèque Nationale de France, Paris, with a Translation, Notes, and Comments*. London: Routledge, 2009.

Johansen, Baber. *Contingency in a Sacred Law*. Leiden: Brill, 1999.

———. "Der *'Iṣma*-Begriff im Ḥanafītischen Recht." In *Contingency in a Sacred Law*, 238–262. Leiden: Brill, 1999.

———. "Legal Literature and the Problem of Change." In *Contingency in a Sacred Law*: 446–64. Leiden: Brill, 1999.

Jones, Alan (tr.). *The Qur'ān*. Cambridge: Gibb Memorial Trust, 2007.

Jones, Linda. "Retratos de la emigración: La (Re)conquista y la emigración de los ulemas a Granada, según *al-Iḥāṭa* de Ibn al-Jaṭīb." In *Biografías mudéjares o La experiencia de ser minoría: biografías islámicas en la España cristiana*, ed. Ana Echevarría Arsuaga, 21–58. Madrid: Consejo Superior de Investigaciones Científicas, 2008.

———. *The Power of Oratory in the Medieval Muslim World*. Cambridge: Cambridge University Press, 2012.

Juda, Jamal. "Die sozialen und wirtschaftlichen Aspekte der Mawālī in frühislamischer Zeit." Ph.D. diss., Universität Tübingen, 1983.

Juynboll, G.H.A., *Encyclopedia of Canonical Ḥadīth*. Leiden: Brill, 2007.

Kassis, Hanna E. "A 13th-Century Polemical Debate between Ibn Rashīq of Mursiyah and a Priest from Marrākush." *The Maghreb Review* 29 (2004): 8–21.

———. "Muslim Revival in Spain in the Fifth/Eleventh Century." *Der Islam* 67 (1990): 78–110.

———. "Roots of Conflict: Aspects of Christian-Muslim Confrontation in Eleventh-Century Spain." In *Conversion and Continuity: Indigenous Christian Communities in Islamic Lands Eighth to Eighteenth Centuries*, ed. Michael Gervers and Ramzi Jibran Bikhazi, 151–60. Toronto: Pontifical Institute for Medieval Studies, 1990.

Kenbib, Mohammed. *Les protégés: contribution à l'histoire contemporaine du Maroc*. Casablanca: Faculté des Lettres et des Sciences Humaines, 1996.

Khan, Zafarul-Islam. *Hijrah in Islam*. New Delhi: Pharos Media & Publishing, 1997.

Koningsveld, Pieter Sjoerd van. and G.A. Wiegers. "The Islamic Statute of the Mudéjars in the light of a New Source." *Al-Qanṭara* 17 (1996): 19–58.

———. "Islam in Spain during the Early Sixteenth Century: The Views of the Four Chief Judges in Cairo (Introduction, Translation, and Arabic Text)." In *Poetry, Politics and Polemics: Cultural Transfer between the Iberian Peninsula and North Africa*, ed. Otto Zwartjes, Geert Jan van Gelder and Ed de Moor, 133–52. Amsterdam: Rodopi, 1996.

Krawietz, Birgit. "The Weighing of Conflicting Indicators in Islamic Law." In *Law, Christianity and Modernism in Islamic Society*, ed. Urbain Vermeulen and J.M.F. van Reeth, 71–74. Leuven: Peeters, 1998.

Kreutz, Barbara M. *Before the Normans: Southern Italy in the Ninth and Tenth Centuries*. Philadelphia: University of Pennsylvania Press, 1991.

Ladero Quesada, Miguel Angel. *Granada después de la conquista: repobladores y mudéjares*, 2nd ed. Granada: Diputación Provincial de Granada, 1993.

Lagardère, Vincent. "Communautés mozarabes et pouvoir almoravide en 519h / 1125 en al-Andalus." *Studia Islamica* 67 (1988): 99–119.

———. "La haute judicature à l'époque almoravide en al-Andalus." *al-Qanṭara* 7 (1986): 135–228.

———. *Histoire et société en occident musulman au moyen âge: analyse du Mi'yār d'al-Wanšarisī*. Madrid: Casa de Velázquez, 1995.

Lambton, Ann K.S. *State and Government in Medieval Islam: An Introduction to the Study of Islamic Political Theory: The Jurists*. Oxford: Oxford University Press, 1981.

Laroui, Abdallah. *The History of the Maghrib: An Interpretive Essay*. Princeton: Princeton University Press, 1977.

———. *Les origines sociales et culturelles du nationalisme marocain (1830–1912)*. Paris: François Maspero, 1977.

Last, Murray. *The Sokoto Caliphate*. New York: Humanities Press, 1967.

Latham, John D. "The Strategic Position and Defence of Ceuta in the Later Muslim Period." *Islamic Quarterly* 15 (1971): 189–204.

———. "Towards a Study of Andalusian Immigration and its Place in Tunisian History." *Les Cahiers de Tunisie* 5 (1957): 203–249.

Lehmann, Jean-Pierre. "Léon Roches—Diplomat Extraordinary in the Bakumatsu Era: An Assessment of His Personality and Policy." *Modern Asian Studies* 14 (1980): 273–307.

Lévi-Provençal, Evariste. *Les historiens du Chorfa*. Paris: Larose, 1920.

———. "La 'mora Zaida", femme d'Alphonse VI de Castille et leur fils l'infant D. Sancho." *Hesperis* 18 (1934): 1–8.

Levtzion, Nehemia. "ʿAbd Allāh b. Yāsīn and the Almoravids." In *Studies in West African Islamic History. I: The Cultivators of Islam*, ed. J.R. Willis, 78–112. London: Frank Cass and Co. Ltd., 1979.

———. "The Sahara and the Sudan from the Arab Conquest of the Maghrib to the Rise of the Almoravids." In *The Cambridge History of Africa*, ed. J.D. Fage, 637–84. Cambridge: Cambridge University Press, 1978.

Lewicki, T. "The Ibadites in Arabia and Africa." *Journal of World History* 13 (1971): 113–30.

Lewis, Bernard. "Legal and Historical Reflections on the Position of Muslim Populations under Non-Muslim Rule." In *Islam and the West*, 43–58. Oxford: Oxford University Press, 1993.

———. *The Muslim Discovery of Europe*. London: Phoenix, 1994.

Lindsay, James E. "Prophetic Parallels in Abu ʿAbd Allah al-Shiʿi's Mission among the Kutama Berbers, 893–910." *International Journal of Middle East Studies* 24 (1992): 39–56.

Linehan, Peter. *History and the Historians of Medieval Spain*. Oxford: Oxford University Press, 1992.

Lirola Delgado, J. and J.M. Puerta Vílchez, *Biblioteca de al-Andalus*, 9 vols. Almería: Fundación Ibn Tufayl de Estudios Árabes, 2004–2012.

———. *Diccionario de Autores y Obras Andalusíes*. Seville: Junta de Andalucía, Consejería de Cultura, 2002.

Lomax, Derek W. *The Reconquest of Spain*. London: Longman, 1978.

López de Coca Castañer, José-Enrique. "Sobre la emigración mudéjar al reino de Granada," *Revista d'Història Medieval* 12 (2001): 241–58.

López Ortiz, J. "*Fatwās* Granadinas de los siglos xiv y xv: la *fatwā* en al-Andalus." *al-Andalus* 6 (1941): 73–128.

———. "La recepción de la escuela malequí en España." *Anuario de Historia del Derecho español* 7 (1930): 1–167.

Madelung, W. "Has the Hijra come to an End?" *Revue des Études Islamiques* 54 (1986): 225–237.

Maghen, Z. "Close Encounters: Some Preliminary Observations on the Transmission of Impurity in Early Sunnī Jurisprudence." *Islamic Law and Society* 6 (1999): 348–392.

———. "Strangers and Brothers: The Ritual Status of Unbelievers in Islamic Jurisprudence." *Medieval Encounters* 12 (2006): 173–223.

Maíllo Salgado, Felipe. "Acerca del uso, significado y referente del término mudéjar." In *Actas del IV congreso internacional encuentro de las tres culturas, Toledo 30 septiembre–2 octubre 1985*, ed. Carlos Carrete Parrondo, 103–112. Toledo: Tel Aviv University and the city of Toledo, 1988.

———. "Consideraciones acerca de una *fatwā* de al-Wanšarīsī." *Studia Historica* 3 (1985): 181–91.

———. "Del Islam residual mudéjar." In *España, al-Andalus, Sefarad: síntesis y nuevas perspectivas*, ed. Felipe Maíllo Salgado, 129–40. Salamanca: Universidad de Salamanca, 1988.

Mansour, Mansour H. *The Maliki School of Law: Spread and Domination in North and West Africa, 8th to 14th Centuries* C.E. San Francisco: Austin & Winfield, 1995.

March, Andrew F. *Islam and Liberal Citizenship: The Search for an Overlapping Consensus*. Oxford: Oxford University Press, 2009.

Marín, M. "Des migrations forcées: les 'ulema d'al-Andalus face à conquête chrétienne." In *L'Occident musulman et l'Occident chrétien au moyen âge*, ed. M. Hammam, 43–60. Rabat: Faculté des Lettres, 1995.

———. "*Šūrà* et *al-Šūrà* dans al-Andalus." *Studia Islamica* 62 (1985): 25–51.

Marlow, Louise. "Friends and Friendship." In *Encyclopaedia of the Qur'ān*, ed. Jane Dammen McAuliffe, 6 vols. 2: 273–5. Leiden: Brill, 2009.

Martin, Bradford G. *Muslim Brotherhoods in Nineteenth-Century Africa*. Cambridge: Cambridge University Press, 1976.

Martínez Enamorado, Virgilio. " 'Donde rigen las normas de Satán': Ibn Antuluh, Ibn Hafsun y el asunto de la propiedad sobre una esclava." In *Espacio, Tiempo y Forma. Serie* III. *Historia Medieval*, 23 (2010): 97–112.

———. *'Umar Ibn Ḥafṣūn, de la rebeldía a la construcción de la Dawla. Estudios en torno al rebelde de al-Andalus (880–927)*. San José: Universidad de Costa Rica, 2011.

Martos Quesada, Juan. "Características del muftí en Al-Andalus: contribución al estudio de una institución jurídica hispanomusulmana." *Anaquel de estudios árabes* 7 (1996): 127–144.

Masud, Muhammad Khalid. "The Obligation to Migrate: The Doctrine of *Hijra* in Islamic Law." In *Muslim Travellers: Pilgrimage, Migration, and the Religious Imagination*, ed. Dale F. Eickelman and James Piscatori, 29–49. London: Routledge, 1990.

Masud, Muhammad Khalid, Brinkley Messick and David S. Powers, editors. *Islamic Legal Interpretation: Muftis and their Fatwas*. Cambridge: Harvard University Press, 1996.

Meier, Fritz. "Almoravids and Marabouts." In *Essays on Islamic Piety and Mysticism*, tr. John O'Kane, 335–421. Leiden: Brill, 1999.

———. "Über die umstrittene Pflicht des Muslims bei nichtmuslimischer Besetzung seines Landes auszuwandern." *Der Islam* 68 (1991): 65–86.

Melchert, Christopher. "The Early History of Islamic Law." In *Method and Theory in the Study of Islamic Origins*, ed. Herbert Berg, 293–324. Leiden: Brill, 2003.

———. *The Formation of the Sunni Schools of Law, 9th-10th Centuries* C.E. Leiden: Brill, 1997.

Meouak, Mohamed and B. Soravia. "Ibn Bassām al-Šantarīnī (m. 542/1147): algunos aspectos de su antología *al-Ḏajīra fī maḥāsin ahl al-ŷazīra*." *al-Qanṭara* 18 (1997): 221–232.

Mercier, Louis. *L'ornement des âmes et la devise des habitants d'el Andalus, traité de guerre sainte islamique par 'Aly ben 'Abderraḥman ben Hodeïl el Andalusy*. Paris, P. Geuthner, 1939.

Messier, Ronald. *The Almoravids and the Meanings of Jihad*. Santa Barbara: Praeger, 2010.

Metcalfe, Alex. *Muslims and Christians in Norman Sicily: Arabic speakers and the End of Islam*. London: RoutledgeCurzon, 2003.

Meyerson, Mark D. *The Muslims of Valencia in the Age of Fernando and Isabel: Between Coexistence and Crusade*. Berkeley: University of California Press, 1991.

———. "Prostitution of Muslim Women in the Kingdom of Valencia: Religious and Sexual Discrimination in a Medieval Plural Society." In *The Medieval Mediterranean: Cross-Cultural Contacts*, ed. Marilyn J. Chiat and Kathryn L. Reyerson, 87–95. St. Cloud: North Star Press of St. Cloud, 1988.

Mezzine, Mohamed. "Les relations entre les places occupies et les localités de la region de Fès aux XVIème et XVIIème siècles, a partir de documents locaux inédits: Les *Nawāzil*." In *Relaciones de la Península Ibérica con el Magreb siglos XIII–XVI*, ed. Mercedes García-Arenal and María J. Viguera, 539–60. Madrid: Instituto Hispano-Árabe de Cultura, 1988.

Miège, Jean-Louis. *Le Maroc et l'Europe (1830–1894)*. 4 vols. Paris: Presses Universitaires de France, 1961.

Miller, Kathryn A. *Guardians of Islam: Religious Authority and Muslim Communities of Late Medieval Spain*. New York: Columbia University Press, 2008.

———. "Muslim Minorities and the Obligation to Emigrate to Islamic Territory: Two *Fatwās* from Fifteenth-Century Granada." *Islamic Law and Society* 7 (2000): 256–88.

Miller, Susan Gilson and Muḥammad al-Ṣaffār. *Disorienting Encounters: Travels of a Moroccan Scholar in France in 1845–1846: The Voyage of Muhammad As-Saffar*. Berkeley: University of California Press, 1992.

Miller, Susan G. and Amal Rassam. "The View from the Court: Moroccan Reactions to European Penetration during the Late Nineteenth Century." *International Journal of African Historical Studies* 16 (1983): 25–38.

Molénat, Jean-Pierre. "Le problème de la permanence des musulmans dans les territoires conquis par les chrétiens, du point de vue de la loi islamique." *Arabica* 48 (2001): 392–400.

———. "Sur le rôle des almohades dans la fin du christianisme local au Maghreb et en Al-Andalus." *Al-Qanṭara* 18 (1997): 389–414.

Molina López, Emilio. "Algunas consideraciones sobre los emigrados andalusíes." *Homenaje al Prof. Darío Cabanelas Rodríguez*, 2 vols., 1: 419–32. Granada: University of Granada, 1987.

———. "Dos importantes privilegios a los emigrados Andalusíes en el Norte de África en el siglo XIII, contenidos en el *Kitāb Ẓawāhir al-Fiqar* de Muḥammad b. al-Murābiṭ." *Cuadernos de Historia del Islam* 9 (1978–9): 5–28.

Monès, Hussain. "Le Malékisme et l'échec des Fatimides en Ifriqiya." In *Études d'Orientalisme dédiées à la mémoire de Lévi-Provençal.* 197–220. Paris: G.P. Maisonneuve et Larose, 1962.

———. "The Role of men of Religion in the History of Muslim Spain up to the End of the Caliphate." In *The Formation of al-Andalus*, ed. Manuela Marin. 2 vols. 2: 51–84. Aldershot: Ashgate, 1998.

Moraes Farias, Paulo Fernando de. "The Almoravids: Some Questions Concerning the Character of the Movement during its Periods of Closest Contact with the Western Sudan." *Bulletin de l'Institut fondamental d'Afrique noire*, series B, 29 (1967): 821–47.

Morand, Marcel. "Rapport presenté à la commission de codification." In *Études de droit musulman algérien*, 481–498. Algiers: Typ. A. Jourdan, 1910.

Motylinski, A. de C. *L'ʿAqida populaire des Abadhites algériens*. Algiers: Fontana, 1905.

Motzki, Harald. "Child Marriage in Seventeenth-Century Palestine." In *Islamic Legal Interpretation*, eds. M. Masud, B. Messick and D. Powers, 129–40. Cambridge: Harvard University Press, 1996.

Müller, Marcus Joseph. *Beiträge zur Geschichte der westlichen Araber*. 2 vols. Munich: G. Franz, 1866–78.

Munson, Henry. *Religion and Power in Morocco*. New Haven: Yale University Press, 1993.

Muranyi, Miklos. *Beiträge zur Geschichte der Ḥadīṯ und Rechtsgelehrsamkeit der Mālikiyya in Nordafrika bis zum 5. JH. D.H.* Wiesbaden: Harrassowitz, 1997.

———. *Materialien zur mālikitischen Rechtsliteratur*. Wiesbaden: Otto Harrassowitz, 1984.

Norris, H.T. "New Evidence on the Life of ʿAbdullāh b. Yāsīn and the Origins of the Almoravid Movement." *Journal of African History* 12 (1971): 255–68.

———. *Saharan Myth and Saga*. Oxford: Clarendon Press, 1972.

O'Callaghan, Joseph F. *Reconquest and Crusade in Medieval Spain*. Philadelphia: University of Pennsylvania Press, 2003.

O'Connor, Isabel A. *A Forgotten Community: The Mudéjar Aljama of Xàtiva 1240–1327*. Leiden: Brill, 2003.

———. "The Mudéjars and the Local Courts: Justice in Action." *Journal of Islamic Studies* 16 (2005): 332–356.

———. "Muslim Mudéjar Women in Thirteenth-Century Spain: Dispelling the Stereotypes." *Journal of Muslim Minority Affairs* 27 (2007): 55–70.

Oswald, R. "Spanien unter den Almoraviden. Die *Fatāwā* des Ibn Rušd als Quellen zur Wirtschafts- und Sozialgeschichte." *Die Welt des Orients* 24 (1993), 127–145.

Peláez Portales, David. *El proceso judicial en la España Musulmana (siglos viii–xii): con especial referencia a la ciudad de Córdoba*. Cordoba: Ediciones el Almendro, 2000.

Pennell, C.R. "Makhzan and Siba in Morocco: An Examination of Early Modern Attitudes." In *Tribe and State: Essays in Honour of David Montgomery Hart*, ed. E.G.H. Joffe and C.R. Pennell, 159–81. Cambridgeshire: Middle East and North African Studies Press, 1991.

———. *Morocco since 1830: A History*. London C. Hurst & Co., 2000.

———. "Tyranny, Just Rule and Moroccan Political Thought." *Morocco: Occasional Papers* 1 (1994): 13–42.

Peters, Rudolph. *Islam and Colonialism: The Doctrine of Jihad in Modern History*. The Hague: Mouton Publishers, 1979.

Pormann, Peter E. "Das Fatwa Die Herrlichsten Waren (*Asnā l-matāǧir*) des al-Wanšarīsī." *Der Islam* 80 (2003): 301–28.

Powers, David S. *Law, Society, and Culture in the Maghrib, 1300–1500*. Cambridge: Cambridge University Press, 2002.

———. "Legal Consultation (*Futyā*) in Medieval Spain and North Africa." In *Islam and Public Law*, ed. Chibli Mallat, 85–106. London: Graham and Trotman, 1993.

Ribera, J. and M. Asín, *Manuscritos árabes y aljamiados de la Biblioteca de la Junta*. Madrid: Centro de Estudios Históricos, 1912.

Roca Traver, F. "Un siglo de vida mudéjar en la Valencia medieval (1238–1338)." *Estudios de Edad Media de la Corona de Aragón* 5 (1952): 115–208.

Roches, Léon. *Dix ans a travers l'Islam: 1834–1844*. Paris: Perrin et cie, 1904.

Rosado Llamas, María Dolores. "Ibn Qaṭrāl: Cadí de Úbeda y Jaén en el siglo XIII." *Boletín del Instituto de Estudios Giennenses* 176 (2000): 1175–1186.

Rosen, Lawrence. *The Justice of Islam*. Oxford: Oxford University Press, 2000.

Rubin, Uriel. "The Life of Muḥammad and the Qur'ān: The Case of Muḥammad's *Hijra*." *Jerusalem Studies in Arabic and Islam* 28 (2003): 40–64.

Sabbagh, Leila. "La religion des Moriscos entre deux fatwas." In *Les morisques et leur temps*. Paris: Centre National de la Recherche Scientifique, 1983.

Safran, Janina M. "Identity and Differentiation in Ninth-Century al-Andalus." *Speculum* 76 (2001): 573–98.

———. "Rules of Purity and Confessional Boundaries: Mālikī Debates about the Pollution of the Christian." *History of Religions* 42 (2003): 197–212.

———. *The Second Umayyad Caliphate: The Articulation of Caliphal Legitimacy in al-Andalus*. Cambridge: Harvard Middle Eastern monographs, 2000.

Santillana, David de. *Istituzioni di diritto musulmano malichita con riguardo anche al sistema sciafiita*. 2 vols. Rome: Istituto per l'Oriente, 1925.

Schwartz, Werner. *Die Anfänge der Ibaditen in Nordafrika: der Beitrag einer islamischen Minderheit zur Ausbreitung des Islams*. Wiesbaden: Otto Harrassowitz, 1983.

Serjeant, R.B. "Ṣanʿāʾ the 'protected' *hijra*." In *Ṣanʿāʾ: An Arabian Islamic City*, ed. R.B. Serjeant and R. Lewcock, 39–43. London: World of Islam Festival Trust, 1983.

Serrano, D. "Dos fetuas sobre la expulsion de mozárabes al Magreb en 1126," *Anaquel de Estudios Árabes* 2 (1991): 162–182.

Sezgin, Fuat. *Geschichte des arabischen Schrifttums* (GAS). 13 vols. Leiden: Brill, 1967–.

Shadid, W. and S. van Koningsveld. "Loyalty to a Non-Muslim Government: An Analysis of Islamic Normative Discussions and of the Views of Some Contemporary Islamicists." In *Political Participation and Identities of Muslims in Non-Muslim States*, ed. W.A.R. Shadid and P.S. van Koningsveld, 84–114. Kampen: Kok Pharos, 1996.

Shinar, Pessah. "ʿAbd al-Qādir and ʿAbd al-Krīm: Religious Influences on their Thought and Action." *Asian and African Studies* 1 (1965): 139–74.

Skinner, Neil. *An Anthology of Hausa Literature*. Zaria: Northern Nigerian Publishing Co., 1980.

Stewart, Devin. "The Identity of 'the *Muftī* of Oran', Abū l-ʿAbbās Aḥmad b. Abī Jumʿah al-Maghrāwī al-Wahrānī (d. 917/1511)." *al-Qanṭara* 27 (2006): 265–301.

Talbi, Mohamed. *L'émirat aghlabide (184–296/800–909)*. Paris: Adrien-Maisonneuve, 1966.

Terem, Etty. "The new *Miʿyar* of al-Mahdi al-Wazzani: local interpretation of family life in late nineteenth-century Fez." Ph.D. diss., Harvard University, 2007.

Turki, Abdel-Magid. "Consultation juridique d'al-Imām al-Māzarī sur le cas des musulmans vivant en Sicile sous l'autorité des Normands." *Mélanges de l'Université Saint-Joseph* 50 (1984): 689–704.

———. "Pour ou contre la légalité du sejour des musulmans au territoire reconquis par les Chrétiens: Justification doctrinale et réalité historique." In *Religionsgespräche im Mittelalter*, ed. B. Lewis and F. Niewöhner, 305–323. Wiesbaden: Harrassowitz, 1992.

Tyan, Émile. *Histoire de l'organisation judicaire en pays d'Islam*. 2 vols. Paris: Librairie du Recueil Sirey, 1938.

Udovitch, Abraham L. "Muslims and Jews in the World of Frederic II: Boundaries and Communication." *Princeton Papers in Near Eastern Studies* 2 (1993): 83–104.

Umar, Muhammad S. *Islam and Colonialism: Intellectual Responses of Muslims of Northern Nigeria to British Rule*. Leiden: Brill, 2006.

Urvoy, Dominique. *Le monde des ulémas andalous du V/XIe au VII/XIIIe siècle: étude sociologique*. Geneva: Droz, 1978.

Vallvé, J. "La emigración andalusí al Magreb en el siglo XIII." In *Relaciones de la Península Ibérica con el Magreb*, ed M. García-Arenal and M.J. Viguera, 87–129. Madrid: Consejo Superior de Investigaciones Científicas, 1988.

Vidal Castro, Francisco. "Aḥmad al-Wanšarīsī (m. 9141508). principales aspectos de su vida." *al-Qanṭara* 12 (1991): 315–52.

———. "El Mi'yâr de al-Wanšarîsî (m. 914/1508). I: fuentes, manuscritos, ediciones, traducciones." *Miscelánea de estudios árabes y hebraicos* 42–3 (1993–94): 317–362.

———. "El Mi'yâr de al-Wanšarîsî (m. 914/1508) II: contenido." *Miscelánea de estudios árabes y hebraicos*, 44 (1995): 213–246.

———. "El muftí y la fetua en el derecho islámico. Notas para un estudio institucional." *Al-Andalus-Magreb* 6 (1998): 289–322.

———. "Las obras de Aḥmad al-Wanšarīsī (m. 914/1508)." *Inventario analítico* 3 (1992): 73–112.

———. "Sobre la compraventa de hombres libres en los dominios de Ibn Ḥafṣūn." In *Homenaje al Profesor Jacinto Bosch Vilá*. 2 vols., 1: 417–28. Granada: Universidad de Granada, 1991.

Wansbrough, John. "On Recomposing the Islamic History of North Africa: A Review Article." *Journal of the Royal Asiatic Society* (1969): 161–70.

Wasserstein, David J. "Inventing Tradition and Constructing Identity: The Genealogy of 'Umar Ibn Ḥafṣūn between Christianity and Islam." *al-Qanṭara* 23 (2002): 269–97.

Watt, Montgomery. *Muḥammad at Mecca*. Oxford: Oxford University Press, 1953.

Weber, Max. *Economy and Society: An Outline of Interpretive Sociology*, ed. G. Roth and C. Wittich, tr. E. Fischoff et al. 2 vols. Berkeley: University of California Press, 1978).

Weiss, Bernard. *The Search for God's Law: Islamic Jurisprudence in the Writings of Sayf al-Dīn al-Āmidī*. Salt Lake City: University of Utah Press, 1992.

———. *The Spirit of Islamic Law*. Athens: University of Georgia Press, 1998.

Wiegers, Gerard Albert. *Islamic Literature in Spanish and Aljamiado: Yça of Segovia (fl. 1450), His Antecendents and Successors*. Leiden: Brill, 1994.

———. "Language and Identity: Pluralism and the Use of Non-Arabic Languages in the Muslim West." In *Pluralism and Identity: Studies in Ritual Behaviour*, ed. Jan Platvoet et al., 303–26. Leiden: Brill, 1995.

Willis, John Ralph. *In the Path of Allah: The Passion of al-Hajj 'Umar: An Essay into the Nature of Charisma in Islam*. London: Frank Cass & Co. Ltd., 1989.

———. "Morocco and the Western Sudan: Fin de Siècle—Fin des Temps: Some Aspects of Religion and Culture to 1600." *The Maghreb Review* 14 (1989), 91–95.

Yanagihashi, Hiroyuki. "The Judicial Functions of the Sulṭān in Civil Cases According to the Mālikīs up to the Sixth/Twelfth Century." *Islamic Law and Society* 3 (1996): 41–74.

Index

www.ingramcontent.com/pod-product-compliance
Lightning Source LLC
LaVergne TN
LVHW010556300926
849162LV00002B/341
* 9 7 8 9 0 0 4 2 8 3 1 9 0 *